Return
of Royalty

WILD SHEEP OF NORTH AMERICA

Return of Royalty
Wild Sheep of North America

By
Dale E. Toweill
and
Valerius Geist

Library of Congress Catalog Card
  Number: 98-071414
ISBN: 0-940864-33-9
Published January 1999

Published in the United States of
America by

Boone and Crockett Club
250 Station Drive
Missoula, MT 59801
(406) 542-1888
Fax (406) 542-0784
www.boone-crockett.org

and

Foundation for North American
  Wild Sheep
720 Allen Ave.
Cody, WY 82414
(307) 527-6261
Fax (307) 527-7117

Return of Royalty

WILD SHEEP OF NORTH AMERICA

By Dale E. Toweill and Valerius Geist
Sketches provided by Ken Carlson

Published by
Boone and Crockett Club and
Foundation for North American Wild Sheep

Missoula, Montana 1999

Foreword

BY DANIEL A. PEDROTTI AND PAUL D. WEBSTER

A great opportunity was presented to the Foundation for North American Wild Sheep (FNAWS) at our 1996 Convention in Reno. Dr. Dale E. Toweill approached me with the idea of having FNAWS publish a book that he and Dr. Valerius Geist were in the process of composing. The book was to be a comprehensive treatise on the wild sheep of North America covering their history from migration to the New World, their decline in the 1800s and today's return of wild sheep to most of their ancestral habitats.

I was overwhelmed at the thought that these two eminent authors, Dr. Dale E. Toweill and Dr. Valerius Geist, would permit us to sponsor and distribute such a prestigious book. Little did I realize that **Return of Royalty** would become the definitive work on the wild sheep of North America.

Realizing that FNAWS had not published books in recent years and knowing of the Boone and Crockett Club's extensive experience and success in publishing and marketing wildlife related books, my first reaction was to ask Dr. Toweill if a joint venture between these two prestigious organizations would be acceptable. He thought it would be a great idea so we contacted Paul Webster who was the President of the Boone and Crockett Club. Paul also recognized this as a tremendous opportunity and agreed that co-publishing such an important book would be good for both organizations.

I subsequently became President of FNAWS and on February 8, 1997, at the FNAWS Convention in Philadelphia, a memorandum of understanding, providing for the co-publication of this book, was signed between Dr. Dale E. Toweill and Dr. Valerius Geist as authors and by Paul Webster, President of the Boone and Crockett Club and Daniel A. Pedrotti, President of FNAWS, as publishers.

We have both reviewed the entire manuscript, in draft form, and our greatest expectations have been fully realized. This is without question the definitive work on wild sheep in modern North America. **Return of Royalty** reads with such sincerity and excitement that it is almost impossible to put down. The history of wild sheep on this continent is well documented and insight into the decline of this magnificent species is provided in detail. The book also tells the wonderful story of wild sheep's return to sustainability through the cooperation and untiring efforts of wild sheep hunters, wildlife biologists, government agencies, and wildlife departments throughout North America.

The details of the decline of most North American big game species during the 1800s, to the brink of extinction, provide a sad testimony to the ethics of early settlers and the greed of market hunters. This westward march of civilization was especially devastating for wild sheep due to the introduction of domestic sheep. These flocks intermingled with our native bighorns and exposed this species that had evolved in the New World without immunities, to insidious diseases by the European domestics. The results were disastrous. Many sub-species were lost entirely. Audubon's bighorns were extinct by 1925, and in 1960 the last of the *texanas*, the native desert bighorns of Texas, were observed in the Trans-Pecos region of west Texas.

Awareness of the need for conservation of the remaining species of big game began in earnest with the formation of the Boone and Crockett Club by Teddy Roosevelt in 1887. However, the successful recovery of wild sheep really began in 1974 at a meeting in Wisconsin where the seeds for the Foundation for North American Wild Sheep were planted by a small group of sheep hunters who wished to return something to the mountains of North America that had given them such enjoyment, namely wild sheep. Thus "Putting Sheep on the Mountain" became the battle cry and today we can enjoy this species in relative abundance.

Return of Royalty chronicles what many have titled "The Wildlife Conservation Story of the 20th Century" with primary focus on the restoration of wild sheep. As you read the following pages that detail the status of wild sheep, state by state and province by province, keep in mind that not only were wild sheep saved but many other big game species benefited as well. Our efforts have also contributed heavily toward the preservation of numerous endangered species and that is a dividend few appreciate.

Finally, let me say, the publication of this book by Boone and Crockett Club and FNAWS as co-sponsors moves us one step closer to one of my most serious wishes— that the great conservation organizations of today will come together with common aims to become the dynamic force that can lead us into the next century. By returning wildlife management to the professionals and educating the non-hunting public in the importance of our "Hunting Heritage" thus inspiring them to help us, we can provide a legacy of abundant wildlife habitat and wild game for future generations. Hopefully, publishing **Return of Royalty** as a joint effort can be the first step toward this goal.

We wish to thank Dr. Toweill and Dr. Geist for a great book and for giving us the opportunity to be part of it.

The authors are deeply indebted to all who worked to make this book a success. Books are born of sometimes vague concepts, and are nourished to completion through hard work and the support of many people.

Our heartfelt appreciation must be extended first to two people who believed in this project and who committed themselves to its completion. Dan Pedrotti, as President of the Foundation for North American Wild Sheep, and Paul Webster, as President of the Boone and Crockett Club, found in our proposal something they believed would benefit the wild sheep resource and the many people who enjoy that resource.

This book is the result of decades of dedicated service by biologists and sportsmen to the conservation— literally, the 'wise management'— of wild sheep. The authors extend a special thank you to the many people, friends and colleagues all, who contributed of their knowledge and expertise with wild sheep: Ted Benzon, Vernon Bleich, Dan Blower, Vic Coggins, Jerry Cooke, Lou Cornicelli, Jim DeForge, Raymond Demarchi, John Ellenberger, Glenn Erickson, Amy Fisher, Ian Hatter, Wayne Heimer, Manfred Hoefs, Brian Horejsi, Kevin Hurley, Bill Jensen, Rolf Johnson, Jim Karpowitz, Raymond Lee, Beth MacCallum, James McKenzie, Stacey Ostermann, Gary Schlictemeier, Helen Schwantje, David Shackleton, Wes Shields, Norman Simmons, Gregg Tanner, Steve Torres, Raul Valdez, Alasdair Veitch, Walt Van Dyke, and William Wishart.

Ken Carlson, one of the nation's greatest wildlife artists and a strong conservationist, provided the cover art and sketches, for which we are deeply grateful. We are grateful, too, for the photographs supplied by biologists and sportsmen that bring color and life to the text: Ted A. Benzon, Craig Biehrle, Rosemary Bisiar, Vernon Bleich, John Boone, Dave Brooks, Harvey Brown, Denver Bryan, Vic Coggins, Jim DeForge, John Ellenberger, Glenn Erickson, Jerry Feist, Michael H. Francis, Duncan Gilchrist, Nadine Gines, Wayne Heimer, Bill Hickey, Manfred Hoefs, Doug Humphreys, Rolf Johnson, Jim Karpowitz, Lon E. Lauber, Raymond Lee, Don L. MacCarter, Burk Mantel, Bob Miles, LuRay Parker, Don Paul, Gregg Tanner, Tom Tietz, Harold Umber, Vic Van Ballenberghe, and Walt Van Dyke. The University of Calgary supplied the photograph of Sir Wilfred Laurier.

Special appreciation is extended to the publications staff at the Boone and Crockett Club.

Earl Morgenroth, First Vice President and George A. Bettas, Vice President of Communications, were instrumental in approving the resources and manpower to begin the project and saw it through to completion. Our very special and heartfelt appreciation is extended to Julie Tripp, Director of Publications and sometimes worker of miracles, for her efforts in layout and design.

Finally, the authors want to express their special appreciation to others who contributed, directly or indirectly, to whatever success we may have achieved through this book. They will know their contribution: Frances Cassirer, Ted Chu, Jay Crenshaw, Jim DeForge, Robert DiGrazia, Glen Gearhart, Rick Furniss, Duncan Gilchrist, Burk Mantel, Justin Naderman, Lou Nelson, Steve Pozzanghera, Dan Pedrotti, Jeff Rohlman, Mike Scott, Randy Smith, Jerry Thiessen, Deyanne Toweill, William L. Toweill, Ken Whitten, and Jack Ward Thomas.

Return of Royalty

WILD SHEEP OF NORTH AMERICA

TABLE OF CONTENTS

Chapter One

ROYALTY IN NORTH AMERICA – THE WILD SHEEP

The grandeur of the high mountains of western North America has held Americans in thrall since the first reports from the Corps of Discovery lead by Merriwether Lewis and William Clark at the very beginning of the nineteenth century. From the earliest days, the wild sheep, more than any other North American animal, has symbolized these great mountains and vistas, elevated above the day-to-day and mundane lowland dwellers. Wild sheep rams (males) are characterized by regal bearing, great curling horns that seem disproportionate to their body, and an ability to negotiate breathtaking cliffs characteristic of their mountain habitats with ease. For these reasons and more, the wild sheep have been termed kings of the crags and monarchs of the high country— royalty— for the past two centuries.

Royalty or not, the remoteness of wild sheep terrain and their dramatic presence have led many to covet the great curling horns of rams, men matching their skills and strength against the vast rugged mountains that wild sheep call home. Especially over the past hundred years, the wild sheep have become perhaps the most highly cherished of all game species in North America. The great Chadwick ram, with horns curling over 50 inches in length on both sides, has been called the greatest North American trophy animal ever taken by a sportsman, and the "grand slam," or harvest of one of each of the four major classes of wild sheep in North America (Dall's, Stone's, Rocky Mountain bighorn, and desert bighorn), has become akin to the search for the holy grail among hunters.

Unfortunately, this fascination with wild sheep nearly resulted in their decimation. Sheep were pursued when they were most vulnerable, on winter ranges and at water holes, for their delicious meat, and were forced to compete for the food needed for survival on low-altitude winter ranges with domestic livestock that could spend the summer and fall cropping that critical forage. Domestic livestock (and especially domestic sheep) that had been bred to improve their resistance to natural pathogens and associated diseases over centuries sometimes passed

DALE E. TOWEILL

California bighorn sheep secure among canyon cliffs of the Owyhee River in southeastern Idaho, result of one of the first truly successful wild sheep transplants.

their diseases and parasites to wild sheep that had few, if any, defenses against these organisms, often resulting in sudden and widespread decimation of herds. By the end of the nineteenth century, it appeared that the royalty of western mountains would soon be little more than a memory in most of the range once occupied by wild sheep. Many believed that wild sheep would become extinct, along with many other species of native wildlife, in the twentieth century.

It was not to be. The greatest environmental success story of the twentieth century is the return of wildlife— and wild sheep— in North America. The wildlife we currently enjoy and take for granted is not merely a gift of nature, but is wildlife restored and returned due to the effort of three generations of North Americans.

THE BASIS FOR NORTH AMERICAN WILDLIFE MANAGEMENT: THE ROOSEVELT DOCTRINE

The process that returned wildlife to North America began with the friendship of two like-minded heads of state at the turn of the century, President Theodore Roosevelt of the United States and Prime Minister Sir Wilfred Laurier of Canada. These men, their friendship and their shared vision of what could be in the future, are the reason why wildlife conservation in Canada and the United States is not only based on identical policies, but is legally supported by treaties for migratory species that cross the boundaries between nations. Wildlife conservation in North America was a farsighted, continental effort from the outset, far ahead of its time, that benefited all parties involved.

The efforts of President Roosevelt and Prime Minister Laurier absolutely depended on others as well. Towering public figures in both nations cooperated in salvaging the remnants of wildlife and setting them on the road to recovery, figures like Sir Clifford Sifton in Canada (Chairman of the Commission on Conservation which, in public hearings, focused on the conservation of forests, fish and wildlife from 1911 to 1919). Sifton was a multimillionaire, the developer of the Canadian west, a civil servant, and political activist. His great historical work was overshadowed by the tragedy of World War I, but continues to bear fruit to this very day. Sifton's counterpart in the United States was none

President Theodore Roosevelt, America's great champion of wildlife and wild places, to whom we owe much for our present quality of life.

other than Gifford Pinchot, the first Chief of what was to become the United States Forest Service. Pinchot, visionary and able lieutenant of President Roosevelt, was able to implement a vision for the protection and management of public resources on lands once slated for disposition by the federal government. These men were aided by William T. Hornaday, perhaps the greatest orator to speak on behalf of wildlife. Hornaday was the director of the New York Zoological Society. C. Gordon Hewett, Canada's Chief Entomologist, was the father of the all-important 1916 migratory bird treaty. Author of the seminal book *"Conserving Canada's Wildlife*," Hewett tragically died in the great influenza epidemic in 1920 and never lived to see his book in print. These are but a few of the many dedicated men and woman to whom we owe a deep debt for the quality of life— and wildlife— we enjoy today.

The efforts of President Theodore Roosevelt on behalf of wildlife were far reaching. These efforts went beyond securing large tracts of public land (as he did with the creation of the U.S. Forest Service) or the creation of an informed, politically effective voice for wildlife (as he did with the creation of the Boone and Crockett Club, the original organization of sportsmen dedicated to restoration of wildlife). Roosevelt gave a unique twist to the North American philosophy of wildlife conservation, one that bears his name to date: the Roosevelt Doctrine. The Roosevelt Doctrine proclaimed that the management of wildlife was to be based on the best science and scholarship available. This represented a profound departure from traditional European wildlife husbandry and game keeping, wherein wildlife was maintained at the pleasure of the social elite, who employed game keepers to look after its needs and provide protection from poachers and predators. The fate of wildlife thus varied with the wishes and whims of its private owners, a condition still present to date. North America's wildlife, kept in public ownership as a shared renewable resource, was managed publicly under public scrutiny, a condition that — in the long run— favored the use of the best information available. As a result of the Roosevelt Doctrine, North America's wildlife was simultaneously protected from self-serving political decisions affecting wildlife management, the pressure of economic market forces, and the arbitrary views and whims of private owners.

The Roosevelt Doctrine spawned within a decade, a new and uniquely North American profession: the wildlife biologist. This in turn led to an organization of wildlife professionals, The Wildlife Society, inclusive of university curricula for the training of wildlife biologists and professional journals for the sharing of knowledge.

The first and most prominent of wildlife professionals was Aldo Leopold, whose musings in his posthumously-published *"Sand County Almanac"* inspire to this day. Leopold, for all his sentiments and poetic prose, was also a hard-headed, practical manager of wildlife as revealed by his classic book *"Game Management"* published in 1933. Leopold deserves much of the credit for establishing the scientific basis for modern wildlife management, making him an icon still revered among professional wildlife managers.

This distinction of "science based" as opposed to "experience based" wildlife management has remained to this day as a distinction between the practices of European and American wildlife management systems. Moreover, North American wildlife management is primarily a conservation activity, based on public policy and debated in legislatures. This is a far cry from wildlife management as practiced in most of Europe, where the mere admonition to manage "with conservation in mind" is purely optional. Wildlife on private estates is commonly managed for its commercial values, or as a result of romantic ideals, and void of any deeper biological understanding.

The Roosevelt Doctrine thus insured that in the struggle of vested interests over the management of public wildlife, the input of science and scholarship must be considered. Because of the many public 'stockholders' in wildlife, wildlife research was to be and remains to this day both publicly accountable and subject to public debate and questioning. As a result, wildlife management and wildlife biologists took a different track than some other professional managers of public resources, such as those concerned with management of stocks of ocean fisheries. The research and knowledge of fisheries biologists and managers is typically concerned primarily with large commercial fishing operations

UNIVERSITY OF CALGARY

Prime Minister Sir Wilfred Laurier of Canada, a friend of President Roosevelt, made possible a continental, enduring system of wildlife conservation across North America.

The Wild Sheep in Indian Petroglyphs

Written records relating to wild sheep in North America extend back much further than the time of European exploration, in the form of pictographs (images painted on a rock surface) and petroglyphs (images physically pecked or hammered into the surface of rock faces). Such 'rock art' is nearly impossible to date, although an excavation at an associated site in California's Coso Range, reported by Harrington in 1957, indicated that use of the area by Indians extended to at least 3,000 years ago, and possibly much longer. Further, the formation of desert 'varnish' on the surface of rocks associated with the designs apparently dates back to about 3,000 years as well. If so, virtually none of the designs are older than 3,000 years of age, and many (based on the technology depicted in associated drawings such as atlatls and bows and arrows) may be much younger.

Whatever the age of such art, bighorn sheep are featured in sites from every western state as well as northwestern Mexico. A survey of sites featuring bighorns in rock art was done by Campbell Grant in 1980; he found that the greatest concentrations of sites are found in southern California's Coso Range, the 'four corners' area (where Utah, Arizona, New Mexico, and Colorado converge), south-central Oregon, and the Columbia River Gorge along the Oregon-Washington border. In the Coso Mountain Range alone, over 100,000 petroglyphs have been discovered, and just over half depict wild sheep. Most are found in historic sheep habitat, and many are concentrated in rocky canyons or near desert springs. However, no one knows whether the drawings are meant to invoke magic (i.e., an aid to hunters seeking to harvest wild sheep, or perhaps an invocation to some deity associated with wild sheep that could provide rain or some other desired outcome), or simply represent the equivalent of prehistoric graffiti. Most archaeologists have assumed that the

JIM DEFORGE

Native Americans, too, were captivated by bighorns and thousands of years ago left evidence of this in petroglyphs such as these in California's Coso Mountains.

drawings were somehow related to hunting success. A buttress for this belief is provided by the location of many drawings at sites where wild sheep could have been ambushed by hunters, and by drawings of men equipped with atlatl or bow and arrows associated with some of the drawings. Excavations of Shoshonean sites, however, indicate that the peoples believed to have created the drawings ate very few sheep— and a lot of rabbits and hares, which are rarely depicted.

Archaeologist Dave Whitley studied the ethnographic history of the Shoshone and Paiute, and developed a new theory. According to Whitley, the petroglyphs are the work of shamans, or medicine men, drawn to specific locations (sometimes far distant from where they lived) to seek rain in an increasingly arid land. The bighorn is believed to have been the spiritual guide of rain-making, and the canyons and crevices openings into his otherworldly home. Whitley believes that the shamans subscribed to the principle of symbolic inversion— that the supernatural world was the opposite of the earthly— so that if moisture was desired, one must travel to a dry and hot place to invoke the spirits. "Killing the sheep" (which could mean simply depicting— and thereby 'capturing'— a sheep, or by depicting the shooting of a sheep) was a Shoshonean symbolism for entering the supernatural in a trance. According to this theory, then, the sites mark places where shamans could invoke a god to provide a desired outcome, and the fact that they occurred in potential wild sheep habitat was an artifact of place rather than a site of past or potential hunting success.

Whatever the stimulus leading to the depiction of wild sheep on stones across western North America, it is clear that wild sheep were important to native peoples. To mention only a few examples, *Panwu* (the Hopi bighorn sheep kachina) and *Kac-ko* (the sheep deity of the Acoma peoples) were important deities. *Panwu* may have been the precursor of the important Navajo yei *Ganaskidi*, the humpbacked god who carried the seeds of all the plants in the world in a feathered bag on his back, depicted as having the horns of a bighorn and being the owner and controller of all sheep. Further to the south, the Papago peoples believed that the horns of bighorn sheep killed by hunters must be venerated, piled together near water holes, to control the wind and to prevent the air from leaving the earth.

GREG TANNER

DALE E. TOWEILL

Petroglyphs of bighorn sheep are abundant among the rocky canyons of most western states, such as these from Washington's Hells Canyon (bottom) and Nevada's Colorado River (inset).

and government departments dealing with these corporations. These fisheries managers, with their complex mathematical models and the subject of their research not readily visible to the public, have often developed into a secluded, aloof elite, far removed from and untroubled by public accountability. Wildlife biologists and managers, on the other hand, operate very much in the public eye, dealing with a renewable public resource visited at least once every year by millions of sportsmen and wildlife enthusiasts. These professionals are held publicly accountable for their findings, not only in professional peer review of their conclusions but in public demonstration of the efficacy of their proposals to meet identified management objectives. In one of the great ironies of science, the wildlife professionals, whose efforts have resulted in the nearly miraculous restoration of wildlife throughout North America, are often accorded less scientific respect than the managers of marine fisheries stocks, many of which have collapsed through overharvest.

Wildlife professionals are part of a very successful system of sustained resource use, more often plagued by problems of success than by problems of failure. Whatever the scientific standing of wildlife biologists, they are often superior ecologists, rich in qualitative knowledge, hands-on management experience, and surprisingly open to new insights about wildlife ecology. While this might be due in part to the accessibility of wildlife to researchers, the role of public accountability for management and public scrutiny of results (in the form of unpredictable questions faced by wildlife biologists in public forums) has no doubt contributed greatly. In Canada, fisheries scientists and their labs are guarded by security personnel, with scientists not freely accessible— a state of affairs as foreign to Canadian wildlife biologists as to their United States counterparts. On the down side, wildlife biologists are (with few exceptions) terrible historians and policy analysts, oblivious of the foundations or the successes of North American wildlife conservation. As a result, many uncritically accept damaging policy initiatives developed by self-serving interests, and few are truly effective in defending North America's highly successful system of wildlife conservation.

This book is a product of the Roosevelt Doctrine in wildlife conservation. Mountain sheep conservation is part of that North American success story. It is by no means an unqualified success, nor is it a done deal— far from it! White-tailed deer and elk, for instance, are doing much better than mountain sheep. However, whitetails thrive by man-made ecological havoc, have very high reproductive rates, and disperse readily— none of which is true of mountain sheep. Elk are habitat generalists, able to benefit from human-caused changes in forest and range management. Wild sheep, unlike whitetails and elk, are habitat specialists with low reproductive rates and poor dispersal capabilities, susceptible to diseases, and difficult to manage. Despite this, there have been tremendous successes in mountain sheep management, and the return of royalty to western North America stands as perhaps the epitome of the accomplishments of wildlife professionals. Despite vexing problems and slow scientific progress, there is room for guarded optimism that the great work of mountain sheep conservation will continue to progress.

FIRST CONTACTS

Tangible knowledge about wild sheep grew slowly. Although explorers were aware of wild sheep from the earliest days, due to their remote and inaccessible habitats little was known about wild sheep biology until relatively recent times. The great taxonomist Linnaeus described the giant sheep in the 1766 edition of his taxonomic work on the basis of the descriptions of Gmelin, a German botanist exploring Siberia on behest of the Russian czar. However, the bighorn of North America had been described much earlier.

Written narratives of wild sheep by European explorers date to nearly the earliest days of western exploration. The Spanish explorer Coronado reported back to the Governor of Mexico in 1540 that he encountered:

"...some sheep as big as a horse, with very large horns." By the time the Jesuit priest Father Picolo published a description of the bighorn in Baja California a century and half later, in 1697, the bighorn was well-known among the Jesuit missionaries toiling in what is now northwestern Mexico and the American southwest. Father Picolo reported that "Its Head is much like that of a stag: and its horns, which are very large, like those of a Ram; Its Tail and Hair are speckled, and shorter than a Stags; But its Hoof is large, round, and cleft as an Oxes."

Not long after publication of Linnaeus' book on taxonomy, the American explorer William Clark of the Corps of Discovery killed a bighorn ewe on the upper Missouri River on May 25, 1805; that same day, his interpreter (and hunter) George Drewyer killed a ram as well. These animals (and another ewe killed by private William Bratten) provided the basis

© NADINE GINES

Bighorn ram skull embedded in an Idaho pine tree, likely very similar to the 'medicine tree' described by Alexander Ross in 1823.

for a lengthy description of the species and its use by the local Indian tribes by Merriwether Lewis, copied by Clark into his journal as follows (spelling as recorded by DeVoto):

"...it [the male] was somewhat larger than the mail of the Common Deer; the body reather thicker deeper and not so long in proportion to it's hight as the common Deer; the head and horns of the male are remarkably large compared with the other parts of the animal ... the horn is of a light brown colour; when dressed it is almost white extreamly transparent and very elastic. This horn is used by the natives in constructing their bows; I have no doubt of it's elegance and usefullness in hair combs, and might possibly answer as maney valuable purpoces to civilized man, as it does to the native indians, who form their water cups, spoons, and platters of it."

Clark was also quick to point out the difficulties in hunting the animal:

"...they feed on grass, but principally on the arramatic herbs which grows on the clifts and inaxcessable hights which they frequent most commonly, and the places they generally collect to lodge is the crannies or crevices of the rocks in the face of inaxcessable precepices, where the wolf nor Bear can reach them, and where indeed man himself would in maney instances find a similar deficiency...they are very shy and quick of both sent and sight."

Other narrative accounts soon followed. Alexander Mackenzie of the North West Company reported bighorn sheep in the area of the Blue Mountains in 1818. Alexander Ross, also of the North West Company, reported a curiosity encountered on the East Fork of the Bitterroot River, near the mouth of Medicine Creek, in 1823— a bighorn skull embedded in a tree. Ross reported:

"Out of the pines...and about five feet from the ground is growing up with the tree, a ram's head with the horns still attached to it! and so fixed and embedded is it in the tree that it must have grown up with it. One of the horns and more than half the head is buried in the tree; but most of the other horn, and part of the head, protrudes out at least a foot. ... The tree was scarcely two feet in diameter. ... Our Flathead Indians related to us a rather strange story about the ram's head. Indian legend relates that as the first Flathead Indians that passed this way one of them attacked a mountain ram as large and stout as a common horse, that on wounding him, the fierce animal turned round upon his pursuer, who taking shelter behind the tree, the ram came against it with all his force, so that he drove his head through it, but before he could get it extracted again the Indian killed him and took off the body but left the head, as a momento of the adventure. All Indians reverence the celebrated tree, which they say by the circumstances related conferred on them the power of mastering and killing all animals."

This skull apparently was very similar to the Idaho skull depicted here, presumably the result of a head and horns propped among the limbs of a growing pine until finally incorporated into the tree itself.

Alexander Ross was also among the first of the fur trappers and traders to relate the hunter's dilemma with bighorn sheep— they just weren't big enough or accessible enough to provide meat in the volume needed by hungry men. Faced with a shortage of food in March 1824, he dispatched his hunters eastward to seek buffalo. Offer of a new gun as a reward stimulated another group of hunters to go into the mountains hunting bighorn sheep, but Ross recorded his disappointment with their success in his diary:

"...those animals are smaller in size than I had been in the habit of seeing elsewhere with very disproportionate heads for the size of their bodies, and still more disproportionate horns to the size of the head. The average weight of these animals was 70 lbs. ...One of the ram's horns brought into our camp measured 49 inches in length..."

The fact is, most of the trappers and explorers didn't bother much with wild sheep, especially if they were near an area where bison might be found. Wild sheep typically occupied steep and rugged terrain far from the beaver streams of interest to these hardy men, and hunting them often entailed great difficulty. The hunter not only had to ascend the mountains to where the animals occurred (an effort that could rarely be accomplished on horseback) and then get sufficiently close for an effective shot with relatively inefficient firearms; he also had to attempt to retrieve the meat and pack it to where his horse and packstock waited. In the meantime, his packstock was vulnerable to any passing Indian raiding parties. Even where sheep occurred and there were few other animals that could provide venison for hungry men, wild sheep often could not be effectively hunted. In 1831, while traveling through the northern Great Basin of what is now southern Idaho, northern Nevada, and extreme eastern Oregon, John Work reported:

"The hunters observe the tracks of some sheep in the Mountains but they appear to have been driven off by some straggling Indians whose tracks are seen." [June 2, 1831, Independence Mountains near the Humboldt River] and later "The tracks of some sheep are to be seen in the Mountains but they are so shy there is no approaching them." [June 5, 1831, South Fork Owyhee River, Nevada]

Perhaps John Kirk Townsend, a physician and skilled naturalist who traveled west with Nathaniel Wyeth's expedition in 1834, best summed up the feelings of most trappers and explorers:

"We saw, to-day, a flock of the hairy sheep of the Rocky Mountains, the big horn of the hunters,…We exerted ourselves in vain to shoot them. They darted from us, and hid themselves amongst the inaccessible cliffs, so that none but a chamois hunter might pretend to reach them. Richardson says he has frequently killed them, but he admits it is dangerous and wearisome sport; and when good beef is found to be found upon the plains, men are not anxious to risk their necks for a meal of mutton."

The primary exception to this general statement was when bighorns were encountered at low elevations on winter range. John Work, who assumed command of Peter Skene Ogden's fur-trapping and exploration brigade for the Hudson's Bay Company, found mountain sheep very numerous near Morgan Creek and the site of present-day Salmon, Idaho, in November and December of 1830. Captain Bonneville reported that bighorns were common and easily killed near the site of present-day Salmon, Idaho, during the winter of 1832, and Osborne Russell selected winter camps in 1835-36 (at Mutton Hill near present-day Pocatello, Idaho) and 1836-37 (at the juncture of the Clark's Fork with the Yellowstone River), specifically in order to be able to hunt sheep.

Russell must be counted as perhaps the first great sheep hunter of the west. In reading his journals, it is evident that Russell took delight in hiking into the mountains to observe and pursue bighorns. His journal abounds with sightings and accounts of sheep hunts throughout the Rocky Mountains and western canyon lands, and Russell often traveled from winter camps distant from sheep ranges to areas where he could avail himself of sheep hunting opportunities. In February 1839, Russell recorded one of his sheep hunts near the present Idaho-Wyoming state boundary southeast of Grays Lake as follows:

"Here we found imense numbers of Mountain Sheep which the deep snows drive down to the low points of rocks facing the South near the river. We could see them nearly every morning from our lodges standing on the points of rock jutting out so high in the air that they appeared no larger than Weasels. It is in this position that hunter delights to approach them from behind and shoot whilst their eyes are fixed on some object below. It is an exercise which gives vigor health and appetite to a hunter to shoulder his rifle at day break on a clear cold morning and wind his way up a rugged mountain over rocks and crags at length killing a fat old Ewe and taking the meat to Camp on his back: this kind of exercise gives him an appetite for his breakfast. But hunting sheep is attended with great danger in many places especially when the rocks are covered with sleet and ice. I have often passed over places where I have had to cut steps in the ice with my butcher Knife to place my feet in directly over the most frightful precipices, but being excited in the pursuit of game I would think little of danger until I had laid down to sleep at night, then it would make my blood run cold to meditate upon the scenes I had passed thro. during the day and often have I resolved never to risk myself again in such places and as often broken the resolution."

Another hunt, in February 1842, required lowering himself on a rope to retrieve his meat:

"About sun an hour high I commenced hunting among the rocks in search of Sheep but did not get a chance to shoot at any till middle of the afternoon when crawling cautiously over some shelving cliffs I discovered 10 to 12 Ewes feeding some distance below me I shot and wounded one reloaded my rifle and crept down to the place where I last saw her when I discovered two standing on the side of a precipice Shot one thro the head and she fell dead on the cliff where she stood. I then went above and fastened a cord (which I carried for the purpose) to some bushes which overhung the rocks by this means I descended and rolled her off the cliff where she had caught when she fell upwards of 100 ft. I then pulled myself up by the cord and went round the rock down to where she fell butchered her hung the meat on a tree then pursued and killed the other After butchering the last I took some of the [meat] for my supper and started up the mountain and arrived at the place where I had slept about an hour after dark I soon had a fire blazing and a side of ribs roasting and procured water by heating Stones and melting snow in a piece of skin by the time supper was over it was late in the night And I lay down and slept until morning At sun rise I started on foot to get my meat..."

The number of travelers swelled after 1840, and particularly after the California Gold Rush of 1849. Mention of wild sheep can be found in many diaries and accounts of this period, but the tone of reference changes— people were focused on gold or property, and sheep were often seen merely as wild meat available to all. Within three decades, much of the west had been altered beyond the recognition of both the Indian and the trapper, and the great sheep herds had begun to disappear.

In other parts of the world, names of other great explorers and zoologists were soon added to the roster of those associated with wild sheep and little-known lands, names unfamiliar to many of us today: P. Pallas, N. A. Severtzov, N. Przewalski, Swen Hedin, N. V. Nasanov, Douglas Carruthers, Roy Chapman Andrews, Theodore Jr. and Kermit Roosevelt, William J. Morden, James L. Clark, Ernst Schaefer, to name only a few. Today George Schaller is perhaps the foremost prac-

Bighorn rams negotiate rocky rims in western Wyoming, as they have for tens of thousands of years. The oldest fossils of bighorn sheep ever found were located in Wyoming's Trap Cave site.

titioner of that grand tradition. The material these explorer-scientists gathered was evaluated by a group of very able scientists, taxonomists and others, professionals such as R. Lydekker, N. V. Nasanov, G. Allan, I. McTaggart-Cowan, V. I. Tsalkin, the Russian trilogy of Heptner, Nasimovich and Bannikov, T. Haltenorth, and P. Pfeffer.

Unfortunately, many of the specimens, observations and conclusions reached about wild sheep were (and remain) clouded by a general lack of knowledge about the biology of wild sheep and their role in the ecology of their habitats. Much of the late nineteenth and early twentieth century literature pertaining to wild sheep deals with just describing and naming the various species and races of mountain sheep encountered, based on a few specimens representing only portions of the animals encountered. The resulting taxonomic confusion was due in large part to lack of knowledge about the seasonal and ontogenetic shedding and growth of the hair coat. Therefore, that members of the same race, whose appearance changed through the seasons as they aged, were classified formally as different subspecies depending on their age and the season they were shot. That early literature reflects great enthusiasm about various ways of quantifying the morphology (body shape and form) of specimens, giving an— apparently —objective means of assessing taxonomic differences. However, we now know that body size and proportions are not merely an effect of the hereditary factors, but are much more an expression of the environment in which these sheep grew up and resided. The problem of misused comparative morphometrics is still very much with us, and it has acquired greater significance as taxonomy has become a legal matter, actionable in courts of law, with the growth of conservation legislation. An analysis of deoxyribose nucleic acids (DNA), both of the nuclear and mitochondrial variety, provides the only way to gain an understanding of sheep phylogeny. Adaptations and phenotypic adjustments to variable environments are poor guides from which to determine relationships.

It was apparent early on that various forms of wild sheep stretched in distribution from Mediterranean islands and Asia Minor in the west, across central Asia and Siberia into North America, and then south into Mexico. This is James L. Clark's famous *The Great Arc of the Wild Sheep*, as described in a book by that name. No wild sheep ever penetrated south into the Andes of South America (and in fact, virtually no mammal of Siberian-Eurasian origin ever penetrated into South America during the Pleistocene). Nor did wild sheep enter North Africa or Arabia (although the distantly-related aoudads did so and spread widely within the Sahara desert, while ibex penetrated south to the highlands of Abyssinia). Even the mouflon, found on the Mediterranean islands of Corsica, Sardinia and Cyprus turn out to be introductions by human hand early in the Neolithic age (about 8,000 years ago), based on recent archaeological evidence. The mouflons on Corsica, Sardinia and Cyprus are thus ancient populations of feral domestic sheep. These small sheep displaced preexisting island faunas of dwarfed large mammals. The origin of these island mouflons, judging from the development of their bibs, manes and horns, appears to be central Persia where free-living (Esfahan) mouflons, with similar social organs, are found. The Cypriot mouflon appears to be derived from Turkish populations. These 'island mouflons' have smaller brain capacity than their counterparts on the mainland, a likely artifact of early domestication. Domestication costs brain.

What was not readily appreciated by early explorers and zoologists (and is still not universally

comprehended by modern taxonomists) is that the Arc of Wild Sheep was composed of sheep that were — biologically— very different animals. This is a critically important point to keep in mind when addressing wild sheep management, because what is known of one form of wild sheep is often not valid for another. Eurasian sheep, for example, are not difficult to manage. North American sheep are!

The profound differences in adaptation are not diminished by the fact that in zoological gardens almost any form of sheep will hybridize with another. This phenomenon is not unknown to keepers of waterfowl, where species mixing in captivity can create the most unlikely mongrels. However, that has not had taxonomic repercussions. Unfortunately it has had taxonomic repercussions in mountain sheep, with some European taxonomists proclaiming all wild sheep to be a single species on the strength of zoo mongrels. Such a view fails to consider the fusion — or lack thereof—of subspecies in nature. To understand the wild sheep, we must first briefly review the history of wild sheep.

THE ORIGINS OF WILD SHEEP

Paleontology has not been a great help in deciphering the past of mountain sheep. There are good reasons for this: in the precipitous and rocky terrain favored by wild sheep around the world, specimens are unlikely to remain intact for very long as moving rock rubble eventually crushes all bone. We have, consequently, very few fossil specimens to go by. Moreover, wild sheep, as classical Ice Age mammals, are a phenomenon of the past two million years in which upward of 20 glaciations came and went. Granted the profound ecological differences between glacial and interglacial periods, large shifts occurred among sheep populations and habitats as glaciers expanded and contracted. As we shall see below, each dispersal of sheep (typically associated with glacial contractions) generates very large-bodied forms. In the absence of supplemental evidence, these 'dispersal forms' are easily confused for another species when compared to the small maintenance-type sheep in established populations. Maintenance forms (typically associated with glacial expansion), are often short of resources due to interspecific competition for food, and very small in body size. The differences in body mass between large and small body forms may be four-fold or even greater. Thus large and small sheep pop up in the sparse fossil record, but little can be said about them except that they were large or small.

We do, however, have zoogeographic patterns to decipher, provided we get a handle on what fea-tures are primitive and which are advanced. Then zoogeography can reveal the flow of evolution. Secondly, the laboratory analysis of various DNA patterns can often reveal the branching and speciation of sheep. Collectively, these two distinct avenues of analyses indicate that mountain sheep are one of the branches of the goat-antelope group, a group which arose long before the Ice Ages in the Tertiary period in tropical southeast Asia. In southeast Asia we find to this day the most primitive of the goat-antelopes, the serow and goral. As with other original members of a family's evolutionary radiation, so these primitive goat-antelopes are aggressive defenders of material resources on small territories, a fact that characteristically shapes their biology about this particular form of competition. They typically form pair bonds or family groups of pugnacious, uniformly-colored look-alikes whose horns are used purely as stabbing weapons. For example, serow have been known to attack dogs and hunters, and even to have killed black bears.

Just as in other mammalian families (our own included) there was a break away by goat-antelopes from the tropical territorial system in dense forests. Species advanced into more open landscapes, where gregarious life provided significant benefits over the old pair-bonds, so essential to territorial defense. In the open these primitive goat-antelopes formed herds, an important means to minimize predation by sharing the risks of attack. In these so-called 'selfish herds,' the bigger herd size resulted in reducing the risks to the individual from an attacking predator— provided that the individual was in reasonable health and did not fall behind during escapes. Life in the 'selfish herd' also changed the kind of weapons required among these primitive goat-antelopes. There was a switch from weapons that inflicted severe damage (by piercing, tearing, or bruising the body's surface) to weapons that allowed bloodless, playful, sporting head-to-head tussling. That kind of change is typical in the evolution of all horned and antlered ungulates. One constraining factor remained: the goat-antelopes and their descendants apparently always selected for habitats that included steep slopes and rock, be it forested, grassed-over, snow-covered, or glaciated.

The evolutionary progression then moved from tropical, to temperate, to cold, to glaciated mountains. This happened late in the Tertiary period and in the Pleistocene (or Ice Ages). This was a step-wise progression which, in part, is preserved to this day. The steps surviving extinction are the serow, thar, aoudads, urials/mouflons, and advanced sheep. Note the progressive increase horn size, accompanied by an eventual loss of long display hairs, among this group of species. The progression indicated is not one of direct ancestor descendant. Too many extinctions took place for that. However, the progression approximates the steps that sheep (and true goats) passed through as a process of continually refining their adaptations to their surroundings. This progression is seen again and again in various families of large mammals. It reflects the changes from tropical resource defender to Ice Age giants living at the fertile, productive edge of glaciers. Primitive goat-antelopes compare with orangutan, gorilla, sun bear, muntjac, and Indian rhinoceros of other taxonomic groups. Goat-antelopes evolved into more modern forms in the harsh and variable environments of the Ice Ages, becoming such advanced species as the extinct shrub-oxen and musk oxen, argalis, bighorns, ibex, and mountain goats. These species are comparable to Ice Age species from other families, such as woolly mammoth, woolly rhinoceros, Irish elk, moose, caribou, and humans— splendid Ice Age species all.

The evolutionary progression discussed above represents changes associated with adaptations typical of species as they move from the climatically benign but biologically competitive hell of the tropics, to the biologically benign but climatically demanding periglacial, Arctic and Alpine zones. It is a journey from a great poverty of material resources (coupled with extreme selection for efficiency) in the tropics to great seasonal abundance of such resources in more northerly climates, and the concomitant evolution of luxury organs, like the extravagant horns of bighorn or argali rams, the magnificent antlers of the Irish elk or moose, the luxurious hair coat of the rutting bison bull, or the shapely fat deposits in human females that captivate our attention and imagination to this day.

Wild sheep are thus a product of their adaptations to steep, open, grassy or tundra-like terrain in areas of increasingly harsher seasonal climates. These harsher climates are also typified by greater soil fertility. Snow and ice accumulated over centuries form glaciers, which devour and pulverize rock in their slow advance downhill, finally depositing the resultant fine particles as fertile silt carried in annual melt waters. Accumulated in stream bends and on floodplains, this fine silt dries and is carried off by air

Mature Dall's sheep rams 'clash' in Alaska's Denali Park. It is usually the younger and slightly smaller ram that initiates the clash, and who gives up after the larger ram catches clash after clash successfully.

TOM TIETZ

currents to settle down among organic matter as fertile loess. Through this process, the world's major bread baskets derive their fertility to this day. Wild sheep in their dispersal along with fellow travelers (in particular the closely related goat and the red deer) followed, and retreated from, the expansion and contraction of glaciers, benefitting from the seasonally abundant forage these areas provided. Consequently, we find sheep, goats and red deer speciating concurrently, side by side. Even today, primitive subspecies of sheep are found with primitive subspecies of goats and red deer—and vice versa.

Somewhere along the line, the wild sheep split into two distinct groups. One remained in close contact with goats while the other moved on, leaving the true goats far behind. We recognize these two groups of wild sheep today as Old World (subgenus *Ovis*) and New World sheep (subgenus *Pachyceros*), respectively. That designation is a bit confusing, as New World sheep occupy a range in eastern Siberia so large as to rival that of sheep in North America. The Old World sheep, in response to competition for resources with goats, partitioned the types of habitat they used. Goats remained on the steepest portions of the mountain, where their body form was best adapted to 'rock hopping' and exploiting small patches of high-quality forage largely inaccessible to most predators, while the sheep adapted to the more gentle rolling slopes, plateaus, and foothills where both food and predators were more abundant. While goats continued to evolve the stocky, short-legged body of rock-jumpers, the Old World sheep, (be they primitive or advanced) adopted the body form and abilities of speedy runners. Technically we call such runners 'cursors.' Old World sheep adapted as a particular kind of cursors, namely, the long-legged cursors. As long-legged cursors, Old World sheep adapted to run swiftly over uneven, broken terrain, whereas the short-legged cursors (such as the saiga antelope and the addax or desert oryx) run over relatively smooth surfaces that permit a minimum of foot and body lift. A comparable long legged cursor in North America, to illustrate the point, is the pronghorn of western plains.

In contrast, the New World sheep —free of competition from goats— opted to remain rock hoppers. Consequently, American mountain sheep have retained compact, ibex-like body shapes and sizes.

Mountain goats are adapted to utilize the very steepest portions of the mountains, and utilize some foods such as cliff-growing alpine firs and dwarf birches, that sheep do not.

Body size in mountain sheep is curvilinear with latitude, as it is with other large mammals. That is, wild sheep increase in size from south to north, but reverse at about 60°N and rapidly diminish in body size with higher latitudes. However, since sheep are mountain dwellers, one must compute altitude into this equation as altitude substitutes climatically for latitude. When this is done, the equation predicts that wild sheep in North America should reach maximum body size in the Rocky Mountains between 48-50°N —which happens to fit reality. That is, south and north of these latitudes sheep decline in body size (excepting some populations which happen to be severely affected by environment, positive or otherwise). Thus bighorns on reclaimed mine sites in west-central Alberta at about 52°N have grown into the largest-bodied bighorns ever, in response to local, favorable conditions. In general however, body size appears to be a function of the duration of time in summer in which sheep are able to live free from want. The longer this time-period, the bigger the sheep. Clearly, northern sheep, experiencing a very short summer and vegetation period, do not have enough time to grow large. Conversely, desert sheep, whose vegetation season may be curtailed by aridity, also do not have enough days with luxurious food to grow large.

Body size of any animal is a reflection of many factors in addition to environment and predators. Another factor that contributed to controlling body size of wild sheep was the need for young animals to be of sufficient size at birth to survive potentially inclement weather at lambing time, and to grow quickly enough in the season period of plenty to survive weaning and a scarcity of resources during its first winter. We suspect that the typical 8-9 pounds of body mass of newborn lambs is an optimum size under northern or high altitude conditions for sheep. New World sheep are notorious for giving birth to only a single lamb of that size. The giant sheep or argali of the Old World sheep group, however, typically give birth to two lambs of that size. Consequently, if one unit of metabolic mass gives rise to one 8 pound lamb, it would seem that a body delivering two such lambs needs to be two metabolic masses, i.e., twice as large. And that's exactly what we find in the giant sheep. Since metabolic body size is a function of weight raised to the three-quarter power, two metabolic sizes translates into absolute body mass differences of 2.45. That's how much larger argalis are, on average, than American wild sheep. Such a large body mass, however, also means that argalis cannot be rock hoppers, reinforcing their ad-

aptations as long-legged cursors. To fuel their large body they need twice the daily food intake and must, therefore, cover twice the feeding area beyond protecting cliffs as compared to New World sheep. Even as long-legged runners, such animals may often be too far from the security of cliffs to insure their safety if surprised by a predator, and their large body mass depresses acceleration. It's therefore safer for giant sheep to abandon rock hopping as a security strategy and to maximize their survival by spotting predators far off and reducing their risk by an ability for speedy, enduring running.

The gestation period of New World sheep is three to four weeks longer than that of Old World sheep. New World sheep share this extended gestation period with elk, each as advanced Siberian Northerners, compared to their more primitive ancestral counterparts from latitudes with shorter winters. This extended gestation period implies that mountain sheep adapted to areas that had much longer and more severe winters than those experienced by Old World sheep and goats, an adaptation usually associated with greater life expectancy. Old World sheep, in contrast, adapted for high reproduction rates, typically associated with shorter adult life expectancy, a trait that furthermore suggests that Old World sheep are better dispersers than American type sheep.

When Old and New World sheep separated is not clear from the fossil record, but it must have been a long time ago, possibly as early as the beginning of the major Ice Ages of the Pleistocene about two million years ago. The fact is that New World sheep moved far to the north, occupying what is now Siberia. Since Alaska and the Yukon during glacial times were a mere extension of eastern Siberia, New World sheep must have entered Alaska at an early date. We have some inkling from the fossil record that elk and caribou were in Alaska at least a million years ago, but they may have been there much earlier. One small jaw bone found at El Golfo de Santa Clara in Sonora, Mexico, and aged at 750,000-900,000 years, appears to be that of a small sheep. This would place it early within the Irvingtonian mammal age. It's not unlikely that sheep did enter North America then, as this was the time of entry by several Siberian species

TOM TIETZ

Pronghorn, like Old World wild sheep, are 'cursors' adapted to running over uneven terrain to escape their predators.

into North America including the ancestors of American mammoths, a number of early and very large shrub and musk oxen, and the hare. There is no evidence, however, that sheep survived after this early entry. New World sheep may have entered the southern portions of North America once again later, although just how late is subject to speculation. Some bones found in the Mojave desert of California and aged at about 350,000 years appear to be sheep bones. It is tempting to suggest that New World sheep were part of an eastern Siberian fauna that entered southern North America at the beginning of the Rancholabrean mammal age only a little before this period in geological time. The eastern Siberian steppe bison entered North America, to evolve into the huge American long-horned bison, the type species of the Rancholabrean mammal age. A primitive Siberian moose also entered southern portions of the continent, giving rise to the stag moose. Conditions for preserving moose and bison in the fossil record are far superior to those preserving mountain sheep. It is thus possible that sheep were a tiny part of the early Rancholabrean mammal age in North America. They certainly were members of the late Rancholabrean age, as disclosed by paleontological digs and compiled meticulously by George T. Jefferson of the Anza-Borrego Desert State Park in California and several colleagues.

The first definitive find of the New World bighorn sheep dates back to the Sangamon interglacial, the last interglacial period preceding the Wisconsinian glaciation of about 100,000 years ago. These early sheep, found in Wyoming's Trap Cave site, are clearly recognizable as bighorns. These sheep would be expected to be colonizers from the southern stock of bighorns. Research into differences in mitochondrial and nuclear DNA carried out by Rob Ramey of the University of Colorado and Walter Boyce of the University of California at Davis and their colleagues indicate a significant gap between the Rocky Mountain and the desert sheep, but considerable similarity between populations of desert sheep. These molecular investigations support the conclusion that there was a split between the main stocks of the Rocky Mountain and desert races of bighorn sheep many thousands of years ago.

In the Wisconsinian glaciation that followed, evidence of bighorns vanished from the Trap Cave deposits, but they reappeared in deposits from tens of thousands of years later with the beginning of the deglaciation. These fossils were found along with those of Colombian mammoth, American cheetahs, big American lions, and the great carnivorous bull-dog bear. Remains of bighorns are also found here and there in Wyoming, Nevada, Idaho, Utah, and California in fossil deposits dating to the height of the last glaciation, about 18,000 to 22,000 years ago. Their bones appear along those of mountain goats, as is the case in life today, as well as with those of the extinct stocky mountain deer *Navahoceros*. They are found in cave deposits, which should hardly surprise anyone as wild sheep do not hesitate entering and exploring caves. Fossil remains are also found in desert regions along with those of the fleet-footed American camel, long-legged American llama, and native American horse species. Bighorn bones have also been found in lake deposits close to mountain slopes, along with bones of shrub oxen and woodland musk oxen. These late glacial sheep appear to be part of a wave of colonization that swept much of western North America and populated the expanse of mountains occupied by sheep within this millennium. This great wave of colonization was apparently complete before the massive extinctions that virtually swept away most of the indigenous and unique large mammal fauna that occupied North America. The late glacial bighorns were much larger than current bighorns, approaching the argalis of Outer Mongolia in size and proportions.

The late glacial was a very good time for bighorns. Not surprisingly, wild North American sheep to this day are glacier followers that do very well indeed living about (and at times on) larger alpine glaciers. That raises the question why sheep had failed to populate western North America earlier. One reason appears to be the severe predation pressure which affected sheep and changed them into bighorns, analogous to the predation pressure that shaped the long-horned Siberian steppe bison into the huge, long-horned, highly cursorial American long-horned bison. This super bison is thus analogous to northern Siberian long-horned bison in the same way that bighorns are analogous to northern thin-horned sheep and snow sheep. North America was home to a diverse, spectacular predator fauna during the late Pleistocene as compared to Eurasia: big American lions of the kind found today in Africa or India (but much larger in body size); Siberian tigers were found in Alaska, and further south occurred two kinds of lion-sized cats— the massive, long-fanged, gregarious saber-toothed cat and the gracile, long-necked, swiftly running scimitar-toothed cat. As opposed to the stabbing saber-toothed cat, the less well-known scimitar-toothed cat probably ran alongside escaping mammoths, horses, camels or bison and with a swift, well-aimed bite sliced open their bellies with its broad, but thin-bladed, razor sharp ca nines, spilling the victims intestines, allowing its prey to tangle in its own gut and die of massive hemorrhage. There were big American cheetahs, mountain lions, jaguars, huge dire wolves, and coyotes in this assemblage of predators in North America, as well as four species of bears, the modern black bear plus three species of short-faced bears (one of which was a huge super-predator of the plains). Grizzly bears were absent, but came into North America from Siberia after the bull-dog bear went extinct post-glacially about 12,000 years ago.

As might be expected given this huge assemblage of predators, Rancholabrean ungulates, fossil and living, show the signs of severe predation pressure in the diversity and sophistication of anti-predator strategies they evolved. While large Ice Age mammals of Euasia appear to have been limited in abundance by shortages of material resources, comparable North American species were likely limited by predation. This suggestion leads to expectations that we can verify in the fossil record, since shortages of material resources (food) will result in gradual dwarfing of species and to a gradual improvement in the efficiency of food pro-

cessing organs. Put another way, Eurasian species should shrink in size over time, and evolve larger and more complex teeth. In contrast, North American counterparts to those species should remain the same size or evolve to be even larger, if food was not in short supply in a predator-limited fauna. Further, we would expect little improvement in teeth or other feeding organs once the Siberian ungulates adapted to North America. As an example, descendants of a moose that entered North America with a primitive snout would be expected to retain that 'primitive' form into modern time, while descendants of moose in Eurasia would be expected to continue evolving ever advanced "moose noses". North American species should also demonstrate ever-increasing improvements and greater diversity in anti-predator adaptations. In this respect North American mammals do not disappoint.

One result of severe predation on horned or antlered species that seek safety in running and are non-territorial is the evolution of extra-large horns or antlers. Predation pressure translates into bigger horns. This has nothing to do with horns as weapons, but horn <u>size</u> as a proxy for successful foraging,

Female wild sheep, like this Rocky Mountain bighorn ewe in Oregon's Lostine River herd, must strive to maximize the growth of their lambs if they are to survive weaning and the coming winter.

15

and horn <u>symmetry</u> as a proxy for superior health. The logic is as follows: runners from open landscapes require large, well-developed babies at birth, and their mothers must provide a rich milk supply so that the young may grow rapidly to survivable size. Therefore, females must be exceptionally good at shifting nutrients consumed from requirements for maintenance and growth into gestation and milk production. Such females should search for a mate whose hereditary make-up would help to insure that their daughters can also grow superior babies and produce more and richer milk. What are the signs of this capability among males? Males with the largest luxury organs, such as large horns or antlers and ornate coats of hair, since these reflect males that can identify and defend, if necessary, the best feeding areas. Large horns and antlers in males show positive correlation with age (i.e., survival) and efficiency in the identification and utilization of resources. Matching those traits with the ability to maximize the size of babies and the richness of the milk produced by females will maximize the likelihood that the animal can pass along its genetic material to future generations.

The increasing size of the horns of bighorns, their very large body size, and cursorial body proportions during the late glacial all speak to severe predation pressure. So do the extreme body shapes of other members of the late Rancholabrean fauna. *Navahoceras*, the big mountain deer found in the southern Rockies, had a body shape much like the mountain goat. This body shape is unique to North America, an expression of extremes in rock climbing ability. The stag moose was farther along than modern moose in fleeing smoothly over low barriers, and was narrowly confined to the edges of the huge proglacial lakes, its escape terrain. Colombian mammoths were exceptionally long-legged (due to their great size and body structure, increasing stride length is the only way for elephants to increase speed). Pronghorns have eyes larger than those of elephants and hooves farther evolved for running than any comparable Old World species.

Among the predators, the high frequency of broken and healed bones in Rancholabrean carnivores speaks to severe contests between predators and prey. So does the surprisingly large brain of the extinct American lion as compared to modern African lions.

Yet another line evidence is found in the behavioral plasticity of the survivors of the Rancholabrean mammal age, in animals such as coyotes, black bears, mountain lions, white-tailed and black-tailed deer, pronghorn and peccary. All of these species have shown remarkable abilities to coexist in a landscape dominated by other species (notably humans), whereas late-glacial immigrants

Although desert bighorns show some remarkable adaptations to arid conditions, they show fewer adaptations than such 'true' desert-dwellers as the aoudad of northern Africa, demonstrating that they are still in the process of evolving to North America's postglacial desert environments.

from eastern Siberia, such as gray wolf, grizzly bear, or wolverine have not.

After contemplating all of the foregoing evidence, it is no surprise that bighorns become a most predictable part of the fossil and archeological record following the demise of the Rancholabrean fauna. They almost certainly spread and multiplied, emerging as a benefactor of the great megafaunal extinctions. Other winners were the white-tailed deer, the pronghorn, the bison, and the peccary as well as the adaptable coyote, black bear, and mountain lion. The archeological record reveals that bighorns and mule deer were a dominant part of the diet of many native tribes of Indians well before Columbus entered this continent in 1492.

Before we continue, let us return briefly to eastern Siberia where we expect the ancestors of our wild sheep. The only fossils of sheep found there so far are of the *Pachyceros* or thinhorn/snow sheep type. However, there are currently no finds older than the last glaciation when these sheep occurred several hundred miles to the south of their current distribution, along with cold-adapted species such as mammoth, reindeer, and arctic fox, and also with roe deer. These sheep occurred even on what is today the island of Sakhalin. Snow sheep also occurred on ranges presently occupied by the giant argalis. There may have been simultaneous overlapping use by both

species, although differences in adaptations between these two kinds of sheep would argue against it. Snow sheep show up among the food remains of ancient people, apparently including even Neanderthal man. Although the fossil-bearing strata that might have preserved records of wild sheep were largely lost where continental or mountain glaciers plowed up the landscape, it seems evident that New World type sheep in Siberia did not disperse southward into warm latitudes to become adapted to hot desert climates as occurred in North America. One can only conclude that Old World sheep and ibex barred the way.

Back in North America, the long exposure to southern conditions generated bighorns that are able to dwell under desert conditions. Various attributes speak of this, above and beyond the ability of desert bighorns to dehydrate and go without water for long stretches of time. The large horns of desert bighorn females speak of severe contests over point sources of standing water, a precious resource in the desert. The extended lambing and rutting seasons demonstrate adaptations to long seasons of high temperatures. Nevertheless, desert bighorns have not gone as far in adapting to desert conditions as, for instance, has the aoudad from the Sahara desert. In Rancholabrean times camels, llamas, and a number of burro-like horse species may have kept bighorns confined to higher, colder and wetter montane elevations. It is thus quite likely that bighorns are relatively recent inhabitants of hot deserts, still in the process of adapting to these climates. Put differently, bighorns became beneficiaries of the great late Pleistocene extinctions that decimated North America's native megafauna. After extinctions removed many competitors for food and space, such as native burros, mountain deer, Conklin's pronghorn, llamas and shrub oxen, and after the extinction of many of North America's great predators including the great carnivorous bull-dog bear and the American cheetah about 12,000 years before the present time, bighorns radiated widely. While it remains unclear just what caused the extinction of many of these ungulates, the decline in ungulate numbers is likely associated with the extinction of several top carnivores. These extinctions coincide roughly with a large cold-pulse, well after the glaciers must have melted into low, flat ice fields. Did frequent meeting of warm Pacific air and cold high Arctic air generate icy rains and ice crusts over southern plains, starving out the large herbivores? Why should plains and desert species be the first to go extinct, followed thousands of years later by forest species? Why did the big mountain deer go extinct while bighorns and mountain goats survived and flourished?

Humans were part of a late glacial wave of eastern Siberian mammals to colonize North America during and after megafaunal extinctions of some 10,000 to 12,000 years ago. Humans may have had little ability to colonize a continent characterized by the huge, diverse Rancholabrean predators and their pugnacious prey prior to that time, but afterwards an increasing body of evidence indicates that they rapidly eliminated the Colombian mammoth, and then preyed on native bison until a long-horned Siberian steppe bison appeared in the south, probably forcing changes in hunting techniques. Bighorns became an important human prey shortly thereafter and before the climatic optimum, or Altithermal period, of 7,000 years ago.

WILD SHEEP IN THE OLD AND NEW WORLD

There are five species of wild sheep, two Old World and three New World species. However, one of the New World species, the Siberian snow sheep, is found in the Old World only. An excellent source on the distribution and present status of these species is the volume **Wild Sheep and Goats and their Relatives** compiled and edited by Professor David Shackleton of the University of British Columbia on behalf of Caprini Specialist Group of the International Union for the Conservation of Nature (IUCN). This Conservation Action Plan, published in 1997, covers not only each subspecies on a country-by-country basis, but also provides an up-to-date taxonomy and deals with crucial policy and management issues. We accept here the taxonomy accepted by the Caprini Specialist Group.

The most primitive of the wild sheep species are the urials of the Old World. The Latin name of this species has been in flux, and nothing is gained by reviewing it. We have called them by their common name, urials. The name proposed by the IUCN group is *Ovis orientalis*, and refers to a species group that also includes the mouflons. Urials have 58 chromosomes, diffuse rump patches, bibs and neck manes and a short gestation period. Like all Old World sheep they are cursors, trading high reproductive rates for duration of life. They typically bear twins but have the short life expectancies, typical of Old World sheep.

The mouflons, very similar to urials, have 54 chromosomes, sharply delineated rump patches, a dark tail, and a neck mane. Unlike most wild sheep, female mouflons have no horns. The mouflons integrate with urials producing hybrid populations at the contact zone in present-day Iran. Sheep in the contact zone have between 58 and 54 chromosomes. Mouflons are the ancestors of all domestic sheep. The European mouflons from Corsica and Sardinia, as indicated earlier, appear to be feral populations of very early domestic sheep transplanted to these islands by the hand of man in the Neolithic or New Stone Age when Mediterranean islands were colonized by humans. The same applies to the small mouflon on

Mouflon sheep are the precursors of all domestic sheep.

Cyprus. European mouflons have been widely introduced throughout Europe and North America.

The third Old World sheep species are the giant sheep of inner Asia, the argalis. These sheep have 56 chromosomes. The development of beards, horns and rump patch characteristics differ between races. This species contains the largest and most spectacular living sheep. In the desert regions of Inner and Outer Mongolia, however, some dwarf argalis are found, barely as large as small Dall's sheep. Argalis of advanced subspecies are found with advanced ibex and elk, while primitive argali races are found with primitive red deer and blue sheep. Argalis occupy the climatically most extreme mountain environments among Old World sheep. Though superficially similar in their social behavior to bighorn sheep, the males, unlike bighorns, are harem herders.

The species of New World sheep living in eastern Siberia are the snow sheep. They are found from the Chuckchi Peninsula in sight of the Bering Straight to central Siberia, a distance equivalent from Point Barrow in Alaska to Baja California. They are by and large the size of Dall's sheep. Some have small rump patches similar to bighorns. Others have a rump patch that is diffuse and encompasses the hind legs. These sheep have neither bib nor neck manes. Their horns have characteristics reminiscent of both bighorns and thin-horned sheep. They live in the coldest of climates, and have evolved long, fluffy hair. They may feed in winter extensively on ground lichens. Some northern snow sheep have 52 chromosomes, the lowest number among all wild sheep.

The second species of New World sheep are the thinhorn or Dall's sheep, inclusive of the dark-colored Stone's sheep. The white Dall's sheep occupy the mountains of Alaska, the Yukon, the western edge of the Northwest Territory and extreme northwestern British Columbia. Dall's sheep distribution surrounds the northern, western and eastern edge of the Stone's sheep distribution, and there is a broad band of integration between the two forms, giving rise to the light saddle-backed or fannin sheep. This zone of integration speaks for a long separation of Dall's and Stones's sheep, and contact during post-glacial expansion of their respective populations. Light-colored snow sheep on the northern Chuckchi Peninsula in Siberia suggest that Dall's sheep spread back into Siberia before the Bering Land Bridge was flooded late in the Pleistocene following glacial melt. However, the dispersal dynamics of the thinhorn sheep in eastern Siberia and Alaska remain presently a mystery. We have reason to suspect that from the Alaska/Yukon/Chukchi region (the old Beringia now submerged by the shallow Bering Straits) very similar animals moved south into North America and west into Asia. Elk, genetically almost identical to our North American elk, are found now far away from Beringia both to the southwest in the Altai and Tien Shan mountains of central Asia and to the southeast across much of North America. Our North American moose is an east

JOHN BOONE

Siberian species which is found as far west as Outer Mongolia and as far east as the Atlantic seaboard. American-type caribou are found in Eastern Siberia and Kamchatka. A variety of snow sheep, very similar to our American wild sheep, is found west to central Siberia. However, excepting the Kamchatka and north Kamchatka forms, the snow sheep have rump patches different from American mountain sheep, and thinhorn sheep have 54 chromosome pairs, two more than snow sheep. Light-colored snow sheep in extreme eastern Siberia suggest integration with Dall's sheep, as do the so-called fannin sheep in the opposite direction, intergrades between Stone's and Dall's sheep. We shall have to wait further research to discover the history of the snow sheep in Siberia and of the thinhorn sheep in northern North America.

To the south, and not overlapping with thinhorn sheep, are the bighorn sheep. They differ from thinhorn sheep in small dental, cranial and rump patch differences as well by having larger horns. Bighorn sheep evolved in their southern distributions into the desert sheep, which are adapted to hot and dry conditions. In the north, bighorn sheep and Stone's sheep approach one another in British Columbia, but do not meet. Like the thinhorn sheep, bighorn sheep have 54 chromosomes. Current research on population genetics in bighorns points to significant regional meta-populations that have little affinity to subspecies described on the basis of comparative morphometrics. However, the latter is a most inadequate taxonomic tool as it confounds genetic with environmental, epistatic and true statistical variation. Taxonomy thus needs to be reevaluated from scratch. The genetic research also indicates considerable random genetic drift, as is expected if natural selection on genetic differences is only expected to be severe in extreme environments, as the ability of phenotypes to adjust is usually able to override genetic differences between individuals. ℛℛ

Captive Kazakhstan argali, showing the large body and long legs of an Old World 'cursor' type sheep.

Chapter Two

CONSIDERATIONS IN WILD SHEEP MANAGEMENT

The first goal of wild sheep management in North America is to retain the present geographic distribution of the species. The second is to expand that distribution as closely as possible to its former size in areas that were occupied prior to widespread extermination of wild sheep in the nineteenth century, at least in those habitats still suited for reintroduction, and even beyond ranges formerly occupied where suitable habitat exists. The third goal is to retain a maximum of the evolved genetic diversity. Of course, these goals simply help to ensure that wild sheep will continue to exist as a sustainable component of the landscape. While this is a necessary condition for the manager of wild sheep populations, it is not sufficient to provide much guidance for management actions. Management practices may differ widely based on the objectives for which a herd is to be managed. For example, a herd managed to provide recreational hunting opportunity of a highly desirable native game animal will differ markedly from a herd managed to provide viewing and photographic opportunities.

Fundamental to developing an approach to management is an understanding of the survival strategy of the species. Research in the 1960s indicated that American mountain sheep (<u>but not Asiatic sheep!</u>) were reproductively 'K-strategists.' This is a short-hand term used by biologists to describe a species adapted to exploitation of climax plant communities, a species who strives to maximize its population size through individual longevity, low rates of reproduction coupled with heavy investment in maternal care, the successful rearing of relatively few offspring, complex social behavior which allows many animals to interact on a regular basis, and a precise strategy for exploiting all available suitable habitat, both in space and in time as conditions change.

North American sheep were historically adapted to deal with severe energy shortages in winter; desert bighorns have developed remarkable strategies to deal with water and resource scarcity in desert environments. Although Dall's, Stone's and

DON L. MacCARTER

North American wild sheep, like these desert bighorns in New Mexico, are 'k-strategists' adapted through low reproductive rates and long livelihood to fully exploit available habitat.

some Rocky Mountain bighorn sheep populations endure long periods of extreme cold and darkness, these animals typically live to quite old ages as compared to many other species of a comparable size, maximizing their opportunity to breed and thus contribute their genetic material to future generations. All North American sheep typically give birth to only a single precocial lamb (in contrast with Old World sheep) born after an extended gestation period. Ewes in extreme circumstances may extend maternal care to yearlings, thereby effectively switching from an annual mode of reproduction to a biannual mode. This extended the sexual maturation of females, and appeared to favor survival of yearling males. Bill Wishart, Beth MacCallum and Jon Jorgenson showed experimentally that in Alberta ewes lived on home ranges that are essentially an ecologically <u>closed</u> system, so that the loss of one member of a home range group redistributed the forage resources to others. Thus, the loss of any individual benefitted the survivors by boosting the potential for reproduction among the surviving ewes, as well as the growth of body and horns in their offspring. This feedback system appeared to be sensitive, and limited reproduction to the minimum. Nevertheless, under very favorable environmental and demographic conditions, wild sheep populations had the potential to double in as little as three years.

Research has demonstrated that there are notable differences in phenotypic (body) size, and especially in behavior and ecology, of individuals within and between populations. Managing all populations alike is thus not warranted if there is opportunity to study and determine the operational constraints and opportunities affecting populations. The complex social system of wild sheep appears to minimize the energetic costs of body maintenance and, left intact, to maximize reproduction, survival, and the growth of body and horns.

Wild sheep maintain their home ranges as kind of a 'living tradition' based on knowledge of seasonal feeding and travel routes passed down from generation to generation. Disruption of those traditions and the mechanisms that operate to ensure their passage to future generations may result in suitable habitat being 'forgotten' and thereby lost to future generations of the affected population, threatening the very existence of some herds. Although wild sheep are very effective in passing knowledge of suitable habitats to members of their population, these animals have great difficulties colonizing new or abandoned ranges. As a result,

diseases (particularly those obtained through contacts with domestic sheep) have had devastating effects on bighorn populations, by destroying both the affected animals and the ability of one generation to pass a knowledge of suitable habitats on to the survivors. Outbreaks of pneumonia in particular have swept away even animals that only days earlier had been the very picture of vibrant health. Desert bighorns have perhaps suffered the greatest losses through diseases, especially distressing because populations of desert bighorns often exist in ranges with low carrying capacity and critical dependence on a few specific seasonal requirements, such as water sources, knowledge of which is absolutely essential to succeeding generations. Desert bighorns have currently the lowest abundance of all races of wild sheep and a distressing record of recovery.

All in all, research has shown that wild sheep could not be treated by wildlife managers like white-tailed deer, which have a much different survival strategy. Instead, wild sheep require a management regime uniquely their own. Just to maintain a static population of wild sheep requires attention to the potential for disruption of home range traditions and of the social systems (as well as to the potential for exposure to diseases), in addition to the more typical concerns about available range and its quality. Moreover, experience has shown that wild sheep populations can easily be lost. Once severely depleted, whatever the cause, wild sheep may fail to recover despite apparently adequate range conditions and protection, leaving behind a suitable range permanently void of sheep.

Once sheep are gone from a region they are surprisingly difficult to restore. There are currently scores of small bighorn populations which fail to expand and whose very viability in reproductive success and survival from year to year is cause for concern. This is true even for fairly substantial populations; Joel Berger has shown that populations of under one hundred animals have relatively high rates of extinction.

Despite the fact that, to untrained eyes, wild sheep appear to be inept at expanding into apparently available but vacant ranges, thereby appearing to act blatantly against their own elementary self-interest, there are some very good biological reasons for this odd behavior. Wild sheep exploit grasslands, an ecologically rather stable habitat, which regenerates itself after wildfires. By contrast, mature forests do not regenerate after a fire into mature forests, but come back as forests only decades or centuries later after several different plant communities have

Fires set back forest development, removing the shrubs and trees that invade grasslands critical as feeding areas for wild sheep. Grasslands typically regenerate quickly, offering succulent forage.

successively occupied the burn site. That's a crucial distinction, one very important to wild sheep. Over the last two million years wild sheep have mastered the strategies required to survive both the long glacial periods (which averaged about 75,000 years in length) as well as the interglacials (which lasted on average about 25,000 years). Climatically, these two periods— glacials and interglacials— are entirely different, and the ecological changes associated with moving from one to another are cataclysmic. The prime difference, as a far as sheep are concerned, is the spread of dense timber during the interglacial period, extinguishing grasslands and sheep habitat in the process. Wild sheep are avid glacier followers, doing very well among open alpine habitats in the vicinity of glaciers, as occurs today in the Yukon and Alaska. When temperatures rise and large continental glaciers melt away, coniferous forests spread over the land once glaciated, and timberlines ascend mountains. Consequently, sheep populations are put into a very precarious position by this change in climate. Their grassland habitats shrink dramatically in area and are fractured into ever smaller, ever more widely dispersed patches. Sheep countermand this fragmentation of critical habitat by keeping track of small pieces of distant habitat, stitching these into functional home ranges via migratory traditions that are passed from one generation to the next, from mother to daughter, from big ram to small ram.

During an interglacial period, when habitat is scarce and fragmented, it makes no sense for youngsters to disperse so that each may search for viable habitat on its own. All available habitat is already known to the resident sheep population, and contained within a migratory tradition. It is much safer for a young sheep to merely follow older animals and pick up their home range knowledge than it is to strike out searching for what is already found— suitable habitat in a sea of dangerous non-habitat. Dispersal is a dangerous activity, one that can destroy the future well-being of populations either through the death of the individual sheep or by isolation that precludes social and genetic interchange. Consequently, daughters follow mothers to their varied and dispersed sites, while sons pick some large-horned ram to follow. The larger the horns of the ram, the better it has eaten or the longer it has lived. In either case, the youngster gains an oppor-

Maintenance and Dispersal Phenotypes

One of the now well-documented findings of animal scientists is that the body dimensions of animals (including humans) changes as a response to diet— and that those changes do not affect all portions of the body equally. Well before the second World War, a group of British animal scientists working on livestock and (independently) a group of German researchers working on red deer discovered the profound effect of nutrition not only on the size, but also on the proportions of the body. Put simply, sheep or deer on a "low plane" of diet were not only smaller, but were shaped differently than sheep or deer on a "high plane" of diet. Moreover, absolute body size was so plastic, so malleable, that the largest "high plane" individuals weighed four to five *times* as much as the 'low plane" individuals.

These findings formed the basis for the "Centripetal Theory of Growth." This theory identified tissues of high growth 'priority' (meaning that such tissues developed well regardless of an animal's individual plane of nutrition) and tissues of low growth priority— tissues which developed well only under conditions of abundant food. The Centripetal Theory of Growth also identified centers of high growth priority that were linked by anatomical regions of low growth priority. For example, wrists are centers of high growth priority as is the thoracic basket (i.e., the skeletal components surrounding the heart and lungs). The forelimbs (the humerus, radius and ulna) are of low growth priority, with a sliding scale of priority radiating outward from both the wrist and shoulder. Thus, a puppy has large paws because these have a high growth priority, but short legs, because the long bones have a much lower growth priority.

As predicted by the Centripetal Theory of Growth, animals on a low plane of nutrition typically have a relatively large thorax and relatively small hind quarters, and legs that seem disproportionately small relative to the body as well as short in absolute measurements. Teeth are tissues of high growth priority and are, therefore, just as large in an individual on a low plane of nutrition as in one on a high nutritional plane. Stated differently, "low plane" individuals thus have *relatively* larger tooth rows; i.e., tooth rows just as large as those in the largest-bodied specimen of their species. Another tissue of high growth priority is the brain stem, while the brain's cortex is of low growth priority. It develops well only under luxury conditions. The basal part of the skull is of high growth priority, but the face of low growth priority. Conse-

HARVEY BROWN

tunity for learning and improving his potential for survival. Thus large horns stand for luxury or safety, pretty good attributes if you can have them. Young rams follow old rams. Young rams, to forestall rejection, act towards big rams as if they were females in heat. This explains why sheep do not produce an annual surplus of young adults that strike out on their own in search of place to live, as do young moose or white-tailed deer. Instead, sheep are able to closely match the production of young sheep to the loss of older animals from the population. Consequently, sheep populations can quickly stabilize at low population numbers within a small geographic distribution.

During the holding phase, the period when geographic distribution is small for whatever reason, wild sheep are typically small-bodied, long-lived, non-adventuresome, notably diseased, quite lethargic, and demonstrate low rates of reproduction. They move between patches of good habitat with great precision, moving to the same patch in successive years at virtually the same date, and over the very same geographic routes. We call sheep of this type 'maintenance' or efficiency phenotypes. When sheep are put into an expanse of prime habitat, by contrast, they grow into large-bodied, spunky, healthy and adventuresome individuals. However, while reproducing at a high rate via large lambs and high survival rates, the average life span of adults declines. Animals become more short-lived on average. This is what's called the 'dispersal' or luxury phenotype. These are the kind of sheep that defy the

Lambs (such as these Dall's sheep) learn routes among security and feeding areas– areas that are often far separated one from another– by following their mothers thus stitching together home ranges as a result of learned traditions.

quently "low plane" individuals have short, child-like (paedomorphic) faces. The spine between thorax and pelvis is so low in growth priority that some "low plane" lambs were born with one lumbar vertebrae less than lambs on a high plane of nutrition.

Experimental work with red deer demonstrated that it took five generations for these animals to reach maximum <u>absolute</u> body and antler size— and when they did so, their <u>relative</u> antler mass stayed the same; that is, antler mass was not directly linked to body size. This work had immediate applications for animal scientists trying to maximize profit from domestic animals. For example, the best way to create a larger-bodied animal, such as a hog, was a matter of lengthening the carcass and increasing the hindquarters, so as to produce more high-priced steaks and chops. The way to do it was to put livestock on a high plane diet, which had the effect of lengthening the loins and increasing both the relative and absolute size of the haunches. Bacon hogs long in the loins produced longer slabs of high-priced bacon. Moreover, the animal scientist also knew that to <u>breed</u> for desirable body conformation, such as long loins and large haunches, required a population of animals who had been fed so as to maximally develop these areas of low growth priority. The individuals with the longest loin or haunches repre-

sented individuals with the highest hereditary potential for desirable carcass characteristics. Conversely, low plane individuals which demonstrated well-developed loins and haunches also revealed greater-than-average genetic potential to appropriate scarce resources to those body parts. Individuals between these phenotype extremes were relatively useless for selective breeding. The net availability of energy and nutrients thus had a profound effect on an individual's morphology, as well on the ability of man or of nature to select for specific traits.

These findings have direct results to management of wild sheep. Field studies of mountain sheep indicated very early these same characteristics were true among wild populations. Within and between populations, mountain sheep clearly varied in a manner congruent with the *Centripetal Theory of Growth*. However, it remained a puzzle why there were low quality and high quality individuals and populations in nature. As we contin-

VALERIUS GEIST

Young rams follow large-horned mature rams and learn from them the locations of the best feeding areas, providing opportunity to maximize body and horn growth.

DON L. MacCARTER

Mature rams, such as this old Rocky Mountain bighorn in New Mexico, are essential to maintaining social organization among wild sheep.

normal expectations for mountain sheep and do disperse and colonize new, vacant land. It takes about five generations, on average, to move from maintenance to dispersal phenotypes. Once an area is colonized, and food quality deteriorates because of competition, sheep change from dispersal to maintenance phenotypes. Their colonization is at an end, and the population goes into a holding phase, retaining the area colonized via a migratory tradition.

The signal which triggers the change in phenotypes is amount of protein in food consumed by the gestating female. High protein content generates large, spunky dispersal (luxury) type lambs; low protein content results in small, lethargic, maintenance (poverty) type lambs. To maximize the likelihood of a sheep population surviving, one needs to insure the food

supply. Extreme maintenance type sheep are a red warning flag for the wildlife manager. Food supply is limited. Consequently, judicious burning of shrubs and trees to generate vigorous sprouting grasses and forbs may be an important management tool; in fact, in extreme cases, may be necessary even to simply maintain the population. Supplying missing minerals in salt blocks is another. So is the creation of watering sites so as to allow sheep to exploit food sources otherwise too distant from water.

Maintenance type sheep appear to engage in a few tricks to maximize reproduction under conditions of adversity and poverty. Under maintenance conditions, a female that bears a surviving daughter is likely to share the same home range with her. In essence, a surviving daughter is a competitor for the same food. A son, however, cannot stay on the depleted home range of the mother, lest he fail to grow into a large-bodied, large-horned ram. Aided by a mother turned hostile at the age of about one year, it leaves the depleted and poverty stricken but secure range of the mother to join up with rams that enjoy better food, but on less secure, more dangerous ranges. Not surprisingly, there appears to be

ued studying sheep it became apparent that the low quality sheep had much lower reproduction than the high quality sheep but that they lived longer, while sheep characteristic of habitats providing abundant resources tended to produce more lambs but to live shorter lives overall. In addition, there were behavioral differences: low quality sheep were relatively lethargic compared to high quality sheep. It took some time to sink in that the differences we had found had nothing to do with "quality", but rather were sensible adaptive adjustments by phenotypes. That is, the phenotype differences had real, adaptive biological functions of value to the species. When this all fell into place, it became evident that the "low plane" animals were *maintenance* or *efficiency* phenotypes, sensibly equipped to survive and reproduce under conditions of resource shortages, while the "high plane" animal was a rare, but highly functional phenotype, a *dispersal* or *luxury* phenotype that was biologically and behaviorally equipped to disperse and colonize new, uninhabited terrain during periods of environmental abundance. An understanding of this switching from maintenance to dispersal phenotype, and back again, is crucial to an understanding of several types of mammalian speciation.

The key to the birth of a dispersal phenotype appears to be the amount of high quality protein in-

gested by the gestating female, which acted to switch the central nervous system of the developing fetus from a low to a high threshold of excitation— that was all that was needed theoretically. The critical experiment verifying this was never done on sheep, but on human beings. Like wild animals, humans also demonstrate perfectly good maintenance and dispersal phenotypes in morphology and behavior; the higher the "energetic income" of a human or mammalian population, the more dispersal type features appear in their phenotypes. Thus the genotype (i.e, the expression of genetic possibility in the individual) was responding to signals from the environment to shape the body form, the phenotype, in an adaptive and ongoing fashion. Phenotype switching or *alternative life strategies* lay at the root of defining health biologically: dispersal phenotypes are far healthier than maintenance phenotypes, but this occurs at a biological cost in terms of both body resources, and above all, in *maternal care,* to produce. Dispersal phenotypes not only reproduce more lambs, but they take care of their lambs in a superior fashion, albeit at a cost in life expectancy. Rams of dispersal phenotypes breed earlier, but also die young. In life they are vigorous, very playful, and very tough or forgiving of disturbances. The differences in morphology between maintenance and dispersal phenotypes is more males surviving to yearling age on poor than on good ranges. Even more surprising: females may skip a year of reproduction, then give birth to a super daughter that is nursed well into her second year. Such a daughter, demanding of high quality food, cannot stay on the depleted ranges of a maintenance type mother, but must strike out in search of better pastures. Therefore, bearing males and super-daughters is a poverty stricken ewe's way of lowering competition for the precious food supply on the well-delineated home range she already shares with her clan of female relatives. Put another way, during maintenance conditions sheep live in an ecologically closed system in which the loss of food required by one results in the gain of another sheep. That's the reason why judicious cropping of adult females as initiated by Bill Wishart in Alberta, a cropping so careful that it does not result in loss of habitat associated with sheep avoiding areas in which they were harassed, is likely to quickly result in larger, healthier lambs with better survival, better body growth and better horn growth. A population shifted towards the dispersal phenotype end of the spectrum is also much more forgiving of harassment, and thus, less likely to abandon and lose range. Careful cropping of female sheep can redistribute existing food among the survivors. However, careful is the operative word! Clearly, a vital goal of wild sheep management is to maintain migratory traditions as much as possible for reasons explained above: sheep that abandon parts of their range tend to do so permanently. Consequently, alienating even surviving sheep from use of traditional ranges also leads to a shrinkage of the range and of the population. This demands that sheep populations, which move widely between small patches of habitat, retain a large segment of old individuals. These old 'patriarchs' are crucial in passing the migratory traditions, the knowledge of where to go at what time, from generation to generation. Old barren females are not surplus to the population, but rather are vital to insure that yearlings are kept together when their mothers hide to give birth to lambs. Old rams are essential to insure that young rams have guides to distant, high quality patches of habitat. That's one reason for a conservative harvest of trophy rams in hunted herds. These old animals are crucial for more than breeding— and for still more than passing on

great— but the behavioral differences are much, much greater. These are the rams with large bodies and huge horns, provided they live long enough. Clearly, sheep populations released on exceptional range will grow the huge dispersal type rams. Once an area is colonized, intraspecific competition for food rapidly reduces body and horn size (unless mortality is also high). When competition for food becomes a limiting factor, growth rates slow, individuals are lest 'wasteful' of energy, and such individuals tend to live to older ages — a very effective survival strategy in variable environments.

Managers can make good use of this information. The body condition and behavior of wild sheep populations can be assessed relative to phenotype, which provides a great deal of indirect information about the environment. In terms of body size, dispersal phenotypes tend to show exceptional horn growth, especially among young rams (the picture is complicated for ewes, where horn growth may be slowed by the demands of pregnancy and lactation). Overall body size is also an indicator— rams with weights over about 250 pounds almost certainly

This captive Dall's sheep demonstrates superior body size and horn growth for his age, and is an excellent example of a dispersal phenotype.

JOHN BOONE

home range knowledge to young rams, as we shall see below!

It is also crucial that migratory corridors be maintained, allowing unimpeded passage by wild sheep. New World sheep will disperse and colonize new or abandoned range under two conditions: the landscape is free of tree cover, or the sheep are of an extreme dispersal phenotype. Dense timber is no insurmountable barrier for these very brave sheep. Normally sheep fear timber, as is easily demonstrated by monitoring heartbeats on free-ranging wild sheep. The heart rate escalates dramatically as the monitored sheep approaches timber. Dispersal phenotypes are bold; maintenance phenotypes are timid. Mountains comprised of long, open ridges with a bare minimum of trees in the valley bottoms are ideal for natural dispersal. Deeply dissected mountains with a dense forest cover in the valleys impede sheep colonization or re-colonization.

The last two decades have seen a significant shift in the philosophy of wild sheep management, in which the damaging and false paradigm that hunting mortality is compensatory has given way to an understanding that hunting mortality has to be closely focused lest damage is done. Wild sheep are very sensitive to energy costs. They have evolved originally to survive long, cold Siberian winters on sparse climax vegetation. One sure way to increase the energy costs of females and disrupt reproduction is to harvest too many rams from a herd. This disrupts the social system that regulates ram society and behavior. Young rams— as opposed to old rams — are very hard on females, and especially on themselves. They continually court and harass ewes, beginning well before ewes come into estrus and continuing long afterwards. While courting, they fail to feed and rest in futile attempts to guard and defend *non-estrous* ewes. Not only do older rams not behave like that, but a contingent of large rams quickly puts a halt to this nonsense by young rams, granting to both— females and young rams— a respite from the energetically costly harassment. Young rams, controlled by the superior abilities of the large ones, revert to feeding and resting instead of squandering their precious energy resources on unproductive activities. These savings, in turn, are vital for their survival during winter, and give them a head start in growing larger body and horn size in

VALERIUS GEIST

The oldest bighorn ram known, at least 21 years of age when photographed, is an example of an extreme maintenance phenotype.

come from dispersal phenotypes, while those with weights under 200 pounds most likely represent maintenance phenotypes, as do populations that produce dwarfed individuals. The ratio of the tooth row length relative to overall skull length is an indicator, since a relatively long tooth row is indicative of reduced skull growth, typical of maintenance conditions. In terms of age, many dispersal phenotypes have a life expectancy of 7 to 10 years, as is true for many California bighorn sheep herds established within the past three decades; maintenance phenotypes often live well beyond 10 years of age. Behavior, too, shows differences— lambs in populations of dispersal types suckle more frequently, and for longer periods of time, than lambs in populations largely composed of maintenance phenotypes. Rams among dispersal-type populations demonstrate dominance (clash) more frequently than do rams in maintenance type populations. Finally, dispersal phenotypes demonstrate relatively reduced frequencies of debilitating diseases. Research has shown that populations may cycle between phenotype on a 30 to 50-year cycle.

Obviously, managers tend to desire dispersal-type populations— active, vigorous, healthy herds that have a tendency to disperse into available habitat. Since dispersal phenotypes are a product of habitats in which lactating ewes provide abundant nutrition to their lambs which then mature on a high plane of nutrition, a key management strategy is to limit wild sheep populations to levels below which nutrition becomes a limiting factor. Limitations on herd size may be accomplished with natural predation (if predators are sufficiently abundant) or carefully regulated sport harvest (directed at both rams and ewes). However, managers also must be aware that maintenance type populations fulfill a critical environmental strategy. Maintenance phenotypes are particularly effective in coping with variable habitats, where environmental conditions are likely to change through time. Populations of maintenance type sheep may be essential to ensure long-term sustainability of sheep populations.

he following spring. That is, young rams that are free to waste energy on unproductive rutting activities have a higher mortality in winter, and suffer poor body and horn growth thereafter.

Moreover, large rams leave the ewes they bred right after the rut, taking many (but not all) young rams with them. The young rams that remain may till harass the ewes into the stressful winter months. Therefore, when the females are imprisoned on tiny feeding areas after the rut by rising snow levels, they may have to share the precious food resources with young rams that failed to go off to wintering areas of their own. Large, old rams are needed to lure away young rams to separate wintering sites so as to free females from food competition. Old rams are the last to come to the females and the first to go, minimizing their time on the female's wintering areas where the rut takes place. That is, the older the ram, the less likely he will remain on the foraging areas of the females he bred (at high cost to himself), and the less likely he will deprive his own children of the food their mothers need during gestation to insure a lamb of survivable size at birth.

These insights have all been translated into management decisions that protect all but the oldest of rams from harvest. Such management decisions led in Alaska, where Wayne Heimer put these ideas to the test, to dramatic increases in lamb production in herds with depleted ram segments, as well as an increase in the ram harvest itself. Here the key was to allow only the taking of rams of full curl status or better by hunters, or rams older than eight years. Shifting the kill to old rams *increased* the overall harvest of rams. Social behavior thus did have a high cost component, and earlier disruptions of social systems had in fact resulted in a decline in total ram harvest as well as in the trophy quality of rams. There were, therefore, sound biological reasons why hunting mortality should mimic natural mortality of rams. However, matters were even more complex, as shown by Heimer's research: Dall's ewes at the limit of northern sheep existence must be allowed to grow to an adequate size, and store sufficient energy, in order to bear a lamb large enough to provide the maternal care necessary to give it a boost so that it reached survivable size. Therefore, ewes should conceive only after reaching a growth plateau at 3-4 years of age. Once reproducing, they need to skip reproduction following a year of lamb-raising in order to restore body resources, an insight Paul Krausman gained through his studies of desert bighorns. Young rams, however, in their excessive chasing of ewes, triggered

TOM TIETZ

premature ovulation in young and lamb-leading ewes, leading subsequently to poor, stunted rams and high lamb mortality.

Wild sheep are subject to many threats to their survival. Even apparently healthy domestic sheep can be deadly to wild sheep, as shown in elegant experiments by William J. Foreyt of Washington State University. In a similar vein, European settlers were deadly to North American Indians in early post-Colombian days. Even in the absence of domestic sheep, free-living mountain sheep may pick up diseases from other forms of livestock, as demonstrated by hematological investigations. Consequently, one management goal is to ensure that wild sheep avoid contact with domestic livestock, and particularly domestic sheep. The less contact with any livestock and exotics, the better for wild sheep. The greatest danger to recovery of wild sheep populations are sudden, dramatic die-offs. The small numbers of sheep remaining may fail to utilize the full area of a range previously used, resulting in a permanently small population. Range lost from the population's traditional memory cannot be readily reacquired by sheep. We have both looked in vain for bighorns where they were once numerous before a die off—and have stood year after year before empty ranges.

Another logical goal of wild sheep management is the reintroduction of sheep to localities

The bighorn ram detects the reproductive condition of the ewe with the aid of scent and a specialized sensory organ, the Jacobsen's organ, located in the upper palate.

Inset: Contact between wild and domestic sheep, as shown here in Idaho's Hells Canyon, can result in transmission of disease organism that may cause death among wild sheep, often as widespread and irreversible die-offs.

Bighorn ewes, like these in Oregon, must have access to adequate food during winter if they are to give birth to healthy, vigorous lambs in the spring.

where they once existed, or other suitable habitat now vacant. This has been carried out with reasonable success for bighorns. Thinhorn sheep still cover much (though not all) of their historic ranges. They were severely depleted by market hunting during episodes of gold digging fever, but were able to recolonize much of the range lost. There have been a few transplants of Stone's sheep in British Columbia. Bighorn sheep did not recolonize much of their lost range, and much bighorn sheep management today is associated with active programs of reintroduction. These programs are all based on the availability of good habitat and assurances that the sheep can be kept away from livestock, domestic sheep in particular. A second proviso is that the reintroduced wild sheep are not barred from spreading from the area of release to other promising areas, as the abundant forage is likely to produce dispersal phenotypes initially. There are several ways of aiding dispersal phenotypes in their movements. Cutting strips of timber to facilitate movement between potential habitats, as is being done by Wyoming Game and Fish, is one way. Another way, promising but untried, would be to deliberately lead lambs to promising patches. That would be doing no more than ewes and rams do anyway. It has worked very well on caribou, but has yet to be

DALE E. TOWEILL

V. COGGINS

30

tried on bighorns. We suspect it will work very well. Yet another management thrust should be to restore sheep to disturbed sites that have been restructured into custom sheep habitat. The success of a few such operations indicates that biologists can indeed mimic high quality sheep habitat with environmental design, effectively creating or recreating wild sheep habitat.

While in the northern reaches of New World alpine climax plant communities serve as the primary sheep habitat, in areas occupied by Stone's and bighorn sheep low elevation ranges may be enhanced by controlled burning. Here forest fires adjacent to traditional sheep range may create additional feeding opportunity, albeit of a transient nature as forest successions will soon obliterate the temporary grasslands. In some areas the return of forest may, however, be a very slow process. Consequently, well-planned controlled burning can be used to generate significant and long lasting sheep range.

Predation on wild sheep can be a worrisome management problem. The ability of bighorns to escape gray wolves, as compared to other prey species, is remarkable (as shown in the studies of Ludwig Carbyn in Jasper National Park). Research indicates at least that wolves will preferentially feed on other species before tackling the difficult task of capturing sheep on cliffs. Grizzly bears and coyotes are capable predators of lambs. Ewes defend lambs against attacks by golden eagles, and are often successful. However, where sheep lead a precarious existence due to severe climatic factors, as is the case for many northern sheep populations, predation can be detrimental, and predator control has been shown to increase sheep populations.

The matter of saving a maximum of genetic diversity requires considerable research. Patterns of spatial DNA distribution indicate that genetically distinct meta-populations of sheep do exist, which, however, do not match existing subspecies. This demands detailed regional genetic studies. Eventually this research may lead to management actions that restore lost alleles to populations. It will inform scientists and managers about the minimum effective size necessary for breeding populations to maintain genetic diversity, and it will allow the appropriate genetic stock to be selected for purposes of reintroduction.

There are many aspects to consider in management, including how to ensure that wild sheep populations are able to coexist with some types of unavoidable industrial activities. Because wild

DALE E. TOWEILL

sheep are big-brained learning machines, capable of 'sponging up' information and acting on it with deadly logic, they can be taught to coexist with people. There is nothing 'natural' in sheep automatically fleeing from people. That's a consequence of their experience, not of inherited tendencies (as may be the case with small-brained tropical creatures). Our sheep are 'soft wired,' a characteristic of northern mammals that succeeded in dealing with the vagaries of change imposed by seasons, as well as horrendous ecological changes from glacial to interglacial conditions. Maintaining wild sheep populations that freely associate with humans may not match the romantic notion of how sheep ought to behave, but that romantic notion is based on gross ignorance of wild sheep behavior, and is potentially damaging ignorance to boot. Nothing will lead more quickly to the elimination of sheep than forcing them to avoid vital seasonal home ranges (even if they must share them, in part, with humans). That robs sheep of critical habitat, and habitat not used might as well not exist from the standpoint of wild sheep welfare.

Managers of desert bighorn sheep are faced not only by a huge decline from earlier historical numbers, but also by puzzling failures of populations to recover, or even to decline further. Here lies a great challenge, the effort to decipher what retards recovery in these populations.

Predators—and accidents—lead to the loss of many wild sheep each year, a worrisome problem for wildlife managers attempting to establish herds with only a few animals.

Managing Nursery Herds of Wild Sheep

By William Wishart

Nursery herds are the reproductive units, held together by common actions designed to safeguard lambs.

LURAY PARKER/WG&F

If you drive through ranch country you may have seen a bumper sticker that reads "Eat More Lamb - 50,000 Coyotes Can't be Wrong". Obviously, coyotes like to eat sheep, as do other carnivores. As a consequence, wild sheep have had to seek rocky escape cover in mountains or canyons to avoid being eaten. Their chosen terrain is comprised of meadows within easy access to the safety of cliffs or rocky escarpments. In winter these "islands" are reduced in number to those with south or west-facing slopes that stay free from snow - islands that can confine ewes and lambs for long periods during the winter due to accumulations of snow. Because of this confinement, overgrazing becomes a problem, particularly when this species has the potential to double its population every three years.

The nursery herd, comprised of ewes, yearlings and lambs, lives separately from rams except during the breeding season. Managing the nursery herd by regulating its numbers is essential to the well-being of the total population. During a long-term research program on a mountain sheep herd in Alberta it was found that a resident population of 100 bighorns could be held at 100 animals in a rapid state of growth by manipulating an age/sex ratio to achieve a ratio of 20 lambs and 40 ewes per 40 rams. This required an annual removal of about 20 percent of the ewes.

When ewe removals ceased, the population gradually doubled, aged and then the numbers steadily declined. During the population rise following the cessation of ewe removals, there were a number of symptoms of overpopulation. Body mass of young ewes decreased, and this corresponded to an increased age at breeding. The young ewes (primarily) stopped breeding: first the yearling ewes, followed by the 2-year olds, and then the 3-year olds. The reduced contribution of lambs from young ewes was reflected in the declining percentage of lambs to adult ewes. In addition, horn size in yearling and 2-year-old rams decreased significantly as the nursery herd increased. This observation of poor initial horn growth in rams on overstocked ranges has been noted in other studies. Thus, the first few annual rings on a ram's horn can provide a status report on the nursery herd of its origin.

Alberta has managed its bighorn nursery herds since the 1960s by removing ewes through hunting seasons or translocations. Alberta bighorn populations are in good numbers, producing large rams, and the herds continue to thrive under this management system. A rancher would liken this approach to a cow/calf operation, except he would remove the annual calf increment. Both management systems are dealing with 'closed' or 'island' populations.

In summary, wild sheep have a very high reproductive potential, possibly in response to short-term density fluctuations in their evolution. Certainly this capability has served the species well when they have invaded and heavily utilized newly-formed food sources, the result of fires or avalanches, thereby suppressing forest succession in their favor. With this high reproductive potential, wild sheep should be managed as though they are about to over populate the island. This can be achieved by removing ewes, keeping in mind that a nursery herd requires no more than 30 ewes (2 years of age and older) to produce 20 lambs each year. Clues indicative of overpopulation can be reflected in poor lamb crops, poor growth rates in young ewes, and poor early incremental growth in ram horns.

Managers of wild sheep populations must develop their management strategy to best take advantage of their particular situation. Obviously, the primary concern is to do everything possible to ensure that the population retains knowledge of its environment. That means that if wild sheep are present, even at very low numbers, it is vitally important to retain those animals and the store of knowledge they possess regarding their environment. It is also very important to assess the condition of the population, to determine whether it is dominated by 'dispersal' or 'maintenance' phenotypes, with all that implies not only about the health and vigor of individual animals but social behavior and dispersal ability as well.

Often, managers are faced with apparently suitable habitat, but no sheep. Either populations formerly present have been extirpated, or there is no record that available habitat was ever occupied by wild sheep. Guidelines for managers faced with this situation first appeared a quarter century ago, the result of deliberations of wild sheep researchers and managers whose findings were published in the landmark book *The Wild Sheep in Modern North America*. Briefly paraphrasing the original recommendations: (1) conduct background research to determine whether wild sheep formerly lived in the area of concern, and if so, which subspecies, (2) comb old records to attempt to determine the factors that contributed to the elimination of sheep from the area, (3) attempt to determine the plant communities present when wild sheep existed, and survey the area to determine if suitable forage still exists, (4) determine the present land status and ensure that necessary cooperative agreements between wildlife and land management agencies and private landowners are complete, (5) undertake an active predator control program to allow newly-introduced animals opportunity to learn travel routes and the location of security and escape terrain during initial phases of herd establishment, (6) select transplant stock from an area as ecologically similar as possible, to allow the animals to transfer their knowledge of forage plants, terrain, and other factors, (7) if stock from an ecologically similar terrain is unavailable, build an enclosure to habituate animals to their new surroundings prior to release, and (8) if animals are to be introduced to an area where winter and summer ranges occur in different areas or different elevations, release the animals in the most critical habitats (i.e., a portion of winter range that also offers some potential lambing habitat, for example). Transplants that featured pregnant ewes (captured within the first trimester of pregnancy if possible to minimize risks to both ewe and fetus) from the same herd have been most successful, since these animals know each other and are therefore likely to form a cohesive social group, and social bonds are strengthened in the first year as nursery groups form. If animals from widely separated herds are used, they should be held in an enclosure for two years to establish social bonds. Transplants should feature young animals (less than 3 years of age) which will (hopefully) live for a number of years in their new surroundings, building a store of knowledge to pass along to their offspring. Transplants should total at least 20 animals, if possible, with a ratio of one ram for each three ewes (at least 12 animals if an enclosure is used). Finally, new herds should be supplemented at least every five years with additional stock until established.

Managers, particularly those of herds managed to provide hunting, are often urged to supplement their herds with 'new blood' to promote hybrid vigor and stimulate horn growth among rams. Any such proposal is based on two fallacies, and should be viewed with extreme caution. The first fallacy is that there is little evidence that adding genetic diversity will either result in hybrid vigor or increased horn growth (although it may benefit the long-term survival of the population). Wild sheep live in what is essentially a closed society, where all members have access to all of the range known to their social group (i.e., ewes and lambs or rams). Adding individuals does not increase the habitat available to the population; rather, it simply increases competition for whatever components of the habitat (food, water, etc.) are in short supply. With more competition, each individual is likely to be worse off after the supplement than before, unless supplemental animals are added to the population in such a way that they can add information about habitats available but unused. This can be done by introducing the new animals to an area of nearby but unutilized

BURK MANTEL

Successful hunter with mature California bighorn sheep from southwestern Idaho's Owyhee River canyon herd–a herd reintroduced to Idaho in 1963.

habitat, letting them expand until the growing herd merges with the resident herd, bringing with them new knowledge that can be passed along to future generations of wild sheep. The second fallacy is based on the expression of genetic potential. Animals that live under suboptimal conditions cannot express their full genetic potential for growth that is not essential for survival, such as luxury organs like large horns, because the vast majority of nutrient intake is used for body maintenance. Only when all basic requirements of body maintenance have been fulfilled are there 'excess' nutrients that can be used for luxury organs. That is why these organs are so important as behavior signals— they clearly identify those individuals that have been successful in either survival to an old age, finding abundant excess nutrition, or both. The seeming lack of such individuals in any given population, therefore, is often not an expression of lack of genetic potential but rather is an indication of a maintenance phenotype, i.e., a population just hanging on under less-than-optimal conditions. The likelihood is much greater that such a population will find living conditions <u>worse</u> with the introduction of additional animals than better!

Many herds will be established specifically to provide recreational hunting opportunity. Properly managed, hunting can promote reestablishment of reintroduced herds by producing transient disturbance in the occupied area, thereby pushing sheep into adjacent but unoccupied habitat. Hunting is a legitimate use of wild sheep as a renewable resource, based on traditions as old as man himself. Hunting provides a highly desirable type of outdoor recreational opportunity, one that will yield income to the managing agency to offset (at least partially) the costs of providing that opportunity. Hunting opportunity can be used to accomplish any of three objectives:

1. Maximize opportunities for hunter to pursue a highly desirable species; i.e., maximize hunter days afield.
2. Maximize opportunities to harvest an animal for meat.
3. Maximize the opportunity for a hunter to harvest a highly desirable trophy.

The first objective is possible where populations of wild sheep are large, healthy, and well-distributed. The success of this approach demands that occupied sheep habitat is widely available and well-dispersed. Such a regime must be carefully managed to ensure that harassment of sheep is minimized and that hunters do not con-

DALE E. TOWEILL

centrate on small or isolated portions of the habitat, causing sheep to vacate home ranges or abandon essential habitats. Such hunting should feature harvesting of both sexes. It would probably have to be regulated so that each hunter could shoot only a certain sex and age class of animal to avoid overharvest of the mature animals essential to maintenance of home range use and travel traditions.

This approach to hunting of wild sheep maximizes the risks to the sheep resource, and (since it maximizes the amount of stress placed on sheep during the hunting season) may cause abandonment of large portions of habitat. If not carefully regulated, this approach may result in disruption of the social structure of populations. It is unlikely to prove acceptable to hunters, many of whom will find that encounters with other hunters will degrade their hunting experience. The potential for damage to the sheep population in the hunted area could be offset in part by maintaining large areas of contigu-

ous but unhunted nearby habitat that can provide sanctuary and source stock to repopulate hunted areas. Little work has been done to determine the level of harvest that would result in the maximum sustained yield from such a hunting program.

The second objective, maximizing opportunities for harvest of a wild sheep, is probably somewhat more acceptable to some hunters than the first. Under this objective, the number of hunters would be carefully regulated relative to the desired harvest level, and the hunt would be scheduled at a time that would allow maximum hunter access to the sheep. Since the focus of this effort would be to maximize opportunities for harvest, this hunt would have to feature hunting for animals less than about three years of age in order to maintain survival of the mature segment of the population essential to passing along traditions of habitat use. Some hunters would chafe at the requirement for selective harvest focused on younger-age animals. This kind

of hunt could easily become essentially a game-cropping operation, suitable for subsistence hunting but outside the tradition of sport hunting and unacceptable to many sportsmen.

The third alternative is the one most familiar to North American hunters. It is widely applied because it is compatible with relatively small as well as large populations, it minimizes risks to female portions of the population, and it can generate economic returns vastly disproportionate to harvest when compared with the two alternatives discussed earlier. Under this objective, hunting is focused on a small segment of the mature ram population, as indicated by horn size. Hunter quotas are typically carefully controlled, with the number of hunters allowed to participate increasing as potential for hunter success declines (usually due to difficulties associated with hunter access to areas occupied by harvestable sheep). The greatest risk associated with this type of hunting is that harvest is focused di-

Managers use many methods to capture bighorn sheep for transplant and reintroduction. Here, a helicopter is used to haze California bighorn sheep into a 'drive net' which collapses onto and entangles the animals long enough for managers to blindfold and hobble them.

V. COGGINS

Wild sheep may quickly habituate to the presence of people, such as this researcher, if not also hunted or harassed by people.

rectly on that segment of the population that is most significant in terms of passing along traditional knowledge of habitat use and maintaining social stability in wild sheep populations. Therefore harvests must be carefully limited to minimize potential for adverse impacts. Some general guidelines for this type of hunting exist:

1. Focus harvest on the oldest segment of the population. This will need to be evaluated for each herd, since dispersal phenotypes do not live as long, on average, as maintenance phenotypes. Experience in Alaska has shown that harvests could be increased when the minimum harvestable age was raised from three-quarter curl to full curl.

2. Maintain a total harvest that is less than 75 percent of the natural annual recruitment rate. For most herds, that will mean less than 10 percent of the mature rams in a herd, and it will mean that a number of rams approximately equal to or slightly greater than the number of legally harvested rams will die a natural death. This is essential to ensure that harvest does not eliminate that segment of the population necessary to ensure the social well-being of herds.

3. Allow harvest of a carefully-limited number of adult ewes to keep the ewe/lamb portion of the herd below carrying capacity, and thereby increase the growth rate of lambs.

4. Schedule hunting seasons to ensure that hunters are not afield when sheep are on critical portions of their annual range, i.e., winter range, to minimize the risks of range abandonment or shifts to less favorable forage areas during critical periods.

Not all herds of wild sheep will (or should!) be managed for hunting. Some will exist in parks, refuges, or sanctuaries managed to maximize opportunities for enjoyment by photographers or naturalists; others may be remnant or newly-introduced herds of insufficient size to withstand hunting pressure. As highly adaptable organisms, wild sheep can quickly habituate to the presence of people and the sounds of human activity if that presence is not threatening to their livelihood and well-being. However, habituating sheep to human presence is clearly incompatible with management for hunting, and besides being unethical this is a self-defeating exercise. This does not mean that it does not occur. Many hikers seek out opportunities to view wild sheep in areas where they are hunted. Both authors have experience conducting research on wild sheep in areas where they were hunted, and share concerns that lengthy association with researchers in the field may increase the vulnerability of some wild sheep to hunters. While periodic and irregular contact between humans and wild sheep causes little harm, ethical behavior requires that efforts be made to avoid or minimize subjecting hunted wild sheep to routine or regular contact with humans.

Habituating sheep to tolerate human presence requires finding situations that bring people to the sheep. Once a situation where that may be accomplished is determined, it is necessary to educate people about sheep behavior so as to minimize potential for injury to either sheep or humans. Direct contact between humans and wild sheep is undesirable, and carries risks of injury to both parties. Feeding of wild sheep by humans and exposure to pets carries great risks to wild sheep, and every effort should be made to avoid any potential for this to occur. Much more desirable is the development of viewpoints that allow humans to watch sheep interact among themselves and with other species of wildlife. ℛℛ

Chapter Three

THE THINHORN SHEEP

When Alaska and Eastern Siberia were a land undivided, when the Seward Peninsula and the Chukotskiy Peninsula were but one low, hilly ridge separating the Arctic and Pacific Oceans, and when St. Lawrence, St. Matthew's and Wrangle were mere hills rising above the plains (not islands in the Bering Sea), mountain sheep occupied the foothills of the mountains from the central Yukon to the Putorana Mountains deep within north-central Siberia. To-day these sheep are called snow sheep in Siberia and thinhorn sheep in North America. However, this division is somewhat artificial as these sheep were but a short time ago the very same stock, as were the moose, the elk, the caribou, the grizzly bear, the marmots, the wolves, and the people. The rising ocean levels, fueled by the rapid melting of the great continental glaciers, crept over the vast plateau to create the shallow sea— a sea that, in modern times, occupies the Bering Strait and separates Eurasia from North America while uniting the Pacific and Arctic oceans. No longer would mammoth wander from the Canadian Arctic islands westward to Mongolia and beyond, into western Europe. That was the spread of the great 'mammoth steppe' with its inhospitable dusty climate, but productive loess soils and virile herds of ungulates and predators. Of these, the northern sheep were an integral part, even though they failed to spread all the way across the continents. Instead, they were contained by mountain ranges with cliffs and steep slopes that offered escape terrain, and blocked in their expansion by some mighty rivers that drained from the big glaciers. Snow sheep extend from east to west in northeastern Siberia, a distance equivalent from Point Barrow in Alaska to the tip of Baja California in Mexico.

Mountain sheep differentiate readily from one another, locally forming quite distinct populations. They do not disperse readily, but cling closely to

DENVER BRYAN

Stone's sheep are named not after rocks, but after the hunter-naturalist Andrew J. Stone who brought back the first specimen from the headwaters of the Stikine in British Columbia.

39

acceptable escape terrain. They are, however, not slavish about sticking to home ranges (as are deer). Wild sheep will travel long distances between good chunks of habitat, keeping such travels alive as a living tradition passed on from generation to generation. It should therefore surprise no one that we find these sheep segregated today into regionally distinct clusters of populations: the primitive, big-horn-like snow sheep in Kamchatka; the dark Stone's sheep of northern British Columbia and the Yukon; the colorful Yakut snow sheep of the Verkhoyansk Mountains; the white Dall's sheep of Alaska, the Yukon and Northwest Territories; the dark Okhotsk snow sheep of the Stanovoi and Djugjur Ranges; or the little band of poorly known Putorean snow sheep so distant from the nearest neighbor, stranded now far, far away to the west from others of their kind.

These northern sheep differ in pelage markings, having surprisingly variable rump patches (an important social signal among wild sheep). Kamchatka snow sheep have small, discrete, primitive, rump patches. Those of Stone's sheep are very large, but also discreet. Those of the Yakut snow sheep, however, spread out diffusely over the haunches not dissimilar to the rump patch of the Marco Polo argali. Many snow sheep have a conspicuous white front, contrasting with a dark nose and dark horns. Some populations even differ from others in their genetic makeup, reflected in chromosome numbers. In North America, thinhorn sheep have 54 chromosomes, while some Siberian populations— about which we still have much to learn— have 52 chromosomes. However, in basic body structure, behavior and ecology these are much the same sheep, the striking differences in 'uniform' not withstanding. On the Siberian side they are labeled snow sheep, as descriptive and lovely a name as they come, and on the North American side we call them thinhorn sheep, by contrast with their southern brethren, the bighorn sheep.

These northern sheep are not large, as sheep go, with most older rams weighing about 200-220 pounds. By and large, the northern sheep become smaller with latitude as one goes north. They also become smaller with increasing aridity, also a factor in more northerly ranges. The dryer, colder and more northerly the mountains, the smaller the sheep. In moist northern British Columbia, however, some Stone's sheep exceed many bighorns in size, and Dall's sheep may become just as large in a few populations in the western Yukon.

The ecology of the northern sheep forms a continuum, depending on how far they are in win-ter from the massive eastern Siberian high pressure area. Jakut snow sheep that live within this cold cell are adapted to extremely low temperatures and soft snow. Dall's sheep live largely in the winter air currents skirting the east Siberian cold cell. Their habitat is less dry and cold, but more windy than that experienced by their Siberian brethren. Stone's sheep live further away still from the massive Siberian cold cell, and experience more warm, moisture-laden air coming in from the Pacific. Therefore, they may live in areas with deep snowfall, great summer moisture and very turbulent air masses. Snow sheep, Dall's sheep, and Stone's sheep thus live a little differently depending on the distance from the East Siberian cold cell (and the associated climatic conditions characteristic of their habitat). Nevertheless, the variety of ecological conditions these northern sheep encounter is much less than that experienced by bighorn sheep. These may live very much like northern thinhorn sheep at high latitude and altitude, but they also survive in the southern hot deserts of western North America within a flora deeply marked by the constant grazing pressure of extinct American ungulates such as camels, llamas, horses, elephants and ground sloths within the past million years.

What unites these northern sheep is their requirement to live where snow is no great hindrance in accessing feed during a very long winter. In east-central Siberia these conditions are met through the low layer of fine, powdery snow under extremely cold, but calm conditions. Here green vegetation is frozen suddenly at the beginning of the long winter. A high pressure cell insures great cold and calm, and therefore low precipitation comprised primarily of fine, powdery snow. Sheep feed heavily here on lichen, acting much like caribou or reindeer with which they may temporarily share the range. Sheep have little trouble pawing away the fine, dusty snow which preserves the nutritional quality of the herbs and lichens close to the ground. Despite the climatically inclement conditions, snow sheep may reach surprisingly high population densities.

The ecology of Dall's sheep was ably summarized by Wayne Heimer, longtime student of their

WAYNE HEIMER

North America's wild sheep are intelligent, highly adaptable animals, and given both security and time to adapt, can adjust to alterations in their habitat as evidenced by these Dall's sheep near the Alaska Oil Pipeline.

Mature Stone's sheep ram starting to shed his winter coat.

41

habits and management. He sees the snow shadow effect of mountain ranges and the air currents which flow down valleys, clearing snow from vegetated slopes as they go, as the key to Dall's sheep survival. Dall's sheep can exist only where snow depth does not exceed about 18 inches, the average length of Dall's sheep legs. Although these sheep do paw through the snow blanket for forage, they rely primarily on windswept slopes for survival in winter. In most cases Stone's sheep range and Dall's sheep range are located in the snow shadows of mountains that clear the moisture from clouds sailing in from the Pacific driven by maritime winds. The southern Stone's sheep may be faced with rather heavy snowfalls and deep blankets of heavy snow. They, too, paw some snow. However, some populations of Stone's sheep may owe their survival to the periodic appearance of warm katapatic winds, or Chinooks, to remove the snow. There are also cold wind currents at high elevations, and in areas where these cold winds dominate, Stone's sheep imitate Dall's sheep, i.e., congregate on high, windswept slopes. So do bighorns far to the south, though only at high elevation. Stone's sheep also live at low elevations along Chinook funnels. These violent warm winds blow and melt snow off mountain slopes after Pacific storms have unloaded massive snowfalls that strand the sheep— till the Chinook comes.

Even within (and certainly among) the differing climatic influences and area ecology, sheep populations differ greatly in how they exploit mountains. Neighboring populations may feature quite different sheep. For instance, all northern sheep are glacier followers, who do exceptionally well close to massive mountain glaciers. Here the fertile silts liberated by glacial action act as fertilizers, so that the seasonal flush of vegetation growth provides forage rich in nutrients, thereby playing a crucial role in sheep ecology. Salt licks form at the end moraine, providing popular mineral sources that attract sheep as well as other wildlife. In summer salt licks may be so vital for the normal growth and development of lambs that nursery groups of female sheep literally park for weeks on end beside a mineral lick.

HARVEY BROWN

Ewes invest a great deal of effort in raising lambs, even selecting alternate-year breeding in some situations so as to raise large-bodied, healthy 'super-daughters.'

Dall's sheep often select resting areas on bare, rocky slopes which provide prominent perches for viewing their surroundings.

All northern sheep have yearling rams that are hard to differentiate from females. This is due in part to the thinner horns grown by thinhorn sheep as compared with bighorns (where the larger diameter of the horns of even small rams differentiates them from ewes at a young age). However, although behavior of thinhorn and bighorn sheep in the New World differs in emphasis or style, it is built of identical elements. By and large the actions of thinhorns are expressed more ceremonially than those of bighorns, which are rather rough. We know very little about the social behavior of the snow sheep. Social behavior is normally very conservative, much more so than the external appearance of animals.

DALL'S SHEEP

Dall's sheep are the white thinhorn sheep of Alaska, the Yukon, the western Northwest Territories and the extreme north western portion of British Columbia. The name of these sheep has a peculiar history. This is what Wayne Heimer, Alaska's longtime Dall's sheep research biologist has to say about it: "It was the explorer/naturalists who gave Alaska's white sheep their rather intriguing name, Dall's sheep. One of these early explorers, a fellow named Nelson, had an interest in mammals, and named many of them throughout Alaska. Nelson offered the first Latin scientific name for these white sheep in 1884. It was simply 'Ovis' (the sheep genus) plus 'montana' (for mountains) as the species name. Nelson also offered the 'dalli' subspecies name in honor of another Alaska explorer, William H. Dall. W. H. Dall was primarily a mariner and river traveler, and there's no record of him ever having been in Dall's sheep country. In 1897, another namer of animals, J. A. Allen, changed the species name from 'montana' to 'dalli' and it has remained so ever since.

Dall's name continues to be associated with Alaska's white sheep because the accepted rules of scientific naming call for it. These rules say that the species name (in this case 'dalli', the latinized form of Dall) should be 'de-latinized' and its possessive form (Dall's) used as the scientifically accepted 'common name.' Under these rules, the scientifically correct common name should be 'Dall's sheep.'

However, rules of science (or more specifically, rules of grammar) to the contrary, the most commonly used form of the name is not the possessive form, but the grammatically incorrect 'Dall sheep.' When rules of grammar or logic conflict with common usage, it is the latter that has typically won out historically. In this book, however, we shall adhere to the grammatically correct possessive form.

DESCRIPTION

The most striking aspect about Dall's sheep is their white color. However, a few dark hairs may creep into the tail or 'saddle' in populations which are in the proximity of pigmented Stone's sheep populations. Why Dall's sheep (or mountain goats) should have evolved white coloration is at present an open question. It is a fact that Dall's sheep penetrate well beyond the Arctic Circle and thus may live during winter in continuous night. Arctic wolves also evolved a white coloration under these conditions, as did Peary's and Greenland caribou, polar bears, Arctic hares, and ptarmigan (though musk oxen did not). It may well be that detecting a white form visually at night in a snowy expanse is particularly difficult, and thus a survival advantage is conferred to all-white species subject to predation. However, that is pure speculation. Be that as it may, white Dall's rams with amber horns are esthetically most appealing, no matter what the setting.

The reputation of Dall's sheep for small body size is a consequence of the far northerly distribution of most populations, and the fact that many occupy the dry rain-shadow sides of mountains. Locally, however, and given favorable conditions, Dall's sheep can grow very large, matching large bighorns in body mass. Body size is not fixed genetically, but is very sensitive to environmental conditions and is an excellent indicator of environmental quality. Because Dall's sheep live in the most extreme climatic conditions of all North American mountain sheep, it is their populations which run a delicate energy balance in winter, and thus show an extreme in adjustments in their reproductive biology. Females may reproduce only once every two years, suckle yearlings instead of expelling them, and grow slowly to sexual maturity. (While we suspect that

Inset: Dark colored Stone's ram picks his way across rocky talus.

Dall's sheep often congregate at mineral exposures or 'salt licks,' affording managers opportunities to capture a number of animals at a time by dropping a suspended net over the entire group.

MICHAEL H. FRANCIS

WAYNE HEIMER

44

Population estimates for thinhorn sheep (Dall's sheep and Stone's sheep) in North America. These animals are often scattered thinly across vast, rugged mountainous areas, precluding annual census or precise estimates of population size.

State or Province	Dall's Sheep	Stone's Sheep
Alaska	50,400- 64,300	Few
British Columbia	500	14,500
Northwest Territories	14,000- 26,000	Few
Yukon Territory	18,000	4,000
TOTAL	**82,900-108,800**	**18,500**

such reproductive characteristics apply to some high elevation bighorn herds also, the matter remains to be verified.) Dall's sheep are also unique as they are the only North American sheep to live north of the Arctic circle, and thus live in conditions of perpetual winter night over a period of weeks or months.

STONE'S SHEEP

Stone's sheep are dark thinhorn sheep occupying the southern portions of that species range. About 14,500 live in northern British Columbia, and 4,000 in the south-central Yukon Territory. They get their name not from stones, but from the noted hunter-explorer Andrew J. Stone of Missoula, Montana, who brought back the first specimen from the headwaters of the Stikine River in 1896. In recognition of his contribution, J. A. Allan of the American Museum of Natural History named this new sheep *Ovis stonei* in 1897. Thus the grammatically correct spelling of its common name is not Stone sheep, but Stone's sheep, honoring an explorer, not rocks. Dall's and Stone's sheep were thus named at the same time. Both are 'good' subspecies.

DESCRIPTION

Stone's sheep average somewhat larger in body size than Dall's sheep, a consequence of living at lower latitudes. The coat color and patterns may vary greatly between individuals in the same band, as well as between regions. In the south and west the sheep tend to be very dark, virtually black in color. The head is always lighter than the body, the rump patch is white, large and extends well above the root of the tail. The belly is at least partially white and so are the margins of the legs. These white margins tend to be particularly generous in Stone's sheep when compared with those of bighorns. Eastern populations tend to have light heads and necks. Otherwise, the coat pattern and color variability defies a succinct summary. Some sheep have a white belly, some have

a dark belly band or virtually no white, some have snow sheep-like faces, some have a light neck, some have white faces, etc. Weight, horn size and shape also vary widely. While American sheep are very similar in biology, Stone's sheep differ from bighorns by being less "juvenile" in their behavior, emphasizing ceremony over overt aggression and sex.

Subsequent to Allen, Charles Sheldon published (in 1911) an account of the distribution of Stone's sheep in **The Wilderness of the Upper Yukon**. Carl Rungius, destined to become a legendary wildlife artist, accompanied Sheldon and illustrated the timeless book. Sheldon showed a change in coloration from south to north, with more sheep becoming lighter. His was no statistical statement, but a recognition that there are dark and light sheep in all populations and that the respective frequencies of these color variations shifts as one travels from south to north. In the Cassiar

MANFRED HOEFS

study area discussed in the book *Mountain Sheep: A Study in Behavior and Evolution*, about three percent of the sheep were light. None were pure white, as even the lightest had a black tail and silvery hair on its back. The last evidence of Stone's sheep integrating with Dall's sheep in the Yukon are black hairs in the tails, back, around the eyes, and across the bridge of the nose of otherwise white sheep in the western Yukon, central Alaska, and southwestern Northwest Territories. As Stone's sheep become lighter, they tend to isolate pigmentation in a saddle. This variant was formerly declared a separate species *Ovis fannini* by W. T. Hornaday. Today we consider 'fannin sheep' merely as light-colored Stone's sheep. Since these sheep intergrade with the all-white Dall's sheep across a broad area, the 'hunter's definition' of Stone's sheep includes thinhorn sheep that show black hairs intermingled with white anywhere except on the tail.

Sheldon put Stone's sheep on the map, but while they remained unknown to science, they were a trophy that generated legends. In 1936 L. S. Chadwick and Roy Hargrave hunted down the magnificent Stone's ram that has the longest horns not only of all American sheep, but of any sheep in the subgenus *Pachyceros*. Both horns measure over 50 inches. The Chadwick ram is by far the most famous trophy ever taken in North America. *RR*

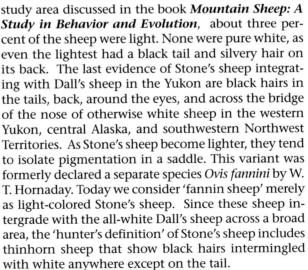

The white coat of Dall's sheep is shared with other northern mammals like snowshoe hares, Arctic wolves, and polar bears, and may provide survival advantages to animals that must endure long winter nights in a snow-covered environment.

Alaska

ince the United States purchased Alaska from Russia about 130 years ago, Dall's sheep have been ignored, exploited, and managed by varying approaches. Present-day management practices range from total protection in state-created viewing areas and Congressionally-established national parks, through biologically sound harvest management on state and federal lands, to highly permissive management for subsistence uses on other federal lands. How this spectrum of management practices evolved is a fascinating, sometimes rough-and-tumble, human adventure in the biology and politics of wildlife conservation in Alaska.

The opportunity to hunt has been the historic linchpin of North American wildlife conservation. Where hunting opportunity has been maintained, wildlife populations thrive through active management programs. Worldwide experience has shown that where public hunting is not allowed, public interest in wildlife suffers and wildlife conservation becomes an exclusive, expensive 'government function' instead of an individual human activity. Broadly stated, preserving hunting opportunity is, at present, the key to maintaining Dall's sheep abundance and use through conservation. Without special effort, funding and aggressive input from Dall's sheep hunters, Dall's sheep management would probably be on a less secure course than it is in Alaska today.

Dall's sheep populations were basically untouched when Alaska was purchased from Russia in 1867, except for those populations heavily exploited by aboriginal hunters. During this period, aboriginal use of Dall's sheep was part of the nomadic seasonal cycle or as a backup source of meat when other sources failed. Aboriginal overharvest of Dall's sheep may have been responsible for the scarcity of Dall's sheep documented in the Brooks Range during the late nineteenth and early twentieth centuries. In addi-

August storms bring snow and a prelude of long winter nights to Dall's sheep habitat in Alaska's Brooks Range.

WAYNE HEIMER

Abundant feed and restrictive harvest management allow many Dall's sheep rams to grow to maturity – and a few to reach exceptional size, such as these tremendous rams.

46

Inset: North America's wild sheep evolved as glacier-followers, feeding on the highly nutritious forage associated with long summer seasons and enduring long, cold winters. Alaska's Tok Glacier provides nearly ideal habitat for Dall's sheep.

Dall's sheep habitat in the Alaska Range provides a mix of rich alpine basins, a variety of slope aspects allowing sheep to take advantage of opportunities to regulate their body temperature depending on weather conditions, and abundant security terrain.

tion to aboriginal hunters and explorer/naturalists, Dall's sheep were exploited by the trappers, miners, market hunters, and homesteaders who followed. Some sheep populations were virtually decimated because of harvesting by humans during the early twentieth century.

The first closed seasons and restrictive bag limits were established in 1926. The bag limit was restricted to two rams. The regulation was consistent with the 'males only' seasons characteristic of early conservation efforts. No systematic population monitoring or regulation program existed, and managers applied their local knowledge of Dall's sheep over what today would be unthinkably huge areas. Thus the territory-wide closure of Dall's sheep hunting in 1942 was based on the as-

sumption that harsh weather which decimated sheep populations on the Kenai peninsula occurred throughout Alaska. When the harvest season was reopened in 1943, the general bag limit was more conservative (one ram) except in the Brooks Range where the limit remained at two rams. In 1951 bag limits were reduced still further and, via federal regulation, only rams with horns describing a 3/4 curl were legally harvested. The bag limit remained two legal rams in the Brooks range until 1970, when the need to limit overall ram harvest for conservation purposes apparently outweighed providing additional opportunities for resident Indians and Eskimos. It was common knowledge, but ignored by authorities, that natives never limited their harvests to rams as specified by regulations 20

WAYNE HEIMER

48

Area	Population	Map
Kenai Mountains	1,500-1,800	1
Chugach Mountains	6,000-7,000	2
Wrangell Mountains	15,000-22,000	3
Talkeetna Mountains	2,000-2,500	4
Alaska Range	11,000-14,000	5
White Mountains	400-500	6
Tanana Hills	500	7
Brooks Range	14,000- 16,000	8
TOTAL	**50,400- 64,300**	

Current population estimates of Dall's sheep in Alaska.

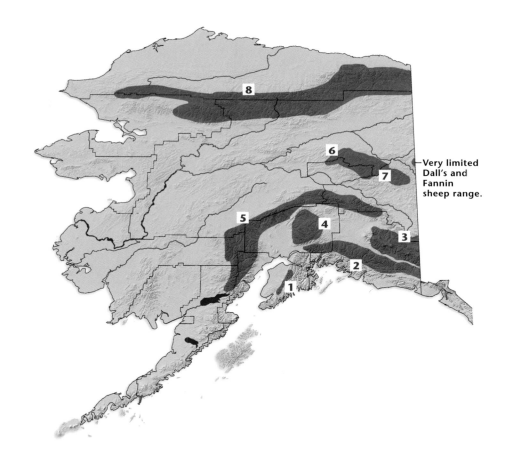

Very limited Dall's and Fannin sheep range.

years earlier. The 3/4-curl regulation was poorly suited to Dall's sheep biology and caused subtle, long-term negative effects to the heavily hunted populations where mature rams were completely removed. It took the newly formed State of Alaska decades to discover and rectify this situation.

Following our discovery that the negative effects of ram overharvest could be reversed by harvesting only mature rams, and that hunters could actually harvest more rams as a result, Dall's sheep hunters proposed in 1989 an end to the 50-year span of 3/4-curl ram harvest. This proposal was the first to factor the subtleties of animal behavior into harvest management of big game in Alaska, and perhaps the entire United States. Consequently, it was highly controversial. As a result of compelling public testimony, the Alaska Board of Game passed the present regulations limiting ram harvest to full-curl or eight-year-old rams, or rams with horns broomed on both sides. After the change to full-curl ram harvest, lamb production doubled, and immature ram survival increased dramatically. Eventually, harvests of full-curl rams exceeded those sustained by the same populations as under the 3/4-curl rule. It took 49 years of Alaska statehood to rectify the biologically incorrect 3/4-curl regulation established by a well-meaning, but biologically naive Federal Territorial Government.

In the 1980s some 80 million acres of state lands were transferred to federal control, resulting in loss of 25 percent of the sheep hunting opportunity in Alaska and in federal recognition of subsistence harvest priority for rural residents of Alaska. Subsistence seasons on Federal lands are typically lengthy and bag limits are liberal, including ewes and lambs. Subsistence harvest reporting is presently voluntary. As anecdotal evidence accumulates, it's beginning to look like this liberal approach to management is inconsistent with Dall's sheep conservation.

During the last five years, Dall's sheep populations throughout much of Alaska have declined because of difficult weather. Predator pressure, primarily exerted by wolves on adult sheep, is an additive factor. This predation may slow population recovery because it increases what we call the 'environmental resistance' to population growth. Despite public opposition from some quarters, predator reduction is the only management-alterable factor which has not been already manipulated in favor of Dall's sheep.

Today, hunting prospects are still good. Some outstanding rams have been harvested from unlikely places. In 1990, two new "top ten" Boone and Crockett rams were harvested from the Brooks Range, which had formerly been assumed incapable of producing 'high book' rams. The Chugach Mountains adjacent to Anchorage continue to produce outstanding rams and a high quality hunting experience, as does Alaska's oldest trophy management area, the Tok Management Area.

British Columbia

Two races of thinhorn sheep are native to British Columbia: Stone's sheep and Dall's sheep. Dall's sheep occur in only low numbers in the province, being restricted in their distribution to mountains in the extreme northwest. Stone's sheep, on the other hand, occur in relatively large numbers, being found in most of the mountain ranges in the northern one-third of the province.

The population of Dall's sheep in British Columbia is estimated at 500, with all Dall's sheep located in the area west of Bennett Lake. The Bennett Lake dividing line between Dall's sheep and Stone's sheep is a rather arbitrary line, chosen by the Wildlife Branch for management purposes to separate the pure white Dall's sheep from those sheep to the east in the Atlin Lake area. The sheep occurring in the Atlin Lake area are intermediate in coloration between the classic pure white Dall's sheep and the dark Stone's sheep, and were once considered to be a separate species of thinhorn sheep, the fannin. Although for management purposes these sheep are considered as Stone's sheep, it should be noted that for Boone and Crockett's records-keeping purposes, Atlin Lake is deemed to be the dividing line between Stone's sheep and the mostly-white Dall's sheep to the west.

The number of Stone's sheep in the province is currently estimated at 14,500, representing approximately 70 percent of the North American population. The most southerly of the Stone's sheep herds occur in the Rocky Mountains to the north of the Pine River. The largest numbers, however, are located in the mountains in the Muskwa, Kechika, and Spatzisi river drainages. These areas contain high, level grassland ranges which are swept relatively free of snow by the wind in winter.

Although thinhorn sheep herd numbers fluctuate considerably from year to year and have shown increasing or decreasing trends over a number of years, populations have generally remained stable over the longer term. The overall factor controlling the distribution and abundance of thinhorn sheep is the availability of quality winter ranges in proximity to adequate escape terrain. Fluctuations in numbers are mainly related to winter weather conditions and to the level of predation by wolves.

MANAGEMENT AND CONSERVATION

Wildlife Branch, British Columbia Ministry of Environment, is the agency responsible for the management of mountain sheep in the province. Many other government and non-government agencies, however, contribute significantly to the management and conservation of provincial sheep populations.

Thinhorn sheep management activities in British Columbia have, to a great extent, been concentrated on setting hunting regulations and monitoring hunter harvests. In this regard, compulsory reporting and horn inspections of hunter kills have been required since 1975. However, other important management activities carried out in various areas include population surveys, range enhancements, habitat protection, and transplants.

Thinhorn sheep population surveys have mainly involved helicopter surveys carried out during the winter on a selective herd basis. Most of the survey work that has been undertaken has been concentrated on herds in the Muskwa-Kechika and Spatsizi areas.

Active habitat manipulation is difficult on most thinhorn sheep ranges, as critical winter habitat mainly involves remote windswept alpine tundra areas. Some sheep populations, however, utilize more accessible and improved shrub or grassland areas as winter habitat, and these can sometimes be improved by prescribed burning. In this regard, range burning has been carried out with good success in the Muskwa-Kechika and Stikine River areas.

Habitat protection activities for thinhorn sheep populations have mainly involved attempts to mitigate the impact of resource development.

Sanctuary Ridge on the Spatsizi Plateau– classic winter range for Stone's sheep in northern British Columbia.

VALERIUS GEIST

Terminus Mountain, the termination of the Rocky Mountains along the Rocky Mountain trench. The low timberline, fertile sedimentary rock, southeastern exposure make this ideal habitat for numerous, large-bodied Stone's sheep.

The most usual mitigative measure used has been the changing of proposed resource access road locations to avoid important sheep habitat.

A limited number of thinhorn sheep transplant projects have been undertaken in recent years. During the years 1990 to 1993, 28 Stone's sheep were transplanted from north of the Peace River to locations south of the Peace River. However, this transplant program has not been fully successful, due mainly to the lack of extensive good quality habitat. During the years 1994 and 1995, approximately 24 Stone's sheep were successfully transplanted from the east of Atlin Lake to an area immediately west of Atlin Lake. In 1996, eight Stone's sheep were successfully translocated within the Toad River drainage of the northern Rocky Mountains.

Recreational hunting of thinhorn sheep is of considerable importance to both resident and nonresident hunters, and contributes significantly to the northern and provincial economies. The northern British Columbia guiding and outfitting industry is particularly dependent upon the income generated from nonresident sheep hunters. The hunting of thinhorn sheep is carefully regulated through the use of a full curl/age regulation (rams must be eight years of age or older, or have horn tips which extend above the bridge of the nose), guide quotas, and (in selected areas) by Limited Entry Hunting (LEH) restrictions. The latter restrictions regulate hunting by resident hunters, and mainly pertain to sheep hunting as permitted in several northern provincial parks. The hunting season for thinhorn sheep in British Columbia extends from August 1 to October 15.

VALERIUS GEIST

Inset: Ghost Mountain, winter range of Stone's sheep in the Gladys Lake Ecological Reserve.

Dark-colored Stone's sheep ewes in security habitat below tree-line in northern British Columbia's Stone Mountain Provincial Park.

DALE E. TOWEILL

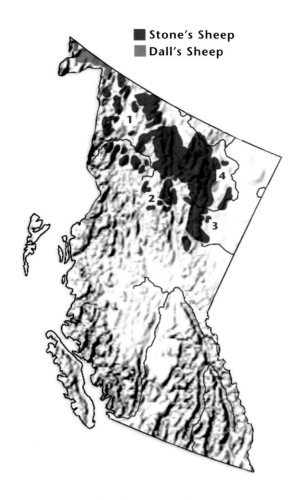

Stone's Sheep
Dall's Sheep

Estimates of thinhorn sheep numbers in British Columbia in 1996.

Region	Dall's Sheep	Stone's Sheep	Total	Status	Map
Skeena	500	4,800	5,300	Stable to increasing	1
Omineca	0	800	800	Stable	2
Peace	0	300	300	Stable to increasing	3
Liard	0	8,600	8,600	Stable to increasing	4
Provincial Total	**500**	**14,500**	**15,000**		

Nonresident big game hunters are required to be accompanied by a licensed outfitter when hunting within the province. Nonresident thinhorn sheep hunters can choose to be guided by any available licensed guide outfitter who has been assigned a sheep quota. A list of provincial guide outfitters who can guide for sheep is referenced in a pamphlet titled, **Guide Outfitters of British Columbia**, available from the Wildlife Branch (British Columbia Ministry of Environment, Victoria, BC V8V 1X4). Those guide outfitters listed as available for sheep hunting in Peace/Liard, Omineca and Skeena regions would all guide for thinhorn sheep. Nonresident sheep hunting license fees can also be obtained by writing to the address above.

The number of hunter days spent hunting thinhorn sheep in British Columbia is approximately 7,000 days per year. Although resident hunters account for most of the provincial thinhorn sheep hunter days, approximately 60 percent of the harvest is by nonresident hunters. This apparent inconsistency is the result of the differential success rates between resident and nonresident hunters. Success rates for the largely unguided resident hunters approximates 20 percent; success rates for nonresident hunters approximates 70 percent.

Over the past 10 years the harvest of Stone's sheep rams has averaged approximately 430 sheep per annum. The harvest of Dall's sheep in the area has been low and extremely variable, with harvest varying from none to 12 sheep annually. All of the Dall's sheep hunting by resident hunters is carried out under LEH hunting regulations.

The annual harvest of thinhorn sheep represents approximately 3 percent of the estimated provincial thinhorn sheep population. This relatively low harvest level is a reflection of the remote locations of the sheep populations (and associated difficulties in hunter access) and restrictive hunting regulations. In this latter regard, the recent initiation of a one-sheep-in-three-years bag limit restriction applied to hunters in the Omineca and Peace/Liard regions and the maintenance of a lower-than-warranted number of authorizations in LEH hunts in the Skeena Region are problematic. Although some room currently exists to increase thinhorn hunting opportunities, substantial increases in opportunities in the future would appear to depend upon an increase in habitat enhancement work and on thinhorn sheep population responses to wolf control.

Northwest Territories

Mountain sheep of the thinhorn species are found in the extreme western part of the Northwest Territories (NWT), in the Mackenzie and Richardson Mountains. They are virtually all Dall's sheep, although sheep with gray saddle backs do crop up in the extreme south of the distribution in the Mackenzie Mountains, while pure white sheep with black tails are found at the head of the Nahanni River. Recent surveys indicate that some 14,000-26,000 sheep occur in the NWT, almost all in the Mackenzie Mountains. Less than 2,000 Dall's sheep occur in the Richardson Mountains.

Typical Dall's sheep habitat in the Mackenzie Mountains of the Northwest Territories near Keele River.

DALE E. TOWEILL

Small alpine benches not only provide food for Dall's sheep, but enable sheep to scan their surroundings for potential predators and afford an abundance of nearby escape (or security) habitat.

Little is known about the historical distribution and abundance of sheep. There is no evidence of extinctions and there have been no reintroductions. The present distribution appears to be the original one. The Mackenzie Mountains are uninhabited and roadless, and at about 140,000 square kilometers in size, one of the largest and most pristine wilderness areas in North America.

Mountain sheep are found in the rain shadow of the mountains in a rather dry, cold and predictable environment that favors very stable sheep populations. Winter snow levels are low and the snow powdery and cold. Chinook winds prevent icing conditions. Therefore, massive die-offs are unknown. Since the snow is powdery all winter, winds are able to blow the snow off the mountain slopes, exposing meager forage. Sheep have here a relatively low reproductive rate and are slow growing. However, since they are long-lived, rams reach respectable body sizes, and some notable trophies have been collected. From 203 rams taken in 1997,

the average horn length was 90.3 cm (35.5 inches with an average basal circumference of 33.3 cm (13.1 inches). The maximum horn length recorded was 110.5 cm (43.5 inches), and the greatest basal circumference was 39.0 cm (15.3 inches). The mean age of rams taken by non-resident hunters was a high 10.0 ± 1.5 years. In six of the eight years between 1991-1997, rams 12 years and older made up at least 9 percent of the harvest. Although none of the top 25 trophies listed in the Boone and Crockett Club's record book came from the NWT, five of the Gold Medal Award winners for Dall's sheep recognized by the Foundation for North American Wild Sheep since 1978 came from the Mackenzie Mountains of the Northwest Territories. The bulk of the sport harvest is taken by non-resident hunters, with a total recorded annual harvest since 1991 usually somewhat less than 200 animals. In 1997, non-resident hunting licenses were bought by 352 hunters, and 346 harvest returns were submitted. A total of 210 Dall's sheep were reportedly harvested by this group of hunters, along with 168 woodland caribou, 44 moose, 2 mountain goats, 17 wolves, and one wolverine. The subsistence kill is a small fraction of the total harvest. Consequently, Dall's sheep populations are only lightly cropped, and as a result, the average age of trophy rams taken is high despite a 3/4 curl regulation. Sheep have been taken by native people for subsistence use as required, but there are no strong sheep hunting traditions among the Mountain Dene people. Studies have been initiated to learn more about subsistence use.

Full curl harvest regulation has not been introduced because of the light harvest and desirable age structure of the populations. Non-residents strive for full curled rams and there are few sheep kills by residents. The few residents that harvest sheep ap-

R. POPKO

Inset: Dall's sheep lambs are intensely curious.

The rugged Mackenzie Mountains of the Northwest Territories provides a vast expanse of nearly unbroken habitat for Dall's sheep.

pear to be primarily meat hunters which are not interested in trophies and who do not compete for large heads. However, some of the accessible areas are currently being heavily harvested.

The management of sheep, as all other wildlife, is complex as it is shared by three jurisdictions: a federal jurisdiction applicable to Nahanni National Park (4,766 square kilometers) in the southern Mackenzie Mountains; tribal lands under land claims jurisdiction of the Sahtu Dene and Metis (68,000 square kilometers); tribal lands under Gwich'in jurisdiction (8,300 square kilometers) and the remaining lands in the Deh Cho region (where there is no land claims settlement). Lands under land claim jurisdiction are deemed privately owned and wildlife is managed in these areas by a fairly recent (1992 and 1993) co-management process involving native communities through Renewable Resource Boards. For lands not affected by land claims, the primary responsibility for natural resources management lies with the Northwest Territories and the Government of Canada. Renewable Resource Boards (half of whose members are native land claims participants) establish policies and propose regulations for wildlife harvest and allocation, approve wildlife management plans, conduct studies to aid in their deliberations, and approve regulations proposed by governments. Native people have thus a dominant voice in wildlife management through these Boards and the related, but community based, Renewable Resources Councils. An unusual feature of this arrangement is subsistence harvest of wildlife in national parks.

The Mackenzie Mountain region inhabited by sheep is large, pristine and subjected to little hunting pressure. It has been divided into eight zones, each awarded to a licensed outfitter who provides outfitting services. Non-resident hunting was first permitted in 1965, and sheep quickly became the main attraction. There are areas of good habitat within the Mackenzies occupied by good populations. Non-resident hunters report an overall high rate of satisfaction with their hunts. Studies have been initiated to learn more about the sheep, as there is realization that they represent a very valuable resource. The goals are to maintain a sustainable harvest and to have people from local communities involved in management as provided by the land claims process. Since wildlife is under a process of co-management, Sahtu Dene and Metis land claim participants have been trained in data collecting and are currently involved in obtaining data for management purposes.

Yukon Territory

The Yukon Territory has the largest wild sheep population of any jurisdiction in Canada. Both subspecies of thinhorn sheep (Dall's and Stone's sheep) occur in this Territory in near-pristine numbers, largely unaffected by human activities. Dall's sheep inhabit mountain ranges of the southwestern (Coast, Kluane, Ruby and Nisling Ranges), northern (Ogilvie and Werneke Mountains), and eastern (Hess, Selwyn, and Logan Mountains) Yukon, while Stone's sheep ranges extend northwesterly from central British Columbia through the Cassiar and Pelly Mountains to the MacArthur Range. These two subspecies intermingle in a broad band of the central Yukon. Intergrades show a wide range of intermediate pelage coloration. These sheep were at one time considered a separate taxonomic entity, referred as 'Fannin' or saddleback sheep.

Stone's sheep among the rolling, rounded mountains of the McArthur's Stone's Sheep Sanctuary in the central Yukon Territory.

Wildlife management 'formally' began in the Yukon in 1894, with passage of the Northwest Game Act in Ottawa when the Yukon was still a portion of the Northwest Territories. This Act provided the legal base for wildlife protection during the gold rush days of 1897 and the following years, when over 30,000 miners invaded the Klondike region. An amendment to this Act in 1900 granted the Yukon power to make ordinances for the protection of game. The first Game Ordnance, the Yukon Wildlife Act, was passed by the Territorial Council in 1901. Over the following years this Act was often subjected to amendment, revisions, or complete rewrites. The first amendment relative to wild sheep came into being in 1908, when all females of big game animals were protected.

During the first twenty years of its existence the Yukon Game Branch was solely an enforcement agency. In 1972, however, its mandate was expanded to include wildlife management, and the first biologists were hired. Since then, surveys have routinely been conducted to determine the distribution and abundance of big game animals. However, long before 1972, Charles Sheldon made the first attempt to map the distribution of wild sheep in the Yukon and to describe the range of pelage coloration observed between regional populations. Accompanied by biologist W. H. Osgood and wildlife artist Carl Rungius, he made expeditions to the Ogilvie, Werneke, Selwyn and other mountain ranges in 1904 and 1905, during which he collected specimens for the U.S. Biological Survey. His accomplishments in this regard were remarkable, especially considering the tremendous difficulties of travel at that time, long before aircraft were available. Sheldon's map on sheep distribution and color patterns, published in his book, *The Wilderness of the Upper Yukon* in 1911, represents an accomplishment that has not been duplicated on a Yukon-wide scale since.

Inventories of wild sheep populations have been completed in over 80 percent of the known ranges, and for the remaining areas estimates were made using harvest information. Based on this information, compiled in 1989, it was estimated

Dall's sheep ram.

© VALERIUS GEIST

that there were about 22,000 sheep in the Yukon. Most (over 18,000) of these were Dall's sheep; dark Stone's sheep numbered about 1,500 animals, and about 2,500 sheep represented the variably-colored 'Fannins' (also considered as Stone's sheep). This estimate is the best available, although probably optimistic. Since 1984, certain populations are known to have declined (probably due to weather-related influences), although the extent of such declines is unknown. About 25 percent (5,400) of the Yukon's sheep are protected in National Parks or sanctuaries.

Sheep population densities over the Yukon are highly variable. Estimates range from 2 to 30 sheep per square kilometer. The highest densities have been documented in the southwest Yukon, in the Coast, Kluane and Ruby Ranges. This is also the area where trophy quality is the highest, as reflected in entries to the Boone and Crockett Club's Records Program. The 1988 edition lists 24 Yukon entries in the top 100 Dall's rams, 18 of which originated in the southwest Yukon.

The annual harvest has been relatively stable (at 250 to 300 rams taken per year) since the early 1970s. The majority of these (70 percent) have been taken annually by nonresident hunters, who provide about $5 million to Yukon economies through the outfitting industry. About one-third of this amount comes from sheep hunters, and sheep top the list of trophy animals sought by nonresidents. All nonresident hunters since 1933 have been required to employ the services of a licensed guide. Guide areas are exclusive; only 20 currently exist in the Yukon. Harvest of sheep

MANFRED HOEFS

Inset: Fannin, or light-colored Stone's sheep, intergrade from nearly white with scattered dark hairs to sheep demonstrating a pronounced dark saddle.

The rugged but chalky Wernecke Mountains of northern Yukon are home to a few scattered herds of Dall's sheep.

VALERIUS GEIST

Summary of thinhorn sheep distribution in the Yukon Territory.

Mountain Range	Herd Estimate	Map
Southwestern Yukon		
Kluane Ranges	5,000	1
Coast Mountains	3,600	2
Ruby Range	4,000	3
Nisling Range	200	3
Dawson Range	100	3
Central Yukon		
Cassiar Mountains	100	4
Pelly Range	1,300	4
Glenlyon Range	550	4
Anvil Range	120	4
MacArthur Sanctuary	70	4
White Mountains	60	4
Eastern Yukon		
Hess Mountains	840	5
Logan Mountains and Labiche	350	5
Northern Yukon		
Ogilvie Mountains	2,600	6
Wernecke Mountains	2,650	7
Arctic Yukon		
Richardson Mountains	500	8
British Mountains	100	9
Total	**Approximately 22,000**	

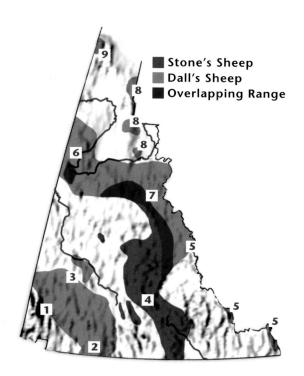

Stone's Sheep
Dall's Sheep
Overlapping Range

is limited to full-curl rams, and all animals harvested must be examined and permanently marked by government officials. In addition to harvest of rams by resident and nonresident hunters, there is some subsistence hunting by native people. Commercial hunting was eliminated in the Yukon in 1951.

Wild sheep management in the Yukon emphasizes trophy production, although a few herds are specifically set aside for wildlife viewing. Recently released Sheep Management Guidelines emphasize ecosystem management and the maintenance of biodiversity. This progressive approach recognizes the special importance of small, isolated populations, habitat conservation, and maintenance of both natural age structures and sex ratios in populations. In a departure from past management guidelines, new policies would allow selective harvest of young rams (and ewes in some circumstances) to meet management objectives, but this provision has not been applied so far.

Management of wild sheep and other wildlife in the Yukon faces many challenges. Most important among these is the territorial status of the Yukon Territory itself. Although wildlife management was transferred to territorial control in 1900, jurisdiction over territorial lands remains with the federal government in Ottawa. Since wildlife is dependent on the land base that provides its habitat, potential problems arising from this division of responsibilities are obvious.

Dall's sheep ewes and lambs in the St. Elias Range, high elevation alpine summer range.

VALERIUS GEIST

61

Chapter Four

THE ROCKY MOUNTAIN BIGHORN SHEEP

ocky Mountain bighorn sheep, with their blocky bodies, thick curling horns, and great agility are the "Kings of the Crags." The most widespread of the various races of wild sheep in North America, they have inspired awe and respect among naturalists and hunters since their discovery in the early 1800s.

DESCRIPTION

The first Rocky Mountain bighorn sheep record dates back to November 29, 1800, when a ram and three ewes were collected by Duncan McGillivray just to the east of present-day Banff, Alberta. Skins and skulls were preserved and later described by David Thompson, the famous Canadian explorer and cartographer.

Rocky Mountain bighorn sheep are striking animals, with dark brown to light brown hair over most of their bodies, strikingly set off by a large white rump patch, white linings along the rear surfaces of all four legs, and white at the front of the muzzle surrounding the nose and lower jaw. Both sexes have horns. Horns of the ewes are short, thin, and slightly curving over their 8 to 10-inch length, while those of the males are much more massive. Horns of old rams curve up and back before dropping to curve forward and curling upward in front of the eye, completing a complete circle (or more) when viewed from the side. The horns diverge slightly from the top of the skull, typically curving either straight down (in younger rams) or slightly inward as they complete their rotation. Bases may exceed 17 inches in circumference, and length may exceed 45 inches.

VIC COGGINS

Rocky Mountain bighorn sheep are synonymous with alpine vistas.

Rocky Mountain bighorns are blocky animals, with heavy compact bodies and relatively short legs. These are cold-adapted sheep, which even today live largely at high latitudes and altitudes and face long, snowy winters. Scientists have found that bighorns are thermal-neutral at 10°F; that is, bighorns in environments above this temperature must actively work to lose body heat. Ray Stemp has shown that bighorn

sheep actually elevate their heart rate in summer to help cool their bodies. Mature rams typically stand about 40 inches tall at the shoulder, and weigh from 160 to 250 pounds, with exceptional animals weighing as much as perhaps 300 pounds. Ewes are smaller, about 36 inches tall at the shoulder, with body weights typically ranging from 115 to 200 pounds.

Bighorn sheep are social animals. Large, mature rams dominate bighorn sheep society. Dominance in ram society is based on horn size.

Older rams typically return to higher elevation pastures with the arrival of spring 'green-up.' Ewes, most of which were impregnated during the November rut, typically move to mid-elevation rugged terrain sometime in March. By this time they have separated from their lambs of the previous season, which now follow any sheep of their choice— often old, barren ewes— and ignore their own mother. These older ewes perform an important social function, keeping the 'short yearlings' together while the pregnant ewes depart from ewe bands to give birth to their new lambs. The adult ewes isolate themselves on small rocky benches or outcrops (following a gestation period of about 175 days) prior to giving birth to an 8 to 10 pound lamb (rarely twins) sometime between late April and mid-June. Lambs are precocious, able to walk and climb shortly after birth, and able to accompany their mother throughout the rugged cliffs within one or two days. Lambs begin eating green grasses and forbs within a few weeks, and ewes with their lambs typically rejoin to form large maternal groups. These groups of 10 to 50 or more animals

TOM TIETZ

Looking at a newborn lamb (inset) it is difficult to envision mature Rocky Mountain bighorn rams–tough and blocky masters of their near-vertical environments.

Not only must Rocky Mountain bighorn sheep master their alpine terrain to be successful, they must also adapt to sudden, severe storms and long winters.

TOM TIETZ

share the advantage of having many individuals alert for predators at all times, reducing the potential for predation on the small lambs. In addition, nursery groups of lambs, cared for by a few ewes, form periodically, allowing most of the ewes greater freedom to forage further away from the security of cliffs and thereby to regain lost body condition. Lambs are usually weaned at about four to five months of age.

RANGE AND HABITAT SELECTION

The range of Rocky Mountain bighorn sheep is provided in the name: these are animals of the Rocky Mountains and associated mountain ranges, south from British Columbia's Peace River through the intermountain west into northern Arizona and New Mexico. Wherever they occur, bighorn sheep are animals that rely on broken, rugged and open terrain. Although bighorn sheep do use the kinds of near-vertical cliffs favored by mountain goats, they more often feed away from these areas into nearby basins and meadows where more food is to be found. Bighorn seldom stray far from rocky escape cover, however, and avoid flat plains, river valleys and forested areas. Annual winter snow accumulations at the high elevation habitats used in the summer may trigger annual migrations to the edges of river valleys and open rolling hills during winter months (especially in northern areas). Bighorns may remain at high elevations throughout the winter if there are locations

Inset: Bighorn rams feast on spring vegetation when available, to replenish body condition and provide nutrients that promote horn development.

Locating food under winter snows can be difficult, forcing bighorn sheep to seek wind-blown ridges where some grasses emerge from beneath the snow.

DON L. MACCARTER

WALT VAN DYKE

where a combination of snow-shadow effects and high winds prevent accumulations of snow great enough to make forage unavailable.

Bighorn sheep were remarkably abundant in the early nineteenth century; Thomas Seton estimated that there may have been up to two million bighorn sheep in North America around 1800. Although this estimate was likely high, many scientists who have examined archaeological evidence and reviewed accounts left by explorers believe that bighorn sheep may well have been the most common big game animal in mountainous regions. Currently, about 35,000 Rocky Mountain bighorn sheep are found in North America.

Alpine summer ranges for Rocky Mountain bighorns typically occur at elevations of 8,000 to 13,000 feet. These areas are generally very limited in distribution except along the British Columbia/Alberta border and southward in Wyoming and Colorado. They are characterized by relatively short growing seasons, but offer a great variety of highly nutritious plants selected by bighorns— sedges, willows, and a wide variety of flowering plants. Competition for food on alpine summer ranges is low. Few native wildlife species heavily use the kinds of terrain favored by bighorn sheep. Domestic sheep use some of the high-elevation pastures, but overall use is limited due to the uncertain weather and the difficulty of retrieving domestic livestock from these areas. However, many bighorn sheep live year-round on ranges found below 8,000 feet, and almost all make at least winter use of such areas. These areas are characterized by a wide variety of grasses (wheatgrasses, bluegrasses, bunchgrasses, and fescues) and shrubs (including snowberry and sagebrushes) used as food by bighorns— and also favored by both domestic livestock as well as elk and mule deer. Most of these ranges have been heavily used by domestic livestock, and many have been damaged by past grazing practices. Competition for food on these low-elevation ranges may be high, especially if also grazed by domestic livestock.

Population estimates for Rocky Mountain bighorn sheep (excluding California bighorns) in North America. Bighorn sheep occupy many remote areas difficult to access, and so the population estimates provided here reflect the most recent information available from biologists and managers nationwide. Numbers are from Buechner (1960), Trefethen (1975), and Thorne et al. (1985).

Location	1960	1975	1985	1998
Alberta	—	9,250	10,000	5,000- 8,000
Arizona	0	0	0	500
BC	—	1,250	3,000	3,000
Colorado	2,500-3,200	—	6,045	6,995
Idaho	2,400-2,800	—	2,805	1,640
Montana	1,400-1,700	2,250	4,600	4,790
Nebraska	0	0	0	57
Nevada	0	16	70	276
New Mexico	0	300	500	600
Oregon	0	55	250	490
South Dakota	22	150	165	375
Utah	Remnant	0	200	850
Washington	0	20	266	200
Wyoming	1,800-2,000	4,500	6,305	6,725
Total	**8,100-9,700**	**19,450**	**34,206**	**31,498- 34,498**

Alberta

When early Europeans entered what was to become Alberta's East Slope around the turn of the nineteenth century they viewed a spectacular panorama of foothills and mountains capable of a high level of wildlife production. The presence of sheep in large numbers, especially in areas where warm winter winds characterized the climate, must have been an impressive sight. While it is unlikely that early explorers like Peter Fidler (1792) and David Thompson (1800) recognized it, the longest stretch of almost continuous bighorn sheep habitat ever found in one political jurisdiction depended on its ecological ties with the river valleys and prairie-to-mountain habitat transition. At the same time, they could not have foreseen the changes that they, by their very presence, were initiating. Until that time in history sheep populations had been confined in numbers and distribution by natural forces, particularly predation by wolves.

But change came quickly as Europeans invaded the area, bringing their firearms and trading them to native Canadians. By the 1880s there were still only 1,500 Europeans in what was to become Alberta, but they had already begun to occupy the foothills and all major passes through the Rocky Mountains. Bighorn sheep on winter-spring ranges were highly vulnerable, and white and native hunters exploited them for subsistence and commercial use. In the next 30 years immigration exploded. Alberta's population expanded to include almost 500,000 Europeans; 264 coal mines were in existence by 1914, and timber, oil, and gas were flowing from the mountains. Work crews were fed on wild game; bighorn sheep populations were decimated. The world record bighorn was shot under these circumstances. Fred Weiler was a meat hunter for early oil exploration crews drilling in what is now Waterton Lakes National Park. In 1911 he shot, perhaps within the same park, what later became known as the famous Baird head. There were no limits on bighorn sheep kill until 1883; then a limit of six per year existed until 1898. Between 1899 and 1900 the legal kill was three per year.

In retrospect, it is likely that entire subpopulations of bighorns with unique and traditional knowledge of winter ranges and movement corridors were eradicated, severely curtailing the gene pool of surviving sheep. It was only the first bottleneck bighorn populations would endure at the hands of man. Today, Alberta bighorns have a very low level of genetic variation when compared with Rocky Mountain bighorn sheep populations in Montana, Idaho, Wyoming, and Colorado.

While critical low elevation ranges extending eastward from the Rocky Mountains were lost forever, as were the exceptional ecological phenomena associated with movements to and from those ranges, summer and fall ranges in the heart of the Rockies remained intact. We do not know if sheep wintered at high elevations historically. But the loss of low elevation and most eastern ranges could have produced today's high-elevation wintering populations of low productivity. Despite claims to the contrary, it is only a remote possibility that bighorn populations have recovered to historical abundance in Alberta after their depletion at the turn of the century.

Estimates of the size of bighorn populations have been unsound: they suffer from lack of consistency in methods, from lack of correction for sightability, typically are statistically unreliable, and have been divorced from the reality of sheep movements (issues we know have a significant bearing on the results.) Thus reported recovery of sheep numbers and estimates of population size reflecting that recovery must be viewed with skepticism. Pre-European numbers probably exceeded 10,000 sheep, and may have periodically reached 20,000, but by the early 1900s mere remnants of these once vast populations remained. Based on the opinions of hunters and guides it was estimated that as few as 1,775 sheep existed in Alberta in 1915. The Alberta Game Act was passed in 1907 and licenses were required as of 1909. Yet bag limits remained at two of either sex between 1909

A 'cirque' or high mountain basin at the head of Misty Creek, Alberta. Areas like this are often favored as feeding areas by bighorn sheep.

VALERIUS GEIST

Rams such as these near Hinton, Alberta, epitomize Rocky Mountain bighorns.

VALERIUS GEIST

VALERIUS GEIST

Chinook winds are critical to the survival of wild sheep ranges in parts of the northern Rocky Mountains. The Palliser Range of Banff National Park, Alberta, is shown here in summer (above) and in winter (below), when cleared of snow by warm Chinook winds.

and 1922, after which legal sport kill (as opposed to native kill) was restricted to males until 1966. A minimum 3/4 curl regulation for males was introduced in 1956; it was increased to 4/5 curl in 1968.

Still, it is highly probable that populations did recover above early 1900 levels. They did so because conservationists and hunters recognized that unrestricted commercial and native hunting had wrought catastrophic consequences on Alberta's bighorn sheep. They had been "forced to the conclusion that the time had passed when wild game was a legitimate part of our food supply"...a "cold, hard, inexorable fact" as recorded by Vreeland in 1916. Population recovery also came at a big cost in biodiversity of wildlife, for wolves were exterminated in southern Alberta and grizzly bears and mountain lions reduced to populations of questionable viability. Sheep populations recovered because habitat, while lost adjacent to the prairies, still remained in unfragmented core areas in the heart of the Rocky Mountains. This habitat still had a significant capacity to produce sheep.

Furthermore, insight and vision had prevailed on some critical areas. Rocky Mountain Park, later to become Banff National Park, was established in 1885; Yoho National Park followed in 1886; Jasper National park in 1907; and Kootenay National Park in 1920. While sheep populations in these parks had not escaped man's early impact, the habitat had remained secure. However, complicating the status of sheep populations in these parks was a provincial management strategy that "milked" trans-boundary sheep populations. Other populations suffered heavy mortality from road and railroad kills; one has been exterminated by road expansion in Banff National Park. Others were depleted or lost during die offs that affected herds in the general

region. Even in national parks there are large areas void of bighorns where they were once seen in abundance.

Although Alberta's hunting and conservation community had repelled the doom of commercial and unregulated hunting, these dangers would reappear almost a century later. But before that, a new threat arrived: domestic livestock. Cattle were exploiting every valley in the Rocky Mountains by the turn of the century. They were followed by large numbers of domestic sheep. This invasion led to contacts that resulted in respiratory diseases and catastrophic mortality among bighorns. By the early 1940s bighorn sheep, whose numbers are speculated to have recovered to somewhere around 4,000 animals, were dying in large numbers in southern Alberta. That die-off led to the closure of hunting seasons.

Coincident with the invasion of bighorn habitat by domestic sheep were major forest fires in the 1930s that burned almost all of Alberta's forested foothills. While this was a natural process essential to ecological renewal and was undoubtedly beneficial to bighorn sheep, it resulted in heightened fire control activity of the Alberta Forest Service. It led to the construction of the Forest Trunk Road through the length and heart of the Rocky Mountains. Begun in 1948 and officially completed in 1963, this road impacted Alberta's sheep country in a way that lasts to this day. Regulatory changes compounded the impact of road access as in 1946 the Game Act recognized the right of aboriginal people to hunt year long on occupied public lands.

Where before horse or foot travel was the only means of access, now anybody could drive into sheep country in a day or less. Aboriginal Canadians exploited roads to kill entire bands of bighorns. Some areas were permanently abandoned by sheep. Widespread demand for sheep hunting led the Alberta Fish and Wildlife Division to try and manage sheep to maximize total kill. In 1966 hunting of females was introduced. It was hoped, among other wishes, that this would alleviate mass die-offs of sheep, but it did not. They happened again in the 1980s in southern Alberta.

Alberta's sheep managers have not been very successful in stemming the threats to habitat integrity. This inability has a historic basis going back to 1930, when public land devolved from federal to provincial control. When the Fish and Wildlife Division took control of game management in the late 1940s the utilitarian interests of griculture, timber, oil, and gas had es-ablished their claim to wildlife abitat under Forest Service control. he ability of the Fish and Wildlife Division to protect habitat is fre-uently frustrated by various claims o the land, including the develop-nent of Olympic ski facilities or nining developments. The bio-cul-ural storehouse of knowledge of he remaining free ranging big-orn sheep continues to be hreatened, as these populations ate low priority compared to vari-ous commercial uses of public lands.

Today, with bighorn sheep numbers estimated at 5,000-8,000, heep management continues to push he limits of sound scientific management nd habitat protection as managers attempt o cope with intense industrial and recre-tional demands on public resources. One

contentious issue among residents is the auction of hunting permits by the Alberta government. Through this process, a few wealthy individu-als may be allowed opportunities denied to others, such as hunting after traditional seasons have been closed and hunting when bighorns are concentrated on rutting ranges and most vulnerable. Perhaps most seriously, the present management course fails to control historic im-pacts on sheep (i.e. depleting genetic and cultural variation) and the ecosystems they depend upon. And after 125 years of increasing human impact, the province still has no habitat protection legislation based on what seems fundamental to the future: designated threshold levels for human activity in moun-tain and foothill ecosystems.

High alpine summer habitat of Rocky Mountain bighorn sheep in northern Jasper National Park, Alberta. Some sheep even winter on these high-elevation wind swept ranges.

Arizona

In 1979, eight Rocky Mountain bighorn sheep captured in Colorado's Rocky Mountain National Park were released near Bush Creek in the Upper Blue River area on the east-central Arizona border. This release consisted of two young rams and six ewes. In 1980, 12 additional Rocky Mountain bighorns (five young rams and seven ewes) captured near Tarryall, Colorado were also released at Bush Creek. The animals quickly took to their new surroundings, producing six known lambs in the first two breeding periods. The animals also began dispersing, seeming to prefer an area just west of the release site near Foote Creek.

The New Mexico Game and Fish Department also transplanted Rocky Mountain bighorn sheep just to the east of this herd, in the Gila Forest along the Arizona-New Mexico state line. In 1964, 10 Rocky Mountain bighorns captured in Banff National Park were released near Turkey Creek, and in 1965, 16 more were captured in New Mexico's Sandia Mountains (which had previously received sheep from Banff) and released along the San Francisco River near the state line. Some of these animals occasionally moved into Arizona. The present population of Rocky Mountain bighorn sheep in Arizona is, therefore, derived from the original transplants directly from Colorado, and indirectly via New Mexico.

Since these original transplants little work has been done with Arizona's Rocky Mountain bighorn sheep. Management efforts and public interest have been directed primarily towards the state's desert bighorn sheep. Other than semi-regular surveys little additional information has been gathered since the original radio-collars ceased functioning. With the opening of a hunting season and the allowance of a 'once-in-a-lifetime' Rocky Mountain bighorn sheep to go along with a 'once-in-a-lifetime' desert bighorn sheep, interest in Rocky Mountain bighorns increased dramatically.

During the summer of 1992, the Arizona Game and Fish Department developed a project to acquire additional information regarding the Rocky Mountain bighorn sheep. This project was designed to help ensure the success of future transplants and to answer several management questions regarding the sheep, such as distribution and movements (especially whether there was still movement across the Arizona/New Mexico state line); habitat types inhabited by Rocky Mountain bighorns; mortality patterns and causes; and health and potential vitamin deficiencies among bighorn sheep. Information concerning the potential for disease outbreaks in the area occupied by Rocky Mountain bighorns is also obtained by examining blood samples from domestic livestock, to determine whether antibodies to known diseases are present.

The Arizona Game and Fish Department retained its interest in transplanting additional Rocky Mountain bighorn sheep to further establish these animals in Arizona, expanding the herd and forming a contiguous population. In 1994 and 1995, 48 Rocky Mountain bighorns were captured in Colorado and released along the Blue River. These animals are currently being radio-tracked to determine their distribution and level and cause of mortality.

Rocky Mountain bighorn sheep populations have been very productive in Arizona. The present population is estimated at over 500 animals. Hunting seasons for these animals were initiated in 1984 when one permit was issued. By 1995, permit numbers had been increased to 10. To date, 52 rams have been harvested.

Rocky Mountain bighorn sheep in Arizona's Black River country.

British Columbia

Currently in British Columbia, Rocky Mountain bighorn sheep are discontinuously distributed in localized populations along the western slopes of Rocky Mountains. This distribution extends northward from the international border to about 54° 50' N. The most continuous section of occupied habitat extends from the international border near Grasmere to just north of Yoho National Park. The general distribution of bighorn sheep is believed to represent their historic range in British Columbia, but current distribution is probably less continuous than in the past. Fossil remains of bighorn sheep in British Columbia date to between 5,000 and 10,000 years ago, but these have not yet been identified to subspecies.

Outside the natural range, there are other populations of Rocky Mountain bighorns in British Columbia resulting from introductions. The first introduction of Rocky Mountain bighorns outside of native range in B.C. was made in 1927 when 99 Bighorn from Banff, Alberta, were transplanted into what was probably historical California bighorn sheep range near Spences Bridge and Squilax in south-central B.C. The largest herd (Spences Bridge) is found between the Fraser and Thompson Rivers north of Lytton. A second introduced herd (also resulting from Alberta sheep) inhabits an area along the south side of the South Thompson River east from Chase to Squilax and south to the Turtle Valley. In addition, there are two more isolated populations of Rocky Mountain bighorn sheep outside their natural range. One inhabits an area near Deer Park at the south end of Lower Arrow Lake, north and west of Castlegar. It originated from 20 sheep captured along the east side of Columbia River near Canal Flats in the East Kootenay in 1985, and from 18 more taken from Stoddart Creek south of Radium Hotsprings in 1987. The other population is a small herd found just north of where Idaho, Washington, and British Columbia, meet. This is the South Salmo herd, and these animals are the result of the northern dispersal of Rocky Mountain bighorn sheep from a herd introduced into the Hall Mountain area of Washington state in 1972 (from Waterton National Park, Alberta).

Besides transplants within the province, British Columbia has provided bighorn sheep for reintroductions to the United States (Colorado, Idaho, Nevada, North Dakota, Oregon, Washington, California, and Utah) where native Rocky Mountain and California sheep populations had been decimated. Today, many of these reintroduced herds have grown sufficiently to provide animals for reintroductions elsewhere.

The British Columbia Provincial Wildlife Branch estimated that there were about 3,100 Rocky Mountain bighorn sheep in the province in 1998. Most populations appear stable, although the subspecies is included in the Province's 1998 Blue List of species at risk. Reasons for this designation include their low absolute abundance, the low number of occurrences (i.e., herds or populations), threats to their habitat, and the long history of major die-offs among Rocky Mountain bighorn sheep populations in B.C. (the most recent in the 1980s). So far these die-offs have been restricted to native herds in southwestern B.C.

The reduction in numbers and distribution of Rocky Mountain bighorns in B.C. is believed to have been caused by over-exploitation around the turn of the century. In addition, disease related die-offs have occurred periodically, typically when animals occurred at high densities on winter range. Large scale die-offs of all age groups have resulted in losses of well over half of the animals in individual herds. Such die-offs have been reported since the 1800s in Rocky Mountain bighorn sheep herds in the East Kootenay portion of the province. Although most die-offs have been associated with pneumonia, a significant die-off in the introduced Rocky Mountain bighorn sheep population near Chase in 1987 was diagnosed by Agriculture Canada as an outbreak of 'hemorrhagic disease.' Other mortality is seen as losses of lambs, usually in the first six months.

Research suggests the pneumonia die-offs have been related to interactions of environmental stress factors that reduce sheep immunity to disease, especially in the presence of infectious microorganisms and lungworm. Disease outbreaks are characterized by acute or chronic pneumonia. Affected animals often die suddenly, others are debilitated and killed by predators. Factors which appear to be associated with all-age die-offs in B.C. include contact with domestic sheep and goats, deficiencies of key trace minerals, changes in sheep diet, poor nutrition, high

Mature Rocky Mountain bighorn ram prepares for winter even as early season snows begin to fall.

population densities, inclement weather, and other stress-producing events. It has been suggested that disease-related mortality may be reduced or avoided by keeping domestic sheep and goats separated from wild sheep, while improving range quality with active range management programs. Treatment of herds with anti-helminthics and supplementing trace minerals has not been successful, by themselves, in preventing disease outbreaks. Research to develop methods of minimizing disease-related fluctuations in population numbers is a high priority.

Although native peoples made relatively little use of Rocky Mountain bighorn sheep in British Columbia, sheep were utilized for more than meat and hides. Drill handles, combs, and knives were made from sheep bones, while the horns of rams were fashioned into ladles, bowls, and ornaments. In some cases, either raw horns or implements made from them made their way to distant tribes through intertribal commerce.

Bighorn sheep in British Columbia are currently managed to optimize population sustainability within ecosystems, while allowing for options and opportunities associated with viewing and hunting. Where bighorn sheep hunting seasons are prescribed, the level of harvest is adjusted to meet hunter demand, within the constraints of conservation and allowance for non-hunting uses. Rocky Mountain bighorn sheep are currently harvested under a general open season "full curl" regulation. If the harvest of large rams exceeds the annual allowable harvest, limited entry hunting is used to further regulate harvest by residents. Quotas or administrative guidelines are used to regulate the guided, non-resident harvest. Ewe and lamb hunting are allowed in some areas where sheep numbers have increased above population management objectives, or where it is deemed necessary to maintain a stable, prescribed balance with habitat carrying capacity. Regulations require that hunters remove

Estimated numbers of Rocky Mountain bighorn sheep in British Columbia from 1985 to 1998. Map scale does not allow distinct herds ranges to be shown.

Location & Herd Name	1985	1990	1998	Comments
Spences Bridge	100	350	400	introduced outside native range
Chase	40	6	20	introduced outside native range
Flathead	?	40	40	includes Middlepass (10), Pollack Creek (5) & Sage/ Kishenina (25) herds
Phillips Creek	35	70	100	
Maquire/Red Canyon	14	50	50	
Wigwam/China Wall	100	200	300	
South Salmo		30	25	also called Salmo/Lost Mountain herd
Deer Park		70	40	also called Deer Park/ Pine Ridge herd
Bull River	37	110	130	
Upper Bull	?	20	30	
Wildhorse River	14	70	50	
Estella	35	80	80	also called Tracy Creek herd
Premier	76	160	120	also called Wasa Creek herd
Marmalade	35	70	70	
Lusier/Blackfoot	?	90	60	
Elko	?	100	85	
Quarrie Creek	?	50	30	
Bingay Creek	?	30	30	
Crossing Creek	?	50	50	
Brule Creek	?	30	30	
Upper Elk	?	30	30	
Ewin Creek	225	225	225	
Imperial Ridge	?	20	20	
Eagle/Brownie	?	25	50	also called Mt. Turnbull herd
Van Nostrand	14	?	60	also called Lussier/Blackfoot or Blackfoot
Whiteswan	40	50	40	
Mt. Glenn	?	20	20	
Nine Mile	?	50	50	also called Gibraltar Rock herd
Columbia Lake	152	250	120	
Windermere	22	70	70	
Stoddart Creek	130+	155	240	includes Kindersley/Luxor/Radium Springs
Assiniboine	65	120	60	also called Simpson River herd
Kootenay/Cross R	?	30	30	also called Kootenay River herd
Kicking Horse Pass	?	15	35	
Sheep Mountain	75	70	70	
Todhunter	25	25	35	
Deadman Pass	?	20	40	
Corbin	?	25	25	
Hamber Park	?	?	?	no estimates available
Kakwa	94	?	100	
Annual Totals	**1,328**	**2,876**	**3,060**	

the edible portions of the carcass to a place of consumption and submit the horns for compulsory inspection. Because Rocky Mountain bighorn sheep are a blue-listed species in British Columbia, they are managed more cautiously than many other ungulates.

Colorado

Bighorn sheep were apparently present in most mountainous areas of Colorado prior to the arrival of trappers, miners and settlers. Early explorers of the area provided accounts of observing bighorn sheep in several areas along the front range of the Rocky Mountains. In later years, hunters and naturalists provided accounts of seeing numerous herds of bighorn sheep in the Manitou Springs and Pike's Peak area, as well as the mountainous areas surrounding South Park. A hunter by the name of Rufous B. Sage described a hunt in which he killed several bighorn sheep in the foothills west of Denver in 1844, but stated that deer were more numerous than bighorn sheep in that particular area. Buechner, in his monograph on bighorn sheep in the United States, provides accounts of bighorn sheep abundance and distribution from early settlers in the Estes Park area near present-day Rocky Mountain National Park. Various accounts provide estimates of sheep numbers in Rocky Mountain National Park as high as 4,000 animals during the middle of the nineteenth century.

It is apparent that bighorn sheep occurred in fairly large numbers in many of the mountainous regions of the state although no reliable estimates of numbers of sheep are available from the mid-1800s. In 1915, a survey of bighorn sheep for Boone and Crockett Club estimated there were 7,230 bighorn sheep in Colorado. Sheep numbers declined from that early estimate to an estimated 3,200 in 1958 and 2,200 in 1970. Market hunting and disease appear to be the main factors causing the decline of bighorn sheep in the late 1800s and early 1900s. Sheep in the Estes Park area were especially vulnerable to market hunting as they would migrate to lower elevations down the Big Thompson and St. Vrain river canyons.

Disease in the form of scabies was first identified in bighorn sheep in the Estes Park area from a

Colorado rams survey their surroundings.

JOHN ELLENBERGER

JOHN ELLENBERGER

hunter-killed animal in 1880. Scabies were thought to have been introduced to bighorn sheep from domestic sheep that began grazing in the area in the late 1870s. Recent research and information indicates that pneumonia, likely introduced by domestic sheep, was probably a more important disease factor than the scab mite. Disease, primarily pneumonia, has continued to plague bighorn sheep into the twentieth century. The most dramatic, recent decline of bighorn sheep occurred in the winter of 1953 in the Tarryall-Kenosha herd when a massive all-age die-off reduced a herd from approximately 1,000 to 30 animals.

When bighorn sheep reached such low numbers in the late 1800s it was feared that they might be extirpated from the state. The Colorado legislature outlawed the hunting of bighorn sheep in 1887. Hunting seasons were not reopened until 1953, when wildlife managers felt that limited hunting was needed to disperse concentrations of bighorn sheep and prevent die-offs like the one that occurred in the Tarryall Mountains. Management in the form of limited hunting, trap and transplant, and habitat manipulation are being used to maintain and augment bighorn sheep populations in the state.

The first transplant of Rocky Mountain bighorn sheep in Colorado occurred in 1945 with 16 sheep trapped in the Tarryall Range and released at Grant on the south side of Mount Evans. This began an intense period of trapping and transplant from the Tarryall Range that lasted for seven years and resulted in establishment or augmentation of many sheep

Bighorn lambs like to run, play and rest together, while the ewes watch their movements closely, but inconspicuously. Heart rate telemetry has shown that ewes are sensitive to losing sight of their lambs, such as these on the slopes of Poudre Canyon.

herds existing in Colorado today. In that seven-year period, 223 sheep were released at 13 different sites. The early use of the Tarryall herd as a transplant source ended in the winter of 1953 as a result of the massive die-off previously described.

The die-off of the Tarryall sheep herd resulted in a sharp decrease of bighorn trapping and transplant activity in the state. No sheep were transplanted until 1964 when 22 bighorns were trapped on Pike's Peak for transplant to South Dakota. Early sheep trapping efforts used a corral trap that wasn't easily moved or portable, and few herds in the state were easily accessible or had population sizes large enough to justify trapping for transplant.

Colorado's rocky Poudre River canyon offers near-ideal habitat for bighorn sheep.

Bear and Jones recommended in 1973 that an intensive trapping and transplant program needed to be reestablished in Colorado to establish new herds and to augment static or declining herds. Concurrent with their recommendations, new techniques for trapping bighorn sheep (portable drop-nets) and new anthelminthic drugs for treatment of lungworm infestations were developed. These breakthroughs not only facilitated trapping, but also increased lamb survival and recruitment. Since the mid-1970s, Colorado has enjoyed an aggressive trapping and transplant program that has seen the augmentation of existing herds and the reestablishment of herds on many historic ranges. The sheep population for the state has grown from a low (in 1970) of approximately 2,200 sheep in 39 herds to approximately 7,100 sheep in 66 herds today.

However, the status of Rocky Mountain bighorn sheep in Colorado is not as promising as it appears at first glance. Human population growth and increases in outdoor recreational activities present significant threats to bighorn sheep populations, in the form of encroachment on, and fragmentation of, bighorn sheep habitats. An evaluation of Colorado's bighorn sheep herds, and its trapping and transplanting program, was conducted by Bailey in 1990. Although bighorn herd size and populations have increased, there is still reason for concern. Approximately 55 percent of the sheep herds and 37 percent of all bighorns in Colorado are a result of some type of transplant activity. Only two of 25 transplants have resulted in sheep herds of more than 100 animals, and a substantial number of transplants have resulted in herds of less than 50 animals. Information from geneticists and conservation biologists indicate that herd sizes should be 150 animals or more in order to persist for long periods of time (i.e., more than 50 years).

The above information indicates that additional work and research needs to be conducted to ensure the long-term survival of our bighorn herds. However, trapping and transplanting is a viable management tool that has been very successful in the past, with over 2,100 Rocky Mountain bighorns having been trapped and moved to sites within Colorado and elsewhere.

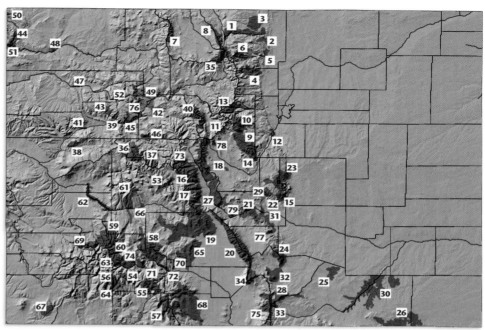

Herd Unit	Type	1981	1988	1998	Map
Upper Poudre	T	162	100	150	1
Lower Poudre	T	60	60	60	2
Lone Mtn.	T	80	20	0	3
Button Rock	T	40	0	0	4
Big Thompson	T	—	100	30	5
Rocky Mtn NP East	I	130	200	140	6
Mt. Zirkel	I	20	0	0	7
Rawahs	I	20	20	10	8
Grant	T	70	100	110	9
Mt. Evans	I	100	75	240	10
Kenosha Pass	I	80	75	150	11
Waterton Canyon	I	16	14	25	12
Georgetown	I	40	112	350	13
Tarryall	I	150	200	225	14
Pikes Peak	I	185	330	300	15
Collegiates North	I	150	160	180	16
Collegiates South	I	90	70	100	17
Buffalo Peaks	I	110	150	200	18
Marshall Pass	I	80	100	100	19
Sangre de Christo	I	200	650	685	20
Texas Creek	I	80	120	190	21
Beaver Creek	I	75	70	80	22
Rampart Rangee	T	60	125	45	23
Greenhorn Mtns	T	17	75	85	24
Apishapa	T	75	40	55	25
Carrizo	T	22	45	55	26
Brown's Canyon	T	40	125	100	27
Spanish Peaks East	T	16	70	150	28
Shelf Road	T	—	75	150	29
Purgatorie	T	—	120	240	30
Copper Gulch	T	—	115	200	31
Mt. Maestas	T	—	75	140	32
Spanish Peaks West	T	—	30	150	33
Mt. Blanca	T	—	25	55	34
Rocky Mtn NP West	I	150	250	175	35
Snowmass West	I	100	188	125	36
Snowmass East	I	120	150	100	37
Battlement Mesa	I	25	30	25	38
Clinetop Mesa	I	25	0	20	39
Gore Range	I	15	25	80	40
Parachute Creek	I	5	0	0	41
Brush Creek	I	0	0	0	42
Rifle Hogback	T	0	28	0	43
N Dinosaur/Ladore	T	80	65	60	44
Glenwood Canyon	T	0	0	15	45
Basalt	T	51	60	75	46
Little Hills	T	15	0	0	47
Cross Mtn	T	40	18	0	48
Derby Creek	T	19	40	65	49
Brown's Park	T	—	45	5	50
S Dinosaur/ Harpers/Yampa	T	—	40	70	51

Herd Unit	Type	1981	1988	1998	Map
S. Fk. White River	T	—	28	75	52
Taylor River	I	70	150	140	53
Cimarron Peak	I	75	65	100	54
Sheep Mtn	I	50	50	100	55
Vallecito	I	30	40	80	56
Blanco Basin	I	50	40	80	57
San Luis Peak	I	175	300	100	58
Ouray	I	200	40	80	59
Pole Mtn	I	54	60	20	60
Dillon Mesa	I	30	50	90	61
Gunnison/ Black Canyon	T	—	50	75	62
Wilson Peak	I	0	0	0	63
Hermosa	I	0	0	0	64
Trickle Mtn	T	425	225	85	65
Lower Lake Fork	T	48	12	20	66
Mesa Verde	T	12	25	10	67
Alamosa Canyon	T	60	100	50	68
Sawpit	T	30	10	10	69
Natural Arch	T	—	75	50	70
Bristol Head	T	—	50	30	71
Blue Creek	T	—	30	40	72
Mt. Elbert	T	—	—	75	73
Rio Grande/ Box Canyon	T	—	—	35	74
Costilla	T	—	—	—	75
Deep Creek	T	—	—	35	76
Hardscrabble Creek	T	—	20	—	77
Mt. Silverheels	T	—	20	25	78
Cedar Springs Gulch	T	—	20	25	79
TOTAL		**4,122**	**6,045**	**6,995**	

Population estimates for Rocky Mountain bighorn sheep in Colorado in 1988. Asterisks denote herds outside of Management Units. Herd names and numbering follow Bailey (1990). T - transplant herd and I - introduced herd.

Idaho

Rocky Mountain bighorn sheep ranged widely in Idaho during the early nineteenth century, and are believed to have been the single most abundant game animal in Idaho's mountains prior to about 1850. Although apparently none occurred in the Selkirk Mountains of north Idaho, bighorn sheep were abundant throughout central Idaho. Lewis and Clark were informed that mountain sheep were common in the Clearwater Mountains, especially in the main divide of the Bitterroot Range on the state line with Montana and west of the Clark Fork River. Three members of the Corps of Discovery saw bighorns north of the Salmon River about 10 miles upstream of its confluence with the Snake River, and Indian petroglyphs of bighorn sheep are relatively common along the Snake River in Hells Canyon. Captain Bonneville reported that bighorns were common and easily killed by hunters near the present town of Salmon in the winter of 1832. Settlers appeared in this area in the 1850s, and reported bighorns abundant, especially in the Lemhi Valley. Bighorn sheep were apparently common near the head of the Middle Fork of the Salmon River in the 1880s, and two trappers reported seeing 2,000-2,500 bighorn sheep there as late as 1897. Bighorns were also numerous in the upper Boise River and Payette River drainages. South and east, in the Lost River Mountains, Abe Leeds (a guide for Thomas Seton) reported thousands of bighorn sheep in the late 1800s. Many bighorns occurred near the head of the Pahsimeroi River east of Mt. Borah in the late 1880s, and bighorns occurred in smaller numbers in the Sawtooth Range during that same period. Bighorns were also common in the 1880s in the present vicinity of Yellowstone and Grand Teton National Parks.

Rocky Mountain bighorn sheep also occurred south of the Snake River Plain. The trapper Osborne Russell and 15 others in his party wintered between the present site of Lava Hot Springs and Chesterfield during the winter of 1835-1836, attracted to the area specifically because of the abundance of bighorn sheep. Bighorns probably occupied all of the mountain ranges in southeastern Idaho until at least the mid-1800s. Further west, in Owyhee County, bighorn sheep were also abundant, but these are believed to have been California bighorn sheep with a closer affinity to Oregon and northern Nevada herds.

DECLINE

Idaho's Rocky Mountain bighorn sheep were a favorite source of food for the fur trappers of the early nineteenth century, and both Captain Bonneville and Osborne Russell offer accounts of wintering near bighorn sheep winter ranges specifically to subsist on 'fat mutton.' Although Captain Bonneville commented on the ease with which bighorns could be surrounded and shot, Osborne Russell cautioned his readers that, "Hunting sheep is often attended with great danger especially in the winter season when the rocks and precipices are covered with snow and ice but the excitement created by hunting them often enables the hunter to surmount obstacles which at other times would seem impossible."

Settlement of Idaho in the mid-1800s resulted in increased harvest of bighorns, and this harvest accelerated sharply following discovery of gold in central Idaho in the 1860s and 1870s. Miners were followed by boom-towns, and boom-towns were followed by market hunters. However, despite initial declines among bighorn sheep herds that wintered in the more accessible areas, bighorn populations apparently remained healthy until about 1870.

John Hawley brought thousands of domestic sheep into central Idaho's Wood River Country in the 1860s. By 1870 the first of a series of die-offs among Rocky Mountain bighorn sheep were reported. George Shoup wrote:

"But, at this time a disease, commonly thought to be scabies, destroyed so many that they became much reduced in number... The sheep appeared to have died upon their winter feed ranges... Their bones were numerous into the 90s."

BILL HICKEY

Female lamb close to 12 months of age near Idaho's Salmon River.

Steep rocky slopes and bunch grasses typify Idaho's Hells Canyon.

83

A second epidemic of scabies and a severe winter around 1890 caused a further decline. In eastern Idaho, Rocky Mountain bighorns disappeared from Swan Valley about 1900, and in 1906, State Game Warden Stephens estimated that only 300-400 bighorn sheep remained in Idaho. A third die-off in the Salmon River country reportedly occurred about 1910, although a few years later, in 1914, the State Game Warden reported that a few bighorns still survived in the headwaters of the Salmon, Boise, and Payette Rivers. The last bighorn reported from Hells Canyon was killed in 1925.

Bighorn numbers along the Salmon River apparently stabilized from 1917-1927. Following a decline in 1928, populations appear to have grown slowly in their former ranges to a population of over 2,000 animals in 1949, the year the Idaho Department of Fish and Game initiated a study of bighorn sheep life history and management. As a result of this study, wildlife managers were better able to identify areas suitable for transplanting bighorns to reestablish herds, and focus on such critical limiting factors as winter range condition and diseases (particularly lungworm infestations). Native bighorn sheep herds along the Salmon River and its tributaries form the core of Idaho Rocky Mountain bighorn sheep populations. Research on the history and status of this herd was published in 1954, documenting periodic increases and declines in population size, a pattern that has persisted. These herds reached their most recent peak about 1990, when nearly 4,000 Rocky Mountain bighorns were believed to occur in Idaho. However, a widely dispersed disease outbreak was documented

Inset: A subordinate ram (middle) rubs his head and pre-orbital gland against the horns of a dominant ram – a common behavior among associates.

Petroglyphs featuring Indians and wild sheep are relatively common along the Snake River in Hells Canyon.

eginning in the winter of 1995-96. Most herds have ubsequently suffered serious declines in population ize. Idaho's population of Rocky Mountain bighorn heep is believed to have plummeted from nearly ,000 in 1990 to about 1,700 in 1998.

Transplants of Rocky Mountain bighorn sheep o reestablish herds in former habitats were initi- ted in 1969. Mahogany Creek in the upper ahsimeroi Valley near Mt. Borah received seven ighorns from near Salmon in 1969, and these were upplemented with 24 bighorns from Banff National ark, Alberta, in 1970.

Rocky Mountain bighorns were restored to lells Canyon in a series of transplants begun in 975, also using animals captured from the Salmon iver herd. These animals were supplemented by ighorns (also from the Salmon River herd) put on he Oregon side of the Snake iver near the mouth of the mnaha River in 1979 and 984, as part of an interstate ooperative venture. In 1984, ocky Mountain bighorns rom Wyoming's Whiskey Mountain herd were trans- lanted to Hells Canyon at raig Mountain, north of the mouth of the Salmon River. nake River herds were supple- nented again in 1997 with ocky Mountain bighorns ob- ained from Spences Bridge, ritish Columbia.

Efforts to reestablish erds along the Continental Di- ide were begun in 1976, with a eries of transplants into the lue Dome and Copper Moun- ain areas. Additional sheep vere moved to Birch Creek outhwest of Challis begin- ing in 1982.

Bighorn sheep restora- ion to the Lost River and ittle Lost River ranges was egun in 1978, using animals aptured from Whiskey Mountain in Wyoming. hese sheep were released into lbow and Jaggles Canyons in he Lost River range, and Bad- er and Little Lost Creeks of he Little Lost River range.

Rocky Mountain bighorn sheep populations in Idaho. Numbers appear in bighorn sheep wildlife management plans and Hebert and Evans (1991).

Area	Unit	1981	1985	1990	1998	Map
Craig Mtn./Redbird	11	10	25	30	80	1
Nez Perce Nat'l Park	14	50	25	15	10	2
Hells Canyon	18, 22	75	130	55	25	3
Selway River	17	125	135	75	50	4
Orogrande Summit	19	150	150	120	60	5
Porphyry Creek	19A	75	50	15	20	6
Bargamin Creek	20	250	220	200	80	7
South Fk. Salmon	20A	325	300	400	140	8
North Fk Salmon	21	150	200	250	150	9
Red Bluff	21A, 28	0	0	0	15	10
Big Creek	26	150	125	250	200	11
Middle Fk. Salmon	27	375	450	800	200	12
Main Salmon	28	250	300	400	150	13
Williams Creek	28	0	0	0	35	14
Eighteen-Mile Creek	30, 30A	0	30	60	30	15
East Fork Salmon	36, 36A	125	150	300	70	16
Morgan Creek	36B, 36	125	200	350	160	17
Lemhi Range	37A, 29	30	30	80	50	18
Mt. Borah/Lost River	37, 50, 51	315	410	395	100	19
Birch Creek	51, 58	40	60	35	60	20
Crooked Creek	58, 59A	40	60	20	20	21
Targhee	61	30	30	—	5	22
TOTAL		**2,690**	**3,080**	**3,850**	**1,710**	

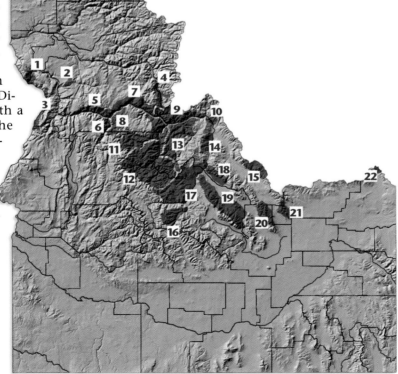

Montana

Rocky Mountain Bighorn Sheep were widely distributed throughout the state of Montana when Lewis and Clark explored the region in 1806. Lewis and Clark frequently mention sighting bighorns along the Missouri and Yellowstone Rivers, but failed to observe them while crossing the Rocky Mountains. However, they did find all big game scarce in this region at that time and subsequent sightings by other early explorers such as Bradbury (1809-11), Franchers (1811-14), and Maxmilian (1832-34) indicate the species was also present within the Rocky Mountains. Couey mapped what has been accepted as the original habitat in his 1950 Montana Fish and Game Commission report titled "The Rocky Mountain Bighorn Sheep of Montana."

Bighorn ewes above the Missouri River breaks.

DAVE BOOKS

In describing bighorns near the mouth of the Marias River, Lewis wrote: "These animals abound in this quarter, keeping themselves principally confined to the steep cliffs and bluffs of the river." The bighorn of the lower Missouri and Yellowstone River breaks were later classified as the Audubon subspecies. The last Audubon sheep was reported killed in the breaks country south of Glasgow, Montana in 1916. Over the years, there has been frequent debate surrounding the separation of the Audubon subspecies. Recently, measurements of 1,238 Rocky Mountain bighorn sheep skulls from collections in the United States and Canada have led Dr. Ramey II (1996) to recommend synonymizing the Audubon subspecies with the Rocky Mountain bighorn. In doing so, Dr. Ramey stated it is difficult to imagine any biogeographic barriers that would have separated Audubon's bighorns from Rocky Mountain bighorn sheep, especially given that during the Pleistocene glacial advance, the area from the foothills east to the plains was open to bighorn dispersal.

Rocky Mountain bighorn rams near the timberline in Glacier National Park.

THE DECLINE

Although bighorn were numerous in Montana during early explorations, wild sheep decreased in number dramatically during the settlement of the west. The causes most often cited were contact with domestic sheep, range competition from livestock, contraction of diseases, and subsistence hunting. Historically, in Montana, contact between domestic sheep and wild sheep has been implicated in several large die-offs of the later. Often, however, poor range conditions, severe weather events, and high number of wild sheep were cited as concurrent factors present during the reported outbreaks of scabies, anthrax, lungworm, and pneumonia related diseases. Couey gives the following picture of events surmised for these early-recorded die-offs. "The bighorns were primarily infested with lungworms (*P. stilesi*) with secondary invasion of *Corynebacterium pyogenes*, although *Pasterella* was always present." Recent research has documented *Pasterella hemolitica*, biotype T, as one of the causative agents for more recent pneumonia related die-offs bighorn herds periodically experience. Montana's largest bighorn sheep herd occurs in the Sun River Drainage within the Rocky Mountains. Die-offs of this population were recorded in 1925, 1927, 1932, and most recently in 1984. Other major die-offs in earlier years were noted in Glacier Park, the Stillwater River, and Rock Creek areas. By 1930 bighorn sheep were reduced to small remnant bands and were considered by some to be an endangered or rare species.

RESTORATION

The present distribution and status of bighorn sheep in Montana is due to regulated hunting and transplanting. Hunting of bighorn was closed in 1915 and remained closed until 1953 when 30 licenses were issued and 20 sheep were taken. The number taken that year was less than 2 percent of the estimated statewide sheep population at that time. Conservative harvests, primarily focused at the larger male (3/4 curl or larger) segment, were the norm until 1974 when adult ewe licenses were first implemented. Since that time, harvest levels have increased to control herd size in several locations. An estimated 141 rams were harvested in 1996.

The use of transplant sites at lower elevations with favorable range conditions, and less frequent winters and/or springs with severe weather conditions have resulted in excellent animal health, and

high lamb and adult survival. These circumstances have resulted in phenomenal horn growth within several transplanted herds within the state. The famed "King" ram, which was found dead near Melrose, Montana, scored 203 5/8 Boone and Crockett points and was only 7 years old. This was the largest Montana ram until Jim Weatherly took a 9-year old ram in Granite County on October 9, 1993 scoring 204 7/8 Boone and Crockett points.

Although the first transplant of 12 bighorn from Banff, Alberta, Canada to the National Bison Range at Moiese occurred in 1922, it was the availability of Pittman-Robertson wildlife restoration funds in 1941 that provided the impetus to begin a transplant program in Montana. During the 40s, 50s, 60s and 70s, new populations of elk, deer (both white-tailed and mule deer), pronghorn, moose, mountain goat, and bighorn sheep were initiated throughout the state with transplants.

Although new populations of bighorn continue to be established through transplant, today most of the historic habitat in Montana (especially on public land) is currently occupied. Augmentation of populations that have previously experienced die-offs continues to be a major use of transplanted stock. A complete history of bighorn sheep transplanting efforts in Montana was recently compiled by J. McCarthy for the 1996 Northern Wild Sheep and Goat Council meeting held in Silverthorn, Colorado. The following provides a summary of that account.

Only two bighorn transplants were made within the state with stock from outside Montana. The herd on the Moiese Bison Range was begun with 12 bighorn from Banff, Alberta in 1922 and the herd in Billy Creek in the Missouri breaks was initiated with 16 bighorn from Colorado in 1947.

From 1941 to 1997, a total of 1,740 bighorns have been transplanted within Montana with stock from herds within the state. The Sun River herd has accounted for 819 animals (47%) of the transplanted stock. Wildhorse Island, Rock Creek and Lost Creek herds have accounted for most of the remaining stock. These three herds are introduced populations initiated with stock from Sun River. The number of bighorn transplanted increased exponentially from the 1940s to the 1970s as experience in capture was gained and personnel were hired to specifically capture and transplant wildlife. Prior to 1960, less than 200 (181) bighorn had been transplanted. During the 1970s alone, over 560 bighorn were transplanted within the state. With the exception of bighorn, the transplant of big game species to initiate new populations in Montana ended during the late 1960s and early 1970s with the occupation of the majority of available habitat. From 1990 to 1997, 462 bighorn were captured in the state. Ninety-four were taken to the states of Washington and Oregon, while the remaining 368 were used to either augment or initiate new populations in Montana.

POPULATION TRENDS

Couey estimated about 1200 bighorn occupied 16 different areas within the state in 1950. Unpublished wildlife division records show estimates by Merle Rognrud, then division bureau chief, of 2,000 in 1957 and 1,500 in 1968 based upon the estimated percent of the population harvested. By the early 1970s, eleven major herds were known to exist in the state and thirteen other areas had been stocked by transplanting. Of those areas with transplanted stock at least four were considered not successful at that time resulting in a total of about 20 herds within the state.

Recent die-offs recorded in the Highlands, Tendoys, and Lost Creek have had a significant impact; however, these herds appear to be increasing again. Today, there are 42 different herds in the state with an estimated 4,890 total population.

MANAGEMENT

A statewide bighorn sheep management plan has not been developed to guide bighorn management in Montana. Regional personnel have written a few regional and specific herd plans. Management direction is currently defined at the regional level with individual wildlife biologists having management responsibility for individual herds. Coordination of activities has been accomplished through collaboration between regional wildlife managers and wildlife division staff.

A population objective has been established for each herd in the state. In the case of newly trans-

G. ERICKSON

Montana's Ural-Tweed bighorn sheep range.

A large band of rams feeds among the Missouri River breaks. Bands of this size are a very good sign, evidence of a hardy population. Rams go where the feed is best, with security a secondary concern!

G. ERICKSON

planted herds, the population objective is tentative. The number of licenses for rams and adult ewes issued is recommended by the area biologist based upon herd composition. Final quotas are established by the Fish, Wildlife and Parks Commission following public comment.

Because of the individual or regional nature of Montana's management program, a variety of management directions have been established for individual herds across the state. This has led to a variety of hunting opportunities for hunters to choose. There are "unlimited" license areas established in the southern portion of the state where a license can be obtained automatically through an annual drawing. Hunter success in these areas for a legal (3/4 curl) ram is low (often less than 3 percent), but a person is provided an opportunity to hunt sheep. The majority of bighorn herds have a 'limited' number of licenses available through the annual drawing. These areas have high (90 percent or greater) success and some areas have consistently yielded Boone and Crockett book rams.

The 49th Montana Sate Legislature authorized the Montana Fish and Game Commission to auction one male mountain sheep license each year to provide money for the benefit of mountain sheep. Since 1986, the commission has selected the Foundation for North American Wild Sheep to auction the license and over 2.1 million dollars has been raised. The funding has been used to support transplants to establish new herds and augment others, to conduct cooperative burning projects with the U.S. Forest Service to control conifer encroachment and improve forage conditions on key winter ranges, to conduct research, and to purchase conservation easements and acquire important habitat.

DAVE BOOKS

Inset: Bighorns on Yellowstone National Park's Cinnebar Mountain.

Montana's Sun River country provides bighorns, such as this ram grazing a high ridge line pinnacle, a nearly ideal mix of rims and grasslands.

Montana Rocky Mountain bighorn sheep population estimates in 1998. N - native, S - supplemented, and T - transplant.

Herd Name	Source	1998	Map
Kootenai Falls	N/S	100	1
Ural-Tweed	N/S	125-150	2
Ten Lakes	N	45- 60	3
Cabinet Mountains	T	144	4
Thompson Falls	T	326	5
Cut-off	T	130	6
Paradise	T	482	7
Nat'l. Bison Range	T	65	8
Petty Creek	T	100-130	9
Bonner	T	50	10
Lower Rock Creek	T	250	11
Ranch Cr./Brewster	T	—	12
Upper Rock Creek	N/S	200	13
East Fk. Bitterroot	T	125	14
Painted Rocks	T	70	15
Nez Perce/Sheepshead	N/S	30	16
Lost Creek	T	150	17
Highland Mtns.	T	50	18
Tendoy Mtns.	T	60	19
East Glacier	N	100	20
Walling Reef	T	90-100	21
Sun River	N	533	22

Herd Name	Source	1998	Map
Beartooth WMA	T	50	23
Taylor/Hilgard Mtns.	N/S	20- 30	24
Spanish Peaks	N	180-200	25
Hyalite Peak	N	30- 50	26
Tom Miner Basin/ Cinnebar	N	75-100	27
Mill Creek	T	Unknown	28
Upper Boulder River	N	25	29
Lower Boulder River	T	60	30
Stillwater River	N/S	35	31
West Rosebud River	N	70	32
Missouri River	T	100-150	33
Micky Brandon Butte	T	150	34
Little Rockies	T	100	35
Blue Hills	T	25	36
Wildhorse Island	T	75	37
Gardiner/Mammoth	N	75- 85	38
Pryor Mtns.	T	100-150	39
Rock Cr./Hellroaring	N	20- 30	40
Sleeping Giant	T	50	41
Elkhorn Mtns.	T	50	42
TOTAL (ESTIMATE)		**4,790**	

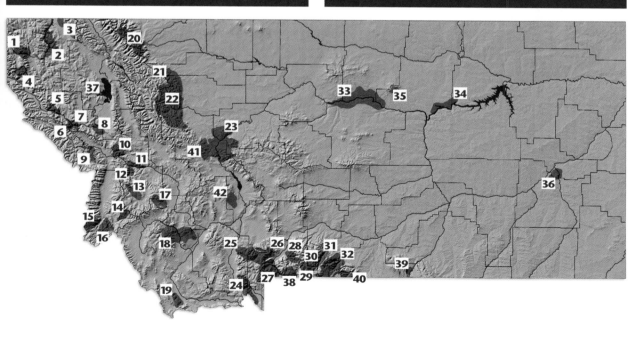

Nebraska

In Nebraska, the Audubon bighorn sheep formerly occurred in the Wildcat Hills, the Pine Ridge, along the North Platte River to eastern Lincoln County, and on the Niobrara River. This subspecies probably became extinct in the early 1900s with its last stronghold in the South Dakota badlands.

In 1981, the Nebraska Game and Parks Commission, with the help of the Foundation for North American Wild Sheep and the Nebraska Chapter of Safari Club International, began a project to reintroduce bighorns into the Pine Ridge. The Pine Ridge escarpment is located in the northwest part of Nebraska and covers an area of approximately 630 square miles. The topography includes rough narrow canyons, open grass areas and high rugged buttes. Ponderosa pine is the dominant tree, although a variety of deciduous trees are located near small creeks and streams.

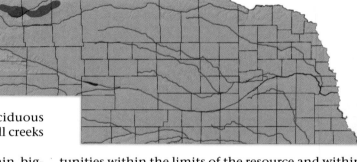

Six Rocky Mountain bighorns, four ewes and two rams from Custer State Park, South Dakota were released into a 500-acre enclosure at Fort Robinson State Park near Crawford. Two additional transplants were made later, two rams from Colorado and one ram and three ewes from South Dakota's Custer State Park. These sheep and their progeny provided a viewing herd and became imprinted to the area.

In December 1988, 21 sheep including seven males, eight females and six lambs were released from the pen. The last 23 bighorns were released in January 1993. The enclosure was then dismantled and removed.

Based on observations during December 1997, an estimated 57 Rocky Mountain bighorn sheep were believed to inhabit Fort Robinson State Park near Crawford. A few sheep, mostly rams, have ranged from the Fort Robinson complex and have been sighted as far east as the Bordeaux Creek drainage southeast of

NEBRASKALAND MAGAZINE/NEBRASKA GAME AND PARKS COMMISSION PHOTO/BOB GRIER

Rocky Mountain bighorn sheep ewes and a lamb in Fort Robinson State Park.

Chadron, south near Belmont, west near Gilbert Baker Wildlife Management Area and north in the Oglala Grassland. No lambs have been observed outside the 22,000 acre Fort Robinson complex. It is possible that presently Nebraska's total sheep population may include over seventy animals.

The management goals for mountain sheep in Nebraska include the establishment and maintenance of free-ranging bighorn sheep in the Pine Ridge area to provide hunting and viewing opportunities within the limits of the resource and within limits that most affected landowners will accept.

A population of 200 animals may represent the necessary minimum to insure desired genetic diversity and sufficient protection from disease and other mortality factors. It is thus uncertain at this time if we can maintain an annual sustainable harvest of mature rams. Since bighorns are polygamous, most of the rams are surplus to production needs, and a few could be removed without detrimental impact upon the population. This will have no appreciable effect on availability of sheep for future desired transplants.

In recent years as many sheep as possible have been wormed annually using fenbendazole in a mash mixture. Fecal samples have been analyzed for lungworm and the number of lungworm larvae found has been found to be insignificant.

Although a few sheep, mostly rams, have been sighted up to 25 miles from the Fort Robinson complex, apparently none have become established. Additional range expansion will probably necessitate transplants. A bighorn sheep habitat evaluation study in the Pine Ridge, utilizing remote sensing technology and the application of habitat modeling, is currently underway.

Nebraska's first-ever bighorn sheep hunting season in modern time is scheduled for November 22 through December 21, 1998. There will be only one auction permit and one lottery permit available for the hunt. The auction permit was purchased for $87,500 during the Safari Club International Annual Hunters Convention in Reno, Nevada. Applications for the lottery permit can be accepted only from Nebraska residents at the present time. The legal bag limit will be one ram with at least one horn of 3/4 curl or greater, as determined by an imaginary line extending downward from the front of the base of the horn through the center of the eye. If that line intersects any portion of the horn, the animal is considered to be at least 3/4 curl.

Bighorn sheep are a unique resource in Nebraska and we receive many positive comments and expressions of interest from landowners, sportsmen and the general public regarding the continued presence of these animals in Nebraska.

NEBRASKALAND MAGAZINE/NEBRASKA GAME AND PARKS COMMISSION PHOTO/BOB GRIER

NEBRASKALAND MAGAZINE/NEBRASKA GAME AND PARKS COMMISSION PHOTO/BOB GRIER

Nevada

Nevada is uniquely situated relative to bighorn sheep distribution in North America. In recent centuries Nevada has also been lacking the kinds of geologic features that would preclude sheep movement. Because bighorns that have been defined as distinct subspecies in the twentieth century all occurred in Nevada (i.e., California bighorns in the northern reaches of the state dominated by the Great Basin desert; desert bighorns in the southern reaches including the Mojave desert; and Rocky Mountain bighorn sheep radiating westward from Utah's Wasatch Range), some intermingling of representatives from all of those subspecies undoubtedly occurred.

Rocky Mountain bighorns were apparently never numerous in Nevada; only remnant populations occurred at the time that white settlers entered the region. Numerous firsthand accounts of sheep observations in northeastern Nevada mountain ranges in the 1920s and 1930s have been documented. E. R. Hall concluded that those same populations were extinct at the time his work, *Mammals of Nevada*, was published in 1946.

Reintroduction of Rocky Mountain bighorn sheep into eastern and northeastern Nevada mountain ranges was begun in 1975, with 16 bighorns from Wyoming released into the northern Snake Range of White Pine County. That initial release was followed with more releases into White Pine County in 1979, 1980, 1981, 1986, 1987, and 1990. Eighty-three Rocky Mountain bighorn sheep obtained from Wyoming and Colorado were reintroduced over this period into the Snake and Schell Creek Ranges.

In 1987, 20 Rocky Mountain bighorns obtained from Colorado's Basalt Ranch were introduced to Pilot Peak in Elko County near the Nevada-Utah border. The resulting herd was supplemented in 1998 with 19 animals from the Badlands herd and 13 animals from the East Humboldt Range.

The Badlands herd in Elko County was originally established in 1989 with 26 Rocky Mountain bighorns from Colorado. These animals were supplemented in 1993 with 22 additional animals from Colorado.

The Ruby Mountains in Elko County received 20 bighorn sheep from Alberta in 1989. The following year, 1990, another complement of 20 Alberta Rocky Mountain bighorn sheep were released into the Rubies.

The East Humboldt Range received 22 Rocky Mountain bighorns from Alberta in 1992.

In 1998, Nevada has an estimated 276 Rocky Mountain bighorn sheep in seven herds.

Lifting a bighorn sheep 'guzzler' into position to provide a source of dependable water in bighorn sheep habitat.

GREGG TANNER

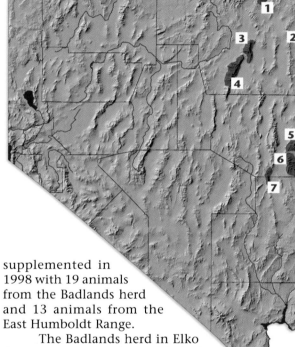

Aerial view of Rocky Mountain bighorn sheep habitat in Nevada's Ruby Dome country.

New Mexico

Historically, Rocky Mountain bighorn sheep occupied six ranges in northern New Mexico. Although local populations may have been large, distribution was limited because New Mexico represents the southern-most extension of this subspecies. By the late 1800s, increasing human populations and introduction of domestic sheep took their toll on native bighorn herds through a combination of unregulated hunting, competition for forage, and disease. As related to Vernon Bailey of the USGS Biological Survey, the last Rocky Mountain bighorn in New Mexico was killed in 1902 in the Culebra Peaks, part of the San Juan Mountains on the border with Colorado. Present populations are the result of transplants.

Few records are available on the early occurrence of Rocky Mountain bighorn sheep in New Mexico. In what is now Bandelier National Monument, the explorer Bandelier saw the last bighorn sheep in 1880, and around 1900, skeletal remains were collected from an old Indian game pit. Biologists have conjectured that over-hunting by Pueblo and Apache Indians caused the loss of the Bandelier bighorns, but no evidence is available to support this belief.

The last evidence of bighorn sheep in the Pecos Wilderness was reported in 1903, when Vernon Bailey found old tracks and signs on Truchas Peaks. Bailey believed that many bighorns were killed on the open alpine slopes, which are easily accessible to hunters on horseback even today. Domestic sheep were traditionally grazed on these summer ranges, however, and their presence probably played a more important role in the loss of this population through the transmission of disease. Domestic sheep probably also contributed to the loss of Wheeler Peak bighorn sheep, reportedly abundant before their elimination between 1870 and 1880. In 1904, Bailey found old bighorn sheep horns at Blue Lake, now part of the Taos Pueblo adjacent to the Wheeler Peak Wilderness.

A total of 194 Rocky Mountain bighorn were transplanted between 1932 and 1993. Of these, 77 bighorn originated from out of state and included bighorn from Banff and Wateron Lakes National Parks in Canada and Whiskey Basin in Wyoming. After the Sandia and Pecos bighorn populations in New Mexico were established with bighorn from Banff, they became sources of transplants for establishing additional populations. Unfortunately, the Sandia population disappeared in 1992. Loss of this population is believed to be related to increased recreational use of bighorn habitat, encroachment of woody vegetation on critical ranges, and illegal hunting.

PRESENT OUTLOOK AND MANAGEMENT PHILOSOPHY

As a result of transplants and careful management, Rocky Mountain bighorn now number about 600, distributed among five ranges in the state. New

Rocky Mountain bighorn ram chews his cud while a companion sleeps.

DON L. MacCARTER

Excellent forage conditions in New Mexico's Pecos Wilderness contribute to good body condition in Rocky Mountain bighorn sheep herds.

Rocky Mountain bighorn sheep herds in New Mexico			
Herd	**Established**	**1998**	**Map**
Wheeler Peak	1993	85	1
Pecos Wilderness	1965	400	2
Manzano Mountains	1977	20	3
Turkey Creek	1964	20	4
San Francisco River	1964	40	5

Mexico's long range objective is to transplant bighorn to all suitable New Mexico habitats, thereby increasing the number of populations to seven and the statewide population to 1,400 bighorn.

HABITAT

Rocky Mountain bighorn are found in two types of habitats: alpine and low elevation. Alpine bighorn in the Pecos and Wheeler Peak Wilderness Areas of northern New Mexico live above timberline year-round at elevations over 10,000 feet and adapt to the winter by seeking out windswept, snow-free slopes to obtain forage. Low elevation bighorn are found in the mountains and river canyons of central and southwest New Mexico below 7,000 feet in the Manzano Mountains, Turkey Creek, and the San Francisco River Canyon. In these areas, they resemble desert bighorn with their sleek coats and wide-flaring horns. All bighorn require wide-open spaces, free of heavy vegetation and seldom far from steep, rocky crags where they seek to elude predators.

Bighorn survival is primarily affected by the severity of the winter in alpine areas and drought in the drier, low elevation areas. Bighorn eat a variety of plants, from lush flowers during the summer, to grasses and shrubs the rest of the year. Although bighorn may obtain sufficient moisture from dew, vegetation, and snow during wet seasons, open available water appears essential during drought periods. Alpine bighorn crave salt in the summer when supplies diminish in the vegetation. Lacking natural salt licks, bighorn in the Pecos Wilderness beg for salty snacks and even lick people and horses for the salty residue. People have taken advantage of their extreme tameness—they have roped, injured, and killed bighorn—but if salt blocks are provided, the Pecos bighorn avoid people and regain their wildness.

Quality bighorn hunting is available in several areas. The auction of a bighorn sheep permit at the annual convention of the Foundation for North American Wild Sheep ensures adequate funding for bighorn management. Nonetheless, restoration efforts continue to be challenged by competing public interests, increasing human encroachment in bighorn habitats, and diseases inadvertently introduced by domestic sheep and goats that are life-threatening to bighorn.

Dark-colored ram in Pecos Wilderness herd.

DON L. MacCARTER

Resting rams in New Mexico's Pecos Wilderness herd position themselves so that no ram looks directly at one another -- and so that predators can be spotted at long distances.

Oregon

Rocky mountain bighorn sheep occurred in the rugged mountains of northeastern Oregon until about the mid-twentieth century. Unlike the California bighorns found elsewhere in Oregon (which were largely decimated by the 1880s), Rocky Mountain bighorns still occupied the high Wallowa Mountains at the turn of the century, and there were reports of individual sheep or small bands in the Blue Mountains along the Wenaha River. However, by 1900 domestic sheep had been introduced to the alpine ranges of the Wallowas, and few bighorns remained. Small herds were reported along the rim of Hells Canyon, on the divide between the Imnaha and Snake River, near the headwaters of the Minam River and in the high country around Aneroid Lake. A decade later, U.S. Forest Service reports indicated that the number of bighorns had declined to about 45 animals in total. Population estimates reached a high of about 60 animals in the early 1930s, but all herds disappeared by 1945.

Summer range for Rocky Mountain bighorn sheep in Oregon's Eagle Cap Wilderness Area.

V. COGGINS

Rocky Mountain bighorn sheep restoration began in 1971, when 40 animals from Jasper National Park, Alberta were transplanted to the Wallowa Mountains and Hells Canyon. Since that time, 328 bighorns have been released at 15 sites (22 translocations through 1996). Sheep from Salmon River, Idaho; Flathead Lake, Montana; Hall Mountain, Washington; Tarryall, Colorado; Cardinal River, Alberta; and Jasper National Park (six different sites) have been used to establish or supplement Oregon herds. Nine separate herds are considered 'Established.' The March 1997 population total was estimated at 525 animals.

Bighorn sheep habitat in northeastern Oregon is canyonland or grassland winter ranges with alpine summer ranges. The lower Imnaha herd typifies the canyonland type, with low elevation steep slopes interspersed with rocky rims. Bunchgrasses dominate the slopes. These sheep move along canyon walls but most do not move to alpine summer range. Big-

"Spot," (right) whose massive horns made him a legend before he died of natural causes, grazes with companions in Oregon's Lostine River area.

horns typically utilize elevations of 1,000 to about 5,000 feet. The Lostine herd in the Wallowa Mountains is migratory, and winters on the Lostine Wildlife Area on steep grassland at elevations of 4,500 to 7,000 feet. In May or June, depending on snow conditions, this herd moves to alpine ranges in the Wallowa Mountains at elevations up to about 9,500 feet. Most northeastern Oregon bighorns have excellent grassland ranges which provide an abundance of feed. Canyonland habitats have short winters allowing excellent animal growth. Forage generally dries out in August and September and, when it does, food quality goes down. Fall rains typical of most years start a flush of green grasses and forbs, allowing sheep to fatten before winter.

V. COGGINS

Disease appears to be the most serious problem affecting Oregon's Rocky Mountain bighorns. Pneumonia outbreaks have decimated most herds: Upper Hells Canyon (1984-85), Lostine (1986-87), Lower Hells Canyon (1995-96), and Wenaha (1996-97). These disease problems are believed to result from direct contact between bighorns and domestic sheep or goats. The Lostine herd declined by about two-thirds as a result of that particular disease outbreak. All rams over age 4 and nearly all of the lambs perished. Lamb survival was poor for three years afterward. This sheep herd has returned to pre-die-off numbers after a ten-year period. The recent 1996 die-off was even more severe, with an estimated 300 bighorn sheep lost

Inset: Bighorn ewes on summer range near Francis Lake.

A three-year old Rocky Mountain bighorn ram surveys his home from the top of the Hurricane Divide in Oregon's Eagle Cap Wilderness Area. Notice that his horns are thicker at the base and flare more than horns of ewes.

DALE E. TOWELL

Rocky Mountain bighorn sheep herds in Oregon.			
Herd	**Year Established**	**1998**	**Map**
Lostine	1971	85	1
Upper Hells Canyon	1971	20	2
Bear Creek/Minam River	1976	20	3
Lower Imnaha River	1979	150	4
Wenaha/Haas/Cottonwood	1983	55	5
Sheep Mountain	1990	70	6
Lower Hells Canyon	1993	25	7
Lookout Mtn/Fox Creek	1993	40	8
Upper Joseph Creek	1995	25	9
TOTAL		**490**	

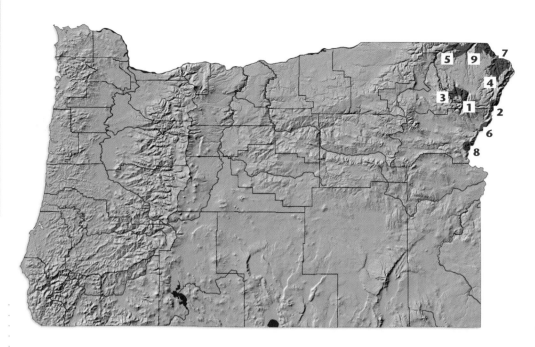

from Oregon, Washington, and Idaho herds. This outbreak is believed to have started from bighorn contact with a domestic goat near Asotin, Washington; before it ended, the die-off had reached herds 40 miles distant. The elimination of grazing by domestic sheep within the Hells Canyon National Recreation Area will allow restoration of bighorn sheep herds to occur in some of the highest quality bighorn sheep range in Hells Canyon.

Predation is another problem affecting survival of both lambs and adults. Carnivore populations (including cougars, coyotes, and bobcats) are increasing, and data from recent studies in California and Alberta indicate that mountain lions, in particular, can depress or reduce bighorn sheep numbers. Mountain lion populations in northeastern Oregon are increasing following a ban on the hunting of these animals with dogs. Predation is believed to be keeping several small herds of bighorns static, and will likely affect some future transplants.

Ram hunting started in 1978 and seasons have been authorized annually since. Strictly controlled hunts allowed harvest of rams with horns that made 3/4 of a curl or larger. A total of 141 tags have been issued, and 126 hunters have harvested rams as a once-in-a-lifetime opportunity (including lottery winners and auction tag buyers). The harvest restriction was changed in 1991 to allow the harvest of any ram. Over the years 17 of Oregon's rams have scored over 180 Boone and Crockett Club 'points' based on size; rams of this size are eligible for records book listing. The largest ram recorded from Oregon to date scored an impressive 184 Boone and Crockett points, indicative of excellent growth potential.

The Foundation for North American Wild Sheep, the states of Oregon, Washington, and Idaho, the U.S. Bureau of Land Management and the U.S. Forest Service have formed a coalition dedicated to restoring the Rocky Mountain bighorn sheep more widely through its historic range in the tri-state Hells Canyon area. Future plans include a major effort to stock unoccupied suitable habitat (the first phase of which was initiated in 1997 with the release of 37 Rocky Mountains bighorns obtained from Spences Bridge, British Columbia, into the tri-state area), continued research on bighorn sheep diseases and disease management, and habitat acquisition, protection, and improvement. The Hells Canyon Initiative has the potential to help consolidate political and financial support necessary to restore this area to support one of the largest contiguous populations of Rocky Mountain bighorn sheep in the United States. This project has the support of the Nez Perce Tribe, many conservation groups, and numerous private individuals that have donated their time, effort and money. This high level of public support should ensure Oregon's Rocky Mountain bighorn sheep herds will continue to expand, providing recreational opportunities for hunters and wildlife viewing opportunities into the future.

V. COGGINS

Ewes and lambs among the rocky recesses of Oregon's Hells Canyon Creek.

South Dakota

Audubon's bighorn sheep were very common in the Black Hills, White River Breaks, and badlands of South Dakota during the early 1800s. In 1833, Maximillian reported that the Manitari Indians went to the Black Hills and surrounding mountainous areas to hunt mountain sheep, killing as many as one hundred or more in one season. In July 1875, members of the Newton-Jenney U.S. Geological Survey shot a sheep along a tributary of Boxelder Creek in the Black Hills. Bighorn sheep were not found very far from the Black Hills, but were reported to be abundant in the badlands near the White River, fifty miles east of the hills.

Due to uncontrolled hunting, the numbers of Audubon's bighorns began to decline during the late 1800s. It was reported that by 1887, mountain sheep were virtually gone from the Black Hills. However, a few still remained in the Harney Peak area within the very core of the hills. It was reported that this band was still present in 1895, but no sheep were found when Thompson Seton visited the area in the summer of 1902. Seton did learn of bands of about 200 Audubon's bighorns that still existed in the White River badlands near Pine Ridge at this time; however, it was reported that the last of the Audubon's bighorns in South Dakota were gone even in the rugged badlands by 1910.

With the last of the Audubon's bighorns gone from South Dakota, no mountain sheep existed in the state until over a decade later when U.S. Senator Peter Norbeck obtained eight Rocky Mountain bighorns from Alberta, Canada in 1922. These sheep were placed into Custer State Park within the Black Hills. This herd grew and sustained itself until a reported soremouth virus eliminated the entire herd by 1961. Again, South Dakota was without bighorn sheep.

In 1964, Rocky Mountain bighorns from Pike's Peak in Colorado were introduced into the Badlands National Park, located in the White River badlands where the last of Audubon's bighorns had existed prior to the turn of the century. This was a result of a cooperative effort between the South Dakota Department of Game, Fish and Parks and the National Park Service. The goal of this effort was to establish a viable herd in suitable habitat within the park, a herd that could serve as a source of transplant stock for movement elsewhere in South Dakota. The original 22 bighorns were placed into a 370-acre enclosure within park boundaries to establish a captive herd. However, reduction of animals due to an unknown disease caused the agencies to release the remaining 16 bighorns into the park in 1967. A 3-year study conducted by the South Dakota Department of Game, Fish and Parks to determine population status of this herd resulted in an estimated herd size of 133-200 animals during winter 1989-90. However, in recent years this population has declined dramatically; causes for the decline are

Mature Rocky Mountain bighorn ram in South Dakota's badlands.

Rocky Mountain bighorn sheep feed near the base of clay walls typical of badlands.

unknown. Badlands habitat is characterized by severe topographic features and weather. Clays walls devoid of vegetation rise several hundred feet, mixed with sod tables dominated by wheatgrass and sparsely distributed juniper trees. The lower flat lands are grazed by other wild ungulates, but little competition or range overlap exists with bighorns on the sod tables. The main range of this herd lies within the Sage Creek Wilderness Area which is devoid of roads and has few recreational hiking trails.

Again, a transplant of Rocky Mountain bighorn sheep was attempted in the French Creek area within Custer State Park in the southern Black Hills. This herd was established in 1965 from 22 Rocky Mountain bighorns obtained from Whiskey Mountain, Wyoming. The herd grew to a population of approximately 150 by 1975 then became static, with no further growth apparent. It now numbers 120-140 animals. Research on the genetic makeup of these animals has indicated limited heterozygosity within the Custer State Park herd, and other research has shown low lamb recruitment due to several factors. Recent wildfires within Custer State Park have burned over 2,400 acres, effectively doubling the acreage suitable for bighorn sheep within the park. However, pioneering movements by bighorns into the new area has been slow and limited. A transplant of genetically unrelated bighorns into the uncolonized areas is planned in the near future. Presently, this is the only bighorn herd within South Dakota that has a limited hunter harvest season, averaging three or four licenses per year.

The youngest herd in South Dakota is located

Inset: Fire, such as this burn in South Dakota's Black Hills, is essential to maintain grasslands necessary to provide forage for bighorn sheep.

Clay walls of the badlands offer security to Rocky Mountain bighorn sheep in habitats once occupied by Audubon's bighorns.

TED A. BENZON

within the central Black Hills in Spring Creek and Dark Canyons. This herd was established in 1991 with 26 Rocky Mountain bighorn sheep obtained from Georgetown, Colorado. An additional five sheep from the Badlands National Park were placed in the canyon in 1992 to supplement the original transplant and provide genetic diversity. Prior to transplanting, extensive habitat work was completed within Spring Canyon. Through a cooperative agreement between the South Dakota Department of Game, Fish and Parks and the National Forest Service, approximately 150 acres of dense pine was clear-cut on the canyon rim, and this was followed by a prescribed burn. An additional 200 acres of pine was clear-cut after the original transplant had occurred. This herd has now divided into three lamb/ewe groups spaced approximately six miles apart, with ram movement between groups. It had grown to approximately 125 individuals by 1997, demonstrating good recruitment and potential. A limited hunting season may be opened on this herd in the near future.

The future for bighorns in the Black Hills looks bright. It may ultimately depend on creating the open habitat within the rugged canyons that typified the Black Hills prior to the 1800s.

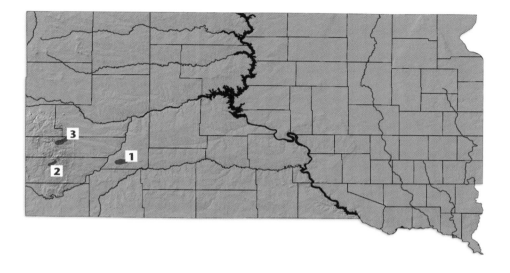

Estimated numbers of Rocky Mountain bighorn sheep in South Dakota in 1998.

Herd Name	1965	1980	1990	1998	Status	Map
Badlands Nat. Park	25	30	175	100	Decreasing	1
Custer State Park	22	150	150	150	Stable	2
Spring Cr/Dark Canyon	0	0	0	125	Increasing	3
TOTALS	**47**	**180**	**325**	**375**		

ROCKY MOUNTAIN BIGHORNS

Utah

Rocky Mountain bighorn sheep are native to the mountain chains of northern Utah. Abundant Indian petroglyphs and bighorn sheep skeletal remains attest to the prehistoric and recent presence of Rocky Mountain bighorn sheep in Utah. In fact, bighorn sheep are depicted more than any other form of wildlife in Utah petroglyphs and pictographs. Early explorers and settlers in Utah recorded observing Rocky Mountain bighorn sheep throughout the state. Jedediah Smith, Osborne Russell, and William H. Ashley reported hunting and observing "mountain sheep" during their travels, and Osborne Russell recorded extensive hunting trips for bighorns in the Wasatch Range in the early 1830s.

Rocky Mountain bighorn sheep declined dramatically in Utah soon after settlement. Factors contributing to their demise by the 1920s include (1) competition with domestic livestock for forage and space, (2) vulnerability to domestic livestock-borne diseases and reduced resistance to native disease subsequent to human-induced stress, (3) habitat conversions away from native grasslands toward shrub lands due to excessive grazing and fire suppression, and (4) unregulated hunting. By the mid-1930s Rocky Mountain bighorn sheep in Utah probably numbered less than 100 individual animals.

Rocky Mountain bighorns in Utah's Rattlesnake Unit.

JIM KARPOWITZ

RESTORATION EFFORTS AND MANAGEMENT PERSPECTIVES

Restoration of Rocky Mountain bighorn sheep to Utah's native habitat began in 1966. Between 1966 and 1970, over 60 bighorns from Whiskey Mountain in Wyoming and Waterton and Banff National Parks in Alberta were released into an acclimation enclosure in the mountains east of Brigham City, Utah. This reintroduction failed due to human disturbance, il-

Biologists survey Rocky Mountain bighorn sheep habitat near Green River.

legal harvest, and disease. Although some of the bighorns escaped the enclosure during the winters of 1971 and 1972 (when hard drifted snows piled up against the enclosure fence) the escapees did not disperse very far. Most remained in the Willard Peak area. All are believed to have died prior to 1980.

The Uintah band of the Northern Ute Tribe introduced nine Rocky Mountain bighorns obtained from Wyoming's Whiskey Mountain into the Florence Creek area of Desolation Canyon in March 1970. This was an area which had been occupied by native Rocky Mountain bighorn sheep until at least into the 1930s. This herd was supplemented in 1973 with 12 Rocky Mountain bighorns from Alberta's Waterton National Park. Tribal fish and wildlife personnel believe the herd is stable or slowly increasing.

Utah Division of Fish and Wildlife Resources initiated release of 27 Rocky Mountain bighorns from Whiskey Mountain in 1980 on Mt. Nebo in the central Wasatch Range. Supplemented by an additional 21 animals (also from Whiskey Mountain) the following year, this herd demonstrated an initial increase in numbers before severe winters and limited winter range precipitated a rapid decline. Domestic livestock, both cattle and sheep, occurred in the area, although no direct contact between bighorn sheep and domestic livestock was documented. This herd disappeared in the late 1980s.

A total of 36 bighorns from Whiskey Mountain were also introduced to Bear Mountain in northeastern Utah in 1983 and 1984. These bighorns were later joined by at least one radio-collared ram from Colorado's Beaver Creek herd on the Colorado-Utah state line. This herd is steadily increasing. Immediately to the south, within Dinosaur National Monument, the Utah Division of Wildlife Resources planted 19 Rocky Mountain bighorns obtained from Colorado's Rocky Mountain National Park. These sheep, separated by only the Green River from Colorado's Ladore Canyon herd, appear to be prospering.

Attempts were made to establish two herds along the Nevada border. The first, in the Deep Creek Mountains, resulted from release of 16 bighorns obtained from Whiskey Mountain in 1984. This herd dwindled to virtually no sheep in 1998. The second, in the isolated Pilot Mountains, resulted from 20 Rocky Mountain bighorns acquired by the Nevada Division of Wildlife from Colorado's Basalt

A mixed band of bighorns rests in bunchgrass habitat typical of Utah's Rattlesnake Unit.

Ranch. This herd is still increasing, and although most animals spend the majority of their time in Nevada, some occasionally wander into Utah.

PRESENT STATUS

As of 1998, two viable herds exist in Utah, one in the Rattlesnake Canyon north of Green River and the other on Bear Mountain on the shores of Flaming Gorge Reservoir in Daggett County. Promising bighorn populations also occur on the Beckwith Plateau, Pilot Mountain, North Slope of the Uinta Mountains, and Dinosaur National Monument. Even so, the future of Rocky Mountain bighorn sheep in Utah remains uncertain. Additional potential reintroduction sites exist in historical ranges. However, these sites (and ranges presently occupied by bighorns) remain exposed to sources of disease, habitat depletion, and pressures from growing recreational demands. Ongoing efforts by the Division of Wildlife Resources and the Foundation for North American Wild Sheep are effectively resolving conflicting land use practices which potentially threaten wild sheep populations in the state. Rocky Mountain bighorn populations can only be made secure in Utah through additional reintroduction, expansion of existing nucleus herds, and directed conservation efforts.

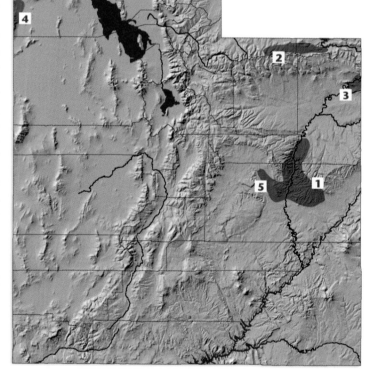

Estimated Population of Rocky Mountain bighorn sheep in Utah, 1997.

Location	Year Established	1997	Trend	Map
Desolation/Rattlesnake	1970	300	Up	1
North Slope/Bear Mtn.	1983	200	Stable	2
Dinosaur	1984	150	Up	3
Pilot Mountain	1987	100	Up	4
Bighorn Mountain	1993	100	Up	5

Washington

Rocky Mountain bighorn sheep occurred historically at the northeastern and southeastern corners of the state— in the Selkirk Range to the north and the Blue Mountains to the south. Skeletal remains have been found along the Pend Orielle River 20 miles upstream from its junction with the Columbia River, as well as at two sites in southeastern Washington, one along the upper Tucannon River and the other near Deadhorse Spring at the head of the middle branch of Asotin Creek. Native populations of Rocky Mountain bighorn sheep were exterminated from northeastern Washington as early as the late 1800s, but those of southeastern Washington persisted much later— at least until 1917.

Washington lacks the high-elevation habitats typical of bighorn sheep ranges in many other states and provinces. Typically, Washington's Rocky Mountain bighorn sheep herds originally occupied hilly to steep grasslands below the 6,000 foot elevation; many of these habitats were timbered at the time of early exploration, and bighorns heavily used the few meadows that persisted among the timber. Herds were apparently sparsely distributed.

Bighorn sheep management in Washington has focused primarily on restoring bighorn sheep to native habitats. One of the first transplants of bighorn sheep was a transplant of six California bighorns to the Tucannon area of southeast Washington— an area originally occupied by Rocky Mountain bighorns. While this herd has done quite well, the entire Blue Mountain area is now believed to have been native Rocky Mountain bighorn range, and all subsequent transplants to the Blue Mountains have featured Rocky Mountain bighorns. In the future, we will convert the Tucannon herd to the Rocky Mountain subspecies.

Reintroduction of Rocky Mountain bighorns in Washington was initiated in 1972 with a transplant of 18 animals from Waterton Lakes, Alberta to Hall Mountain in northeast Washington. This herd has been used as a nursery to stock Joseph Creek, Wenaha-Tucannon Wilderness, and Asotin Creek areas. These herds were later supplemented with bighorns obtained from Thompson Falls, Montana; Sun River, Montana; and Lostine River, Oregon. This herd, although small, has been very productive and has been used since its establishment as a nursery herd, providing bighorns for transplants to many other sites in Washington. Some of these transplants have been very successful. This herd is fed on its wintering grounds, and attracts many visitors for wildlife viewing and photography. Currently, this herd also provides limited hunting opportunity on its dispersed summer range.

In winter 1995-96 Washington herds experienced a major die-off on the Joseph Creek area. Rocky Mountain bighorns contracted a *Pasturella* pneumonia in November 1995. Alerted by reports of sick and dead bighorns, biologists from Washington, Oregon and Idaho cooperated in capturing 72 sheep north of Washington's Grande Ronde

ROLF JOHNSON

Rocky Mountain bighorn ram dashes for cover among rocky outcrops.

ROLF JOHNSON

One and a half year-old ram on Washington's Hall Mountain showing fine horn growth and excellent potential.

Population estimates for Washington's Rocky Mountain bighorn sheep.

Location	Established	1974	1980	1984	1990	1994	1998	Map
Hall Mountain	1972	25	30	65	50	35	35	1
Cottonwood Creek/Lost Prairie/Mountain View	1974	4	20	40	30	55	20	2
Black Butte/Joseph Creek	1977		40	50	95	220	40	3
Wenaha	1983			20	100	90	55	4
Asotin	1991					15	20	5
TOTAL		**29**	**90**	**175**	**275**	**415**	**170**	

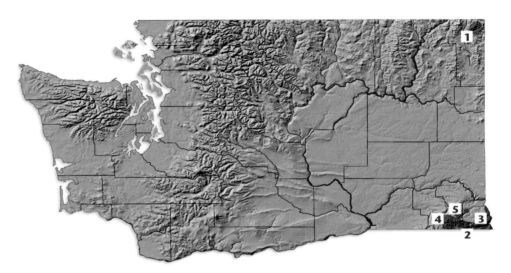

River in an attempt to keep the disease outbreak from spreading. Captured bighorns were sent to the Caldwell Wildlife Veterinary Laboratory in Caldwell, Idaho for treatment. Unfortunately, this effort failed to stop the spread of disease, which spread south of the Grande Ronde River into Oregon. At least 75 percent of the Joseph Creek population and an unknown percentage of the Cottonwood and Wenaha-Tucannon wilderness populations of Rocky Mountain bighorns were lost. All Rocky Mountain bighorns in the Blue Mountains appear to have been adversely affected by the *Pasturella* die-off. Low lamb survival was reported in 1996, but it is hoped that the die-off is over and that these herds will recover. Recovery efforts were initiated in 1997 when nine sheep obtained from British Columbia were placed in the North Fork of Asotin Canyon, as part of the first phase of the Hells Canyon Initiative.

Although a limited hunting program was initiated in 1986 in the Black Butte unit and continued each year until 1996, the 1995-96 die-off forced cancellation of hunting in this unit. The Black Butte, Wenaha Wilderness, and Cottonwood Creek Units were all closed to hunting in 1997 as the impact of the die-off was determined, and no hunting of Rocky Mountain bighorns was permitted in Washington in 1998.

Population estimates for Rocky Mountain bighorns have plummeted since November 1995 because of the *Pasturella*-related die-off. Black Butte bighorn numbers went from about 215 sheep to 50. Wenaha bighorns numbered about 120 before the die-off, but good estimates since then have been unavailable. The Cottonwood Creek bighorn herd numbered 60 prior to the die-off but since then few bighorns have been seen. Only the Asotin Creek herd appears to have been unaffected by the die-off— but this herd is still small, numbering only about 10 Rocky Mountain bighorn sheep. It is believed that Washington currently has about 150 to 200 Rocky Mountain bighorn sheep.

Wyoming

Historical accounts from fur trappers and mountain men provide some of the earliest documentation of what Mandan Indians called "*ahsahta*", the animal we know as the bighorn sheep of the Rocky Mountain West. In Wyoming, the first written record of bighorn sheep dates to 1812, when Robert Stuart and an eastbound party of starving fur traders luckily encountered a small band of bighorns along the Sweetwater River in central Wyoming. All along the North Platte River's rugged slopes and rocky canyons, "innumerable flocks" of bighorn sheep were visible to early explorers.

Thirty years later, the Fremont expedition saw numerous herds of bighorn sheep in the vicinity of a large island in the North Platte River, about 25 miles southwest of present-day Casper. Farther up the Sweetwater River, 4 miles east of Independence Rock, Joel Palmer and his party saw large "droves" of mountain sheep in May 1846.

After Lewis and Clark went their separate ways, Captain Clark named the Bighorn River for the great number of sheep seen at its confluence with the Yellowstone River. The Bighorn Mountains and the Bighorn Basin of northwest Wyoming were appropriately named by fur traders Hunt and Mackenzie for the wild sheep which lived there.

In July 1876, General George Crook and his soldiers climbed to Cloud Peak (elevation 13,165 feet) in the Bighorn Mountains, where they killed 2 mountain sheep, and remarked on the abundant trails left by bighorns. On another sojourn in fall 1876, General Crook took a small hunting party to the summit of Laramie Peak, where they harvested bighorn sheep, deer, elk, and black bear.

In the Wind River Mountains, the first sightings of bighorn sheep were noted by Fremont during his August 1842 climb to the peak (elevation 13,750 feet) that now bears his name. Many parties traveling west along the Oregon Trail through South Pass found and harvested bighorn sheep in the southeastern portion of the Wind River Mountains.

An excellent record of bighorn sheep in the Absaroka Mountains of northwest Wyoming was left by Osborne Russell, an intrepid traveler and mountain man. From the Gros Ventre River to Yellowstone Lake, from Togwotee Pass to the Owl Creek Mountains, bighorn sheep were common in the Absaroka Range, as they are today.

In southwest Wyoming, Baillie-Grohman found bighorn sheep in the rugged breaks of the Green River, along what is now the Wyoming/Utah boundary.

Reliable estimates of Wyoming's bighorn sheep numbers at the turn-of-the-century are difficult to obtain. Inarguably, there were many thousands of Rocky Mountain bighorn sheep in Wyoming, and the now extinct Audubon's subspecies of bighorn occurred along the broken topography of Wyoming's major rivers.

Mountain sheep numbers dwindled as settlement moved westward, altering bighorn habitat along the way. Market hunters focused on bison, elk, pronghorn, and deer, largely ignoring the less accessible bighorn sheep. As the valleys and plains filled with domestic livestock, further encroachment occurred. Domestic sheep found their way into high alpine basins and rougher country where cattle could not forage; competition for feed along with disease transmission from domestic sheep no doubt contributed to a decline in bighorn numbers. Scabies played a major role in the sharp reduction in bighorn sheep numbers throughout Wyoming. In one infamous example, well-known cattleman Otto Franc, founder of the Pitchfork Ranch, observed thousands of bighorns in the foothills along the Greybull River in 1879. During winter 1880-81, there were only a few dozen bighorn sheep still alive, while dead sheep were numerous, victims of scab.

Forage competition, disease transmission, reduced habitat, human encroachment, market hunting, and other factors interplayed to reduce Wyoming's bighorn sheep herds. Significant reductions of mountain sheep occurred, and by the turn of the century, Wyoming's Rocky Mountain bighorn sheep reached their lowest ebb, with perhaps fewer than 1,000 remaining.

Rams in a band stay close together, especially when disturbed and moving.

LuRAY PARKER/WG&F

The rugged Wind River Mountains provided sanctuary and high-quality habitat for Rocky Mountain bighorn sheep during the period of settlement, when populations elsewhere plummeted.

LuRAY PARKER PWGSF

During those lean years, the rugged mountain ranges of northwestern Wyoming remained a stronghold for bighorn sheep. The remote Absaroka, Wind River, and Gros Ventre mountains provided sanctuary and high-quality habitat, as they do today. Elevational movement between seasonal ranges was common, as bighorns summered in alpine basins and wintered on windswept plateaus or descended to more favorable southerly exposures.

Estimates on the number of bighorn sheep in Wyoming are variable. In 1942, Honess and Frost thought Wyoming's mountain sheep numbered 2,500 head, of which 175 lived in small isolated herds while the other 2,300 or more dwelled in the rugged Absaroka, Wind River, and Gros Ventre ranges, "...along the backbone of the continent." In 1960, Buechner estimated 2,255 bighorn sheep in Wyoming, with over 80 percent of those being found in those same three mountain ranges. An active transplant program coupled with improved survey techniques led to steadily climbing bighorn sheep estimates in Wyoming, as many historic ranges were repopulated and helicopter surveys found sheep wintering in alpine and subalpine ranges.

Current estimates by the Wyoming Game and Fish Department, National Park Service, and U.S. Fish and Wildlife Service place Wyoming's bighorn numbers at approximately 6,725 head. Much of the increase in bighorn numbers over the past several decades can be attributed to an active trapping and transplanting program. Beginning in 1934 when 20 bighorns from Flat Creek Canyon near Jackson were relocated to the Bighorn Mountains, over 1,500 sheep have been transplanted within Wyoming, to fill historic but unoccupied habitat. In addition, five western states (Idaho, Nevada, New Mexico, South Dakota, and Utah) have received approximately 400 Wyoming bighorn sheep to further their management programs.

The Whiskey Basin herd near Dubois has served as the principal source for bighorn sheep restoration in Wyoming and the western United States. Considered the largest concentration of Rocky Mountain bighorn sheep in North America, almost 1,000 head roam the grassy slopes in the "Valley of the Wind River". Transplanting bighorns from Whiskey Basin began in earnest in 1956, starting a 40-year legacy of cooperative management by the Wyoming Game and Fish Department, Bureau of Land Management, and Shoshone National Forest. A pneumonia-related die-off in winter 1990-91 severely impacted the Whiskey

Mature ram on open bunchgrass slope in western Wyoming.

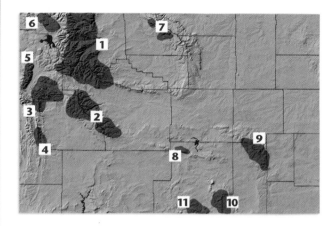

Estimated Rocky Mountain bighorn sheep numbers in Wyoming, winter 1997-98. N - native, S - supplemented, and T - transplant.

Location	Herd Origin	1998	Map
Absaroka Mountains	N	4,165	1
Wind River Mountains	N/T	1,060	2
Gros Ventre Range	N	530	3
Wyoming Range	T	55	4
Teton Mountains	N	100	5
Yellowstone National Park	N	285	6
Bighorn Mountains	T	50	7
Ferris/Seminoe Mountains	T	40	8
Laramie Range	T	250	9
Snowy Range	T	150	10
Sierra Madre Range	T	40	11
TOTAL		**6,725**	

Basin herd, drastically limiting transplant activity in recent years. To date, lingering effects of this die-off (e.g., poor lamb survival) still plague this herd. In 1993, the National Bighorn Sheep Interpretive Center opened in Dubois, focusing much of its educational outreach on the nearby Whiskey Basin herd. Guided tours to portions of the Whiskey Basin unit are available in the fall and winter months, where ethical viewing and fantastic photo opportunities await.

Throughout their range, Rocky Mountain bighorn sheep face a declining habitat base, as human encroachment, fire suppression, and recreational activities erode suitable ranges. As much as any other species, mountain sheep evolved in open, high-visibility habitats where foraging efficiency and detection of predators was enhanced. With the fewest people of any state, Wyoming has not yet experienced the dramatic loss of bighorn habitat due to human development that other states have faced. However, suppression of periodic wildfires has altered the open nature of bighorn sheep habitat, with grassy slopes and benches giving way to sagebrush and conifer canopies. Massive-scale wildfires like the 1988 fires in and around Yellowstone National Park can alter large expanses of habitat, beneficially and adversely. Management of fires, whether lightning- or man-caused, offers a better option to improve and maintain productive bighorn habitat.

Impaired habitats often lead to poor nutritional health of wildlife, and bighorn sheep are no exception. Wild animals with access to high-quality habitats and forage are most able to withstand the effects of disease. *Pasturella*-induced pneumonia and lungworm problems have occurred in the Whiskey Basin herd. Scabies has been documented in bighorns in the

Absaroka and Gros Ventre ranges. Providing high-quality habitat and maintaining the ability of wild sheep to migrate seasonally between ranges is a key component of bighorn management, in Wyoming and throughout their range.

In the large, native herds of northwestern Wyoming, and in some successful transplanted herds around the state, bighorn sheep are hunted on a sustained-yield basis. Hunting seasons are set conservatively, and focus on mature rams. Approximately 300 licenses are issued annually, and ram harvest averages nearly 200 animals per year. Other herds in Wyoming (e.g., Shell Canyon, Wind River Canyon on the Wind River Indian Reservation) are managed for recreational viewing and photography through watchable wildlife programs.

Wyoming is home to the Foundation for North American Wild Sheep (FNAWS), an international sportsmen's organization dedicated to the management of wild sheep throughout North America. Founded in 1974 and headquartered in Cody since 1982, FNAWS has been a leader in supporting transplant, disease, habitat improvement, and research projects for mountain sheep. In addition, FNAWS has championed sportsmen's rights and educational causes in recent years.

Wyoming is proud of its Rocky Mountain bighorn sheep resource. Cooperative efforts between state and federal agencies, conservation organizations, and an informed public will help ensure Wyoming remains a stronghold for wild sheep.

LuRAY PARKER/WG&F

Wyoming's Absoroka Mountains, habitat for many of the state's bighorn sheep.

Audubon's Bighorn

Audubon's bighorn occupied what is now western North Dakota, South Dakota, Nebraska, eastern Montana and Wyoming. Like the California bighorn west of the Rocky Mountains, Audubon's bighorn sheep lacked access to alpine habitats, and lived year-round in the rough terrain afforded by the eroded badlands and river canyons that dissected the plains of the upper Missouri River.

DESCRIPTION

Audubon's bighorns shared the coloration of Rocky Mountain and California bighorn sheep, but unlike the California bighorn was apparently at least as large as the Rocky Mountain bighorn, and possibly larger. This race of bighorn is now extinct, and few specimens or good descriptions survive. Some of the best descriptions are those from the first observers.

When Lewis and Clark started up the Missouri River with the Corps of Discovery on May 14, 1804, there was a sense of anticipation about the new kinds of animals, unknown to science, that they might discover. Merriwether Lewis had been tutored by some of the best naturalists of his time, and was skilled both in reporting his observations and in interrogating those with whom he came in contact about what might lay ahead. Thus in October 1804 they learned from the Frenchman Jon Vallie that about 300 leagues upriver they would reach mountains, and there they would find "... on the Mountains great numbers of goat, and a kind of anamale with circular horns, this anamale is nearly the Size of an Elk...." Later, while spending winter 1804-1805 with the Mandan Indians, Clark reported that "We precured two horns of the anamale the french Call the rock Mountain sheep." Thus it was that a member of the Corps of Discovery, Joseph Fields, was the first to see the Audubon's

GRANCEL FITZ

The finest known surviving specimen of an extinct race. Taken by Howard Eaton in 1880.

bighorn in what is now western North Dakota on April 26, 1805. Despite their efforts, the Corps of Discovery was unable to collect a bighorn sheep until nearly four weeks later, when they had arrived in what is now Montana and the range of Rocky Mountain bighorn sheep.

It was the famous naturalist John James Audubon, following the course of the Lewis and Clark expedition in 1843, who became forever associated with this race of bighorn. Audubon had read the published journals of Lewis and Clark, and traveled west to record the wildlife wonders of the region in paintings. Disdainful of the abilities of the hunters accompanying his party and confident of his own abilities as a hunter as well as a naturalist, Audubon concluded that "...I expect now that we shall have to make a regular turn-out ourselves, to kill both Grizzly Bears and Bighorns." After he and his party did 'make a regular turn-out' in the badlands of what is now western North Dakota, Audubon wrote in his journal of August 13, 1843:

"No one who has not seen these places can form any idea of the resorts of the Rocky Mountain Rams, or the difficulty of approaching them, putting aside their extreme wildness and their marvellous activity. They form paths around these broken-headed cones (that are from three to fifteen hundred feet high) and run around them at full speed... The hunter sometimes, after toiling for an hour or two up the side of one of these hills, trying to reach the top in hopes that when there he will have for a short distance at least, either a level place or good path to walk on, finds to his disappointment that he has secured a point... scarcely large enough to stand on... I was thus deceived time and again, while in search of Bighorns ... From the character of the lands where these animals are found, their own shyness, watchfulness, and agility, it is readily seen what the hunter must endure, and what difficulties he must undergo to near these "Wild Goats." It is one constant time of toil, anxiety, fatigue, and danger. Such the country! Such the animal! Such the hunting!

RANGE AND HABITAT SELECTION

The range of Audubon's bighorn sheep appears to have been very limited. Concentrations seem to have occurred west of the Missouri River, particularly the badlands of the Little Missouri, the badlands and Pine Hills of South Dakota, and extreme northwestern Nebraska. Reports from Audubon and others indicate that Audubon's bighorns were closely associated with rough and broken badlands and canyon country, although it is likely that some (primarily rams) occasionally ventured onto the surrounding plains, as indicated by early (erroneous) reports that these were plains animals driven into rough terrain as a result of hunting pressure.

Little is known of the biology of Audubon's bighorn, except that its demise was probably more a result of over-hunting than other factors. The Missouri River was a gateway to the great frontier in the mid-nineteenth century, and bighorn meat was highly esteemed by trappers and hunters. Based on the limited amount of habitat available, the population was probably never very large. In the decade between 1870 and 1880, survey crews laid out the course of the Northern Pacific Railway pushing west of Bismarck, news of gold discoveries in the Black Hills brought on a gold rush, and the U.S. Army had clashed with the Sioux at the Little Big Horn River and elsewhere in the region. An army fort was constructed on the Little Missouri River, and cattlemen pushed into the country for access to the Great Northern Railway and eastern markets. By 1884 there were as many as 150,000 head of cattle and sheep along the Little Missouri. By 1885 and 1886, when severe winters nearly eliminated the livestock industry in western North Dakota, Audubon's bighorn sheep populations were decimated. Stragglers held on in the badlands and along the Little Missouri River into the 1890s, but populations could not recover. The last known Audubon bighorn sheep date from 1905 in North Dakota, 1918 in Nebraska, and 1924 in South Dakota.

Chapter Five

CALIFORNIA BIGHORN SHEEP

California bighorn sheep, like Rocky Mountain bighorn sheep, entered recent history in 1825. On December 8 of that year, one of the hunters in Peter Skene Ogden's brigade of fur trappers operating out of the Hudson's Bay Company base in Ft. Vancouver killed a bighorn sheep in the Mutton Mountains of eastern Oregon, near the Deschutes River about 45 miles south of The Dalles. Nine months later, on August 27, 1826, David Douglas secured the horns of a California bighorn from an Indian about 6 miles east of The Dalles, and described the species based on those horns and a shirt made from the skin of the animal (which the owner was not willing to give up). Unfortunately, Douglas never saw a live animal, and got the range wrong— he believed California bighorns were animals of the eastern foothills of the Cascade range.

DESCRIPTION

California bighorns are generally slightly smaller than Rocky Mountain bighorns, with a less blocky build. This is to be expected, since body size has been shown to decline in sheep as latitude declines (and, since altitude and latitude are interrelated in their effect on animals, as altitude declines as well). Rams average 181-205 pounds, while ewes average 106-145 pounds. Coloration is similar to that of Rocky Mountain bighorns, with a dark brown to light brown coat, a large white rump patch, white trim on the back of all four legs, and a white muzzle. California bighorns typically show a continuous tail stripe from back to tail, dividing the rump patch.

Taxonomists separate California bighorns from Rocky Mountain and desert bighorn sheep by some specific skull measurements, by a strong tendency for smaller and wider-flaring horns than found among Rocky Mountain or desert bighorns, and by subtle differences identified through protein electrophoresis.

The skulls of Rocky Mountain bighorn rams are larger than those of California bighorns on average, while California bighorns tend to be slightly broader across the nose. Comparisons among Cali-

HAROLD UMBER

Note the typical widely-flaring horns of these young California bighorn rams.

121

fornia and Rocky Mountain rams harvested by hunters in British Columbia clearly demonstrate the slightly smaller skull and horn size of California bighorns. Among 851 California bighorn sheep rams harvested, horn basal circumference averaged 14-inches and horn length averaged just over 32- inches. In a corresponding sample of 442 Rocky Mountain bighorn rams harvested by British Columbia hunters, horn basal circumference averaged 15 1/4 inches and horn length averaged over 34-inches. California bighorn sheep rams harvested in other states (all of which are directly or indirectly derived from stock obtained from British Columbia) averaged somewhat smaller. By comparison, horns of a California bighorn ram killed by John Muir near the turn of the century near the Modoc lava beds of Mount Shasta had a basal circumference of 16 inches and a horn length of 33 inches.

While differences in the average size of skulls differs among populations in British Columbia (and elsewhere), most of the differences may relate more to habitat than to genetics. Most populations of California bighorns occur at lower elevations and in a more southerly distribution than Rocky Mountain bighorns, so that smaller body size would be expected. The length of the tooth row (which is resistant to change) remains essentially the same as in Rocky Mountain bighorns. This is a critical measurement, since length of the tooth row determines the amount of chewing surface available to the animal, which directly relates to the amount of food the animal can process. Smaller horn diameter and length is characteristic; horns of California bighorn rams typically are shorter and more slender than those of Rocky Mountain bighorns, with a more open curl and a greater tendency to diverge away from the face. However, some of this difference may relate to the fact that the dispersal phenotype of California bighorns is likely to predominate in virtually all populations in the United States and many in Canada, based on reestablishment of herds to formerly vacant habitat all within the past few decades. As indicated earlier, sheep with a dispersal phenotype tend to grow more rapidly but to die younger than sheep that live in areas where they have been long established and which are close to the carrying capacity of their range.

Few differences were found that could separate the skulls of female California bighorns from those of Rocky Mountain bighorn ewes. As in Rocky Mountain bighorn sheep ewes, horns are small— much smaller than is typical of the ewes of desert bighorn sheep. Horn length among ewes is believed to reflect competition for scarce resources, and particularly

water. Desert bighorns (but not Rocky Mountain and California bighorns which typically have access to streams in summer and snow in winter) compete for water, and ewes with longer horns can use those horns to fend off competitors. (Incidentally, increased competition for water also likely results in conferring a competitive advantage to fast-growing lambs and a high degree of social intolerance, also typical of desert bighorns but not necessary beneficial to Rocky Mountain and California bighorns).

The fact is, skeletal measurements provide no single, incontestable characteristic that will always separate California bighorn sheep from Rocky Mountain bighorn sheep. Recent research using mitochondrial DNA has indicated, not surprisingly, that California bighorns from British Columbia are much more closely related to Rocky Mountain bighorn sheep than those from remnant populations in California's Sierra Nevada, which are more closely allied with desert bighorns. Some of the differences that have been identified clearly relate to the interrelations of latitude, altitude, and diet; some are related to inherited characteristics associated with small population size, and yet others are related to the fact that nearly all of the California bighorn populations in the United States, at least, represent dispersal phenotypes. Additional taxonomic work is required to clarify the relationships between these and other sheep.

On the other hand, behavioral differences and adaptations to low-elevation habitats among the California bighorns have been shown to be important in reestablishment of herds in once-vacant habitats. All states and provinces currently identify the source stock of their herds, and manage California sheep as a stock or subspecies separate and distinct from Rocky Mountain or desert bighorns. Since the source of stock is known (most from south-central British Columbia, with a very few herds based on residual populations in California's Sierra Nevada) and since barriers exist that preclude interchange between most metapopulations (as opposed to interchange within metapopulations), maintaining this distinction is relatively straightforward. All legally-harvested sheep are permanently marked to allow for future identification of their origin.

RANGE AND HABITAT SELECTION

Prior to settlement, California bighorn sheep were widespread throughout western North America. They occupied nearly all of the relatively dry mountain ranges, basins and canyons west of the Rocky Mountains to the Cascades of British Columbia, Washington, Oregon, and the Sierra Nevada of Cali-

California bighorn sheep are often animals of the arid intermountain west, living in habitats often characterized by sagebrush.

fornia, and were the bighorn sheep characteristics of the Great Basin. Although interbreeding no doubt occurred among bighorn populations where separation from Rocky Mountain or desert bighorn herds was minimal, vast plains, deserts, timbered foothill ranges and major rivers served to isolate populations, allowing them to adapt their bodies and behavior to meet physiological demands imposed by their environment.

California bighorns, like the extinct Audubon's bighorns, were typically sheep of semiarid habitats below 8,000 feet in elevation. Only the few of the Sierra Nevada and Great Basin ranges provided true alpine habitats, such as those favored by Rocky Mountain bighorn sheep. Historic literature offers few clues as to whether alpine areas were extensively used except in the Sierra Nevada of California, where California bighorns still persist. More typically California

CRAIG BIHRLE

bighorns originally occupied habitats described by early biologist Vernon Bailey as "...every canyon, cliff and lava butte as well as many of the rough lava beds... east of the Cascade Mountains."

California bighorn sheep range is believed to have extended from central southern British Columbia southward through eastern Washington and Oregon (exclusive of the Wallowa Mountains and Hells Canyon) southward along the eastern Sierra Nevada of California and eastward into southern Idaho (south of the Snake River) and northern Nevada. Natural boundaries appear to have been the timbered eastern slopes of the Cascade and Sierra Nevada mountain ranges to the east. To the west in British Columbia, California bighorns were separated by approximately 300 miles and several mountain ranges from Rocky Mountain bighorn sheep herds of the Rocky Mountains.

Inset: Young California bighorn rams.

These California bighorns, living in North Dakota's badlands, have access to rich grassland feeding areas.

The scoured badlands and Palouse Prairie of eastern Washington formed a boundary to the tri-state area of the Tucannon and Wallowa Rivers, where Rocky Mountain bighorns occupied the Wallowa and Blue Mountains in northeastern Oregon and southeastern Washington. California bighorns were separated from Rocky Mountain bighorns in eastern Oregon by the timbered foothills of the Umatilla and Blue Mountains, and by the broad Snake River plain from the head of Hells Canyon eastward across southern Idaho. Southward, California bighorns were separated from Rocky Mountain bighorns by the Great Salt Lake Basin of western Utah. The isolated mountain ranges of Nevada were populated by bighorn sheep, most likely California bighorns in the northern one-third of the state and desert bighorns in the southern one-third, but some reports indicate that Rocky Mountain bighorns occurred in central and northeastern Nevada as well.

California bighorns were almost entirely eliminated from this vast area in the late nineteenth and early twentieth centuries, but have been reintroduced into much of their historic range. Bighorn sheep captured in southern British Columbia were the basis for transplants into Oregon, Washington, Idaho, Nevada, Utah, and North Dakota, where California bighorns were introduced into habitats formerly occupied by Audubon's bighorn— the other 'foothill bighorn.'

BIOLOGY

The fundamental biology of California bighorn sheep is identical to that of Rocky Mountain bighorns, with a few exceptions dictated by environment. Most populations were restricted to relatively isolated hills and canyons; with the exception of populations occurring in the Sierra Nevada and on such isolated mountains as Oregon's Steens Mountain or Nevada's Ruby Range, few occupied areas of significant elevational gradients. As a result, few populations exhibited significant seasonal migrations. Ewe/lamb groups most likely occupied the most rugged and broken terrain, while the larger bodied rams radiated further out onto the surrounding Great Basin shrublands and deserts. Although forage was neither as abundant or succulent as that available to Rocky Mountain bighorns at higher elevations, the growing season typically began earlier in the spring and persisted later into the fall. Faced with relatively reduced forage quality but an extended period of availability, California bighorns shifted their breeding period to earlier in the fall (late October and early November), allowing their lambs to be born earlier in April and May, with a peak around the first of May.

Population estimate of California bighorn sheep in North America.

Location	1960	1970	1975	1985	1990	1998
British Columbia	1,185	1,764	1,850	3,240	4,645	3,630
California	390	390	195	300	320	170
Idaho	0	90	50	530	1,205	1,460
Nevada	0	8	30	151	484	1,248
North Dakota	0	120	250	—	232	350
Oregon	24	—	210	1,007	1,805	2,890
Utah	0	0	0	0	0	30
Washington	Remnant	303	400	550	586	745
TOTAL	1,609	2,765	2,985	5,778	9,227	10,523

As is even more pronounced in the desert bighorns, the breeding season was prolonged relative to that of Rocky Mountain bighorns, so that the timing of births was spread out— a strategy that maximized survival of lambs in a more variable climate, and one that afforded the firstborn a greater span of time to grow prior to their first winter. Since horn growth is a function of food intake, there is speculation that this prolonged period of feeding on lower quality forage may well account for the reduced horn size of California bighorns relative to Rocky Mountain bighorns.

California bighorn sheep of today are exposed to virtually the same predators as Rocky Mountain bighorns— primarily golden eagles, mountain lions, bobcats, wolves and coyotes. However, California bighorns were shaped by other predators— American lions, the American cheetah, saber-toothed cats, scimitar-toothed cats, dire wolves, and great bears now extinct— that likely occurred in greater numbers in the low-elevation habitats where these animals evolved than in the higher elevations favored by Rocky Mountain bighorns. Even today, California bighorns face risks associated with their low-elevation habitats. Many ranges occupied by California bighorns are attractive to people— the rocky rims and lava buttes associated with the low-elevation grasslands are often coveted by settlers and livestock-owners. Hikers and other recreationists are attracted to scenic canyonlands associated with rivers and streams in the arid west. The lava buttes and low hill habitats preferred by California bighorns, even when distant from settlements and travel routes, could often be seen for miles across Great Basin deserts, attracting hunters. As a result, California bighorns probably suffered significantly greater losses associated with meat and market-hunting than did either the Rocky Mountain or desert bighorns, whose habitats were more distant from those areas most frequently traveled and settled in the nineteenth century. Many herds continue to be at risk from human harassment.

British Columbia

ew sights in nature match the thrill of observing a band of mature California bighorn rams running headlong down a steep grassland slope towards almost vertical escape terrain. The massive horns and large tan bodies with their white rump patches merge and bump and their cloven hooves throw dust like a small whirlwind as they hurl themselves downslope. Such sights are not uncommonly observed by the dedicated few who venture into the British Columbia haunts of the California bighorn on the Fraser and Thompson rivers and in the Okanagan and Ashnola valleys. Slightly smaller than the Rocky Mountain bighorns whose natural haunts are located in rugged terrain, the California bighorn lives in more open habitat with moderate steep relief. Perhaps a more appropriate common name would have been "grassland bighorn". It is more commonly found in areas with large expanses of open southerly and westerly facing grassland slopes, parkland forests and steep valley walls, from the Chilcotin River in the southern interior of British Columbia to northern California. It is part of a rich and unique fauna including mule deer, cougar, coyote, blue grouse, long-billed curlews, horned larks, and spade-footed toads, to list but a few species. These, however, depend on ecosystems which are periodically and regularly renewed by wildfire.

A band of California bighorn sheep ewes and lambs races to escape the pursuing helicopter–and into the capture net.

GREGG TANNER

Habitat of the Junction herd of California bighorn sheep near Williams Lake, British Columbia.

RECOVERY OF POPULATIONS

The overriding significance of California bighorns in British Columbia to mountain sheep conservation resides in the fact that British Columbian populations served as the source for the successful reintroduction of this subspecies to former ranges in the United States as well as in this province. These reintroductions have been an outstanding success. California bighorns were decimated by Old World disease introduced by their domestic cousins, out-competed for forage by the destructive grazing practices of nineteenth century ranchers, and depleted by market hunters. The outlook for these sheep was bleak in the 1950s, but a few far-sighted biologists, including Lawson Sugden, James Hatter, Patrick Martin, and the late Harold Mitchell, working with their U.S. counterparts and the dedicated efforts of private conservationists, turned the tide. They transplanted California bighorns from the Chilcotin Junction herd (which was first described by Simon Fraser in 1806 at the junction of the Chilcotin and Fraser rivers) to habitats in the northwestern U.S. The recipient state agencies built semi-captive herds to restock additional vacant ranges. Hart Mountain in Oregon, Owhyee Canyon in Idaho, Sinlahekin Wildlife Management Area in Washington, Tuckee Canyon in Nevada, the Badlands area in South Dakota (to replace the extinct Audubon bighorn) and other areas now support viable herds of California bighorns which originated in British Columbia.

The success of these reintroductions encouraged the BC Wildlife Branch to make reintroductions in vacant habitats which historically were known to have supported wild sheep. Several ranges on both the east and west banks of the middle Fraser Canyon north of Lillooet and the Dewdrop Range and Harper Ranch north of Kamloops now support populations of California bighorns in numbers that surprised even the optimists within the recovery teams. Numbers of California bighorns went from an estimated low of 1,200 in BC in 1950 to about 4,000 in 1997. In the meantime populations in the United States recovered to well over 2,000 in the 1990s from a low of about 400 during the 1940s

CONSERVATION AND MANAGEMENT

The conservation of California bighorns in British Columbia has been a unique cooperative effort between government and conservation organizations such as The British Columbia Wildlife Federation, the Guides and Outfitters, the Foundation for North American Wild Sheep, the Wild Sheep Society of British Columbia, the National Audubon Society, the Boone and Crockett Club, and Safari Club International. All have made significant contributions to the well-being of wild sheep to the benefit of hunters and non-hunters alike. The Brit-

127

ish Columbia Habitat Conservation Trust Fund is supported by surcharges on hunting and angling licenses and is another example of hunters and anglers helping to pay for conservation.

Like all wildlife, California bighorn sheep need habitat, and their habitat requires proper protection and management. Fortunately, the majority of California bighorn habitat is located on Crown (public) land, and much of this protected by parks or managed in cooperation with the BC Wildlife Branch. However, key parcels remain in private ownership or on Indian reservations, where control of domestic sheep and enforcement of proper grazing practices is not possible. In such situations only education and good will can prevail to prevent overgrazing or devastating lungworm-pneumonia induced epidemics. There has been an intense program of buying back private land for habitat conservation, including parcels containing important California bighorn habitat.

Another factor which affects California bighorns is the human-induced forest invasion of their grassland ecosystems. The California bighorn is a fire dependent species. Since the 1930s the BC Forest Service has perhaps inadvertently promoted the gradual replacement of grasslands by conifer forests through an intensive fire suppression program and a policy which restricted the use of prescribed fires. While the woody species replacing the herbaceous vegetation utilized as food by bighorns and other species are natural, the rate at which grasslands are being replaced by these communities is not. The BC Wildlife Branch has made attempts to revert the conifer forests to grasslands. However, except for one burn in 1992 in the Ashnola Valley, the effort on other California Bighorn ranges has been largely experimental.

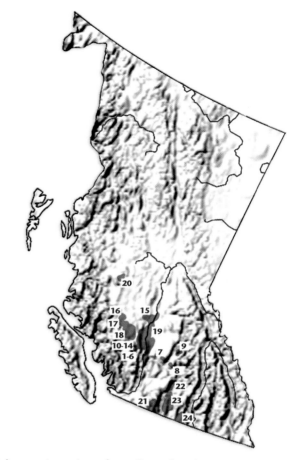

GREGG TANNER

California bighorn sheep habitat in British Columbia features rolling hills interspersed with rocky escape cover.

Prior to the advent of Coordinated Resource Management Planning in British Columbia in 1975, domestic livestock grazing on Crown land was almost always conducted season long. Cattle were turned out in early spring at the first sign of green and not removed until the grassland became dormant in fall. Since that time, new grazing systems such as deferred or rest-rotation, have been applied in most grazing plans. Too often however, economic circumstances prevent full compliance with these plans and the range and the bighorn suffer.

North American sheep are susceptible to introduced diseases and parasites carried by domestic sheep, particularly when wild sheep are subjected to stress. Because wild sheep are frequently stressed by severe winter conditions, particularly when they become overcrowded, there have been massive dieoffs of both California and Rocky Mountain bighorns when they came into contact with domestic sheep. This is thought to be the primary cause for the major declines in bighorn sheep in the western United States in the nineteenth century and for the continuing die-offs of bighorns in British Columbia from the 1920s to the present. The limited south facing, low elevation mountain and canyon grassland slopes utilized by bighorns during winter have been much sought after by the livestock industry.

Following the significant 1974 workshop on North American wild sheep, the long range plans worked out by leading sheep biologists all had one

Estimated numbers of California bighorn sheep in British Columbia in 1998.

Location	1960	1970	1985	1990	1998	Map	Comments (range in estimate for 1998)
Lower Churn Creek/Fraser R.	200	130	350	500	225	1	(200-250) Non-migratory sheep; includes Word, Empire & Lone Cabin herds.
Churn Creek/Camelsfoot Range			250	350	200	2	(150-200) These sheep migrate to Churn Creek and some possibly to Fraser River.
Mt. Sheba/Tyaughton/Relay Mtn.		40		60	80	3	(60-100) Some interchange with Taseko Lake herd.
Fraser River East	50	100	300	600	450	4	(400-500) includes Jesmond, Edge Hills Limestone, Marble Range, winter on Fraser River.
Fraser R. East Lillooet-Kelly Creek					200	5	(175-225)
Fraser River West				175	250	6	(200-300) Fraser River only; non-migratory.
Kamloops Lake		18	150	225	225	7	(200-250) also called Tranquille.
South Thompson			25	75	225	8	(200-250) also called Harper Ranch.
Adams Lake					15	9	(15-20) also called Skwaam Bay.
Mission Ridge		30			35	10	(30-40)
Duffy Lake	25				0	11	Extirpated.
Shulaps	25	65	65	150	165	12	(130-200) non-migratory.
Bendor Range	30				0	13	Extirpated.
Texas Creek		13			0	14	Extirpated.
Junction	200	360	550	500	300	15	(250-350) also called Riske Creek.
Menaiah/Tsuniah	60		70	150	60	16	(50-70)
Yohetta/Tatlow (W. Taseko)		40		50	30	17	(20-40)
Taseko Lake (E. Taseko)	75	125	250	150	40	18	(30-50) 1985 estimate includes Mt. Sheba/Tyaughton/Relay Mtn.
Alkali/Dog Creek	25	35	45	75	175	19	(150-200) supplemented by transplant in late 1980s.
Ilgachuz		8	15		5	20	(0-10)
Ashnola	250	400	350	650	300	21	(275-325) population crashed in the winter of 1990-91.
Shorts Creek	45	75	50	60	5	22	(0-10) population crashed in early 1990s.
South Okanagan (Vaseaux Lake)	200	325	750	700	470	23	(450-500) MU 801=281, MU 809=166, MU 808=20. Population declined in early 1990s.
Granby River			20	175	175	24	(150-200)
TOTAL	**1185**	**1764**	**3240**	**4645**	**3630**		

common theme: the protection of wild sheep from domestic sheep and from harmful grazing practices. Due to economic circumstances, domestic sheep were removed from nearly all Crown ranges in British Columbia managed by the Ministry of Forests. Although no written policy exists against grazing domestic sheep on Crown ranges utilized by wild sheep, it is likely that any proposal to place domestic sheep on or adjacent to wild sheep range would meet with strong public opposition.

California bighorns are currently harvested under a full curl restriction or an any curl/limited entry restriction. Hunting females under strict limited entry regulations also helps to maintain populations in a healthy balance with their environment. Until recently there has been a large demand for transplant animals to restock vacant habitats, and most surplus females and juveniles have been used for that purpose.

THE FUTURE OF BRITISH COLUMBIA'S CALIFORNIA BIGHORNS

It is imperative if the province's California bighorn population is to survive the next century that its habitat be managed with the experiences of the historic die-offs in mind. Otherwise the excellent results of the bighorn recovery programs conducted over the past 50 years will have been in vain and the province will have lost a significant component of its wildlife heritage.

California

California bighorns historically were restricted to suitable habitat in the northeastern part of the state, and to the Sierra Nevada Mountains, a massive range stretching more than 400 miles in the eastern part of California. Although it is uncertain how many populations actually existed, at least twenty were thought to have occupied this vast area.

In the Sierra Nevada, California bighorn sheep ranged as far north as the vicinity of Sonora Pass (Mono County) and nearly as far south as Olancha Peak (Inyo County). The distribution of bighorn sheep within the Sierra Nevada was, however, certainly not continuous. Within the area described above, wintering populations (from north to south) are known to have existed at Lee Vining and Lundy Canyons, McGee and Convict Canyons, Wheeler Ridge, Mt. Morgan, Mt. Tom, and south to Mt. Emerson, Taboose Creek, Mt. Baxter, Mt. Williamson, Mt. Langley, and Olancha Peak. Of these populations, only two have persisted to the present, and three others have been re-established in historic ranges.

California bighorn sheep probably were largely unaffected by humans until the discovery of gold in California in 1849. Following that historical event, fortune seekers flocked to California, and provided a ready market for all forms of wild meat (including that of bighorn sheep). Unregulated market hunting may have played an important role in the extirpation of the small, localized populations. A more onerous problem for bighorn sheep, however, was the introduction of livestock, particularly domestic sheep. During summer months in the late 1800s and early 1900s, herders pastured tens of thousands of domestic sheep in the Sierra Nevada. Grazing by domestic sheep certainly reduced the availability of forage for wild sheep and may have permanently altered the composition of high-elevation plant communities. An even more serious problem was the effect of diseases transmitted from domestic sheep to wild sheep. Although scabies was documented in bighorn sheep following introduction of domestic sheep, pulmonary infections resulting from bacteria transmitted from domestic to wild sheep was probably more serious.

In 1950, Fred L. Jones published a complete account of bighorn sheep in the Sierra Nevada. He confirmed the presence of five populations. Detailed work by John D. Wehausen in the 1970s indicated that only two of these populations persisted until 1970: one at Mt. Baxter, and the other at Mt. Williamson. In northeastern California, bighorns persisted in eastern Siskiyou County, in an area known as Lava Beds, until about 1913.

The first effort to restore California bighorn sheep to an historic range occurred in 1971, when eight females and two males were translocated from British Columbia to a 2 square-mile enclosure at Lava Beds National Monument County. This penned herd provided one male and three females for translocation to the Warner Mountains in Modoc County in February 1980, and in that same year 10 California bighorns from the Mt. Baxter winter range in the Sierra Nevada were also translocated to the Warner Mountains. Unfortunately, all of the bighorns remaining at Lava Beds National Monument succumbed to pneumonia (thought to have been contracted from domestic sheep) in the summer of 1980, and in 1988, the entire Warner Mountains population also died of pneumonia attributed to pathogens contracted from domestic sheep. Currently, no bighorn sheep occupy northeastern California.

Using bighorns captured on the winter range of the Mt. Baxter population in Inyo County, the California Department of Fish and Game has attempted to establish additional herds in the Sierra Nevada. In 1979, 10 bighorns were translocated to Wheeler Crest in Mono County. This herd was supplemented with 10 additional animals in 1980, four in 1982, and four more in 1986.

In 1980, 11 California bighorns were translocated to Mt. Langley in central Inyo County. The Mt. Langley herd was later supplemented in 1982, with an additional 15 animals.

Horns of California bighorn sheep often fail to extend beyond (or even reach) 3/4 curl, regardless of the age of the sheep. Notice how similar the horn shape of this ram on California's Sand Mountain is to the petroglyphs on page 4.

VERNON BLEICH

Ram band picks its way across a boulder-studded slope of California's Sand Mountain.

Finally, in March 1986, 27 California bighorns were translocated to Lee Vining Canyon, Mono County, in an effort to reestablish a population that would summer in Yosemite National Park. Eleven more bighorn sheep were moved to Lee Vining Canyon in 1988.

Currently, there are five populations of California bighorns in the eastern Sierra Nevada Mountains. The California bighorn in this area have recently been found to be unique among bighorn sheep races, and likely warrant taxonomic distinction. Unfortunately in the 1990s, there has been a precipitous decline in numbers of these magnificent animals and less than 100 adult animals remain. Current research has identified mountain lion predation as the primary factor directing this decline. Documented increases in mountain lion predation have substantially reduced the size of these bighorn populations, and has also indirectly made them more vulnerable to natural disasters (hard winters and avalanches) by restricting their wintering to higher elevations (where the forage quality is poorer) to avoid predation. Unfortunately, in 1990 a voter initiative was passed that protected mountain lions, and prevented the California Department of Fish and Game from initiating a short term predator control program to facilitate a population recovery in these fragile bighorn populations.

The Sierra Nevada Bighorn Sheep Interagency Advisory Group, established in 1984 and representing a variety of agencies as well as private citizens, has worked cooperatively to ensure the persistence of California bighorn sheep despite recent losses due to severe winter weather, accidents, and predation. The group recently completed a revised conservation strategy to ensure the continued viability of existing populations and translocation of additional animals to reestablished herds in other historic ranges in the Sierra Nevada. Moreover, the group will work to reduce any potential for contact between bighorns and domestic sheep.

California bighorn sheep rams feed among shrublands.

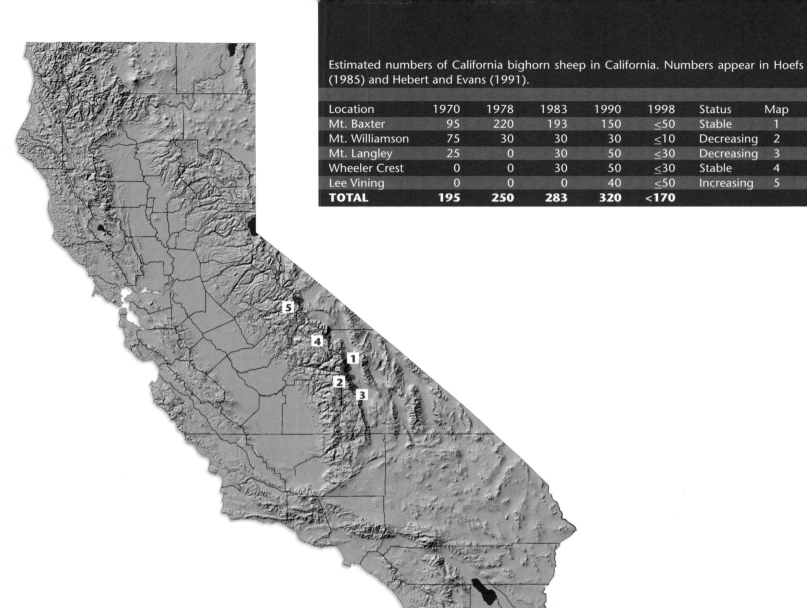

Estimated numbers of California bighorn sheep in California. Numbers appear in Hoefs (1985) and Hebert and Evans (1991).

Location	1970	1978	1983	1990	1998	Status	Map
Mt. Baxter	95	220	193	150	≤50	Stable	1
Mt. Williamson	75	30	30	30	≤10	Decreasing	2
Mt. Langley	25	0	30	50	≤30	Decreasing	3
Wheeler Crest	0	0	30	50	≤30	Stable	4
Lee Vining	0	0	0	40	≤50	Increasing	5
TOTAL	**195**	**250**	**283**	**320**	**<170**		

Idaho

California bighorn sheep occupied the southwestern portion of Idaho, separated from the range of Rocky Mountain bighorns by the vast Snake River plain. In southwestern Idaho, California bighorn sheep ranged eastward from the central Oregon Cascade Range across the northern Great Basin, where Vernon Bailey, a Senior Biologist for the old Bureau of Biological Survey, described their habitat in 1936 as follows:

"Originally mountain sheep occupied every canyon, cliff, and lava butte as well as many of the rough lava beds of Oregon east of the Cascade Mountains...."

His map, developed after a review of many existing trophies and numerous discussions with early settlers and travelers, shows the range of the California bighorn extending to the Idaho border from the current location of Brownlee Reservoir southward to the Nevada state border. It appears that the vast, flat Snake River plain provided a natural barrier to northward movement and intermingling with Rocky Mountain bighorns of central Idaho. California bighorns occupied the canyon of the Snake River itself, and no doubt there was some genetic interchange between Rocky Mountain and California bighorns along the Snake River in the area of Hells Canyon, and perhaps to the east, where Rocky Mountain bighorns were found in the mountain ranges of southeastern Idaho and northeastern Nevada.

Early records tell of massive die-offs of California bighorns: one near the community of Jordan Valley in the winter of 1884-85, another along the Owyhee River (due to 'scab' following the initial introduction of domestic sheep into that country) about 1902. The period between about 1885 and 1940 was a period of tremendous livestock grazing in southwestern Idaho's Owyhee County. Records indicate that the county supported over 100,000 head of cattle in 1888-89, followed by a minimum of 150,000 sheep by 1898. Competition for critical forage no doubt played a role in the loss of California bighorn sheep, as did unregulated hunting. A few California bighorns survived in the drainage of the East Fork of the Owyhee River until about 1920, but all were certainly gone from Idaho before 1940.

California bighorn sheep habitats in Idaho were vacant for a period of at least a quarter century. Then, in 1963, Idaho followed the lead of Oregon in reintroducing California bighorn sheep. Unlike Oregon, however, these bighorns were not transplanted to a remote mountain range but rather to a vast, 300 to 800-foot-deep canyon complex associated with the Owyhee River and its tributaries. This drainage coursed through sagebrush covered plains in southwestern Idaho (and southeastern Oregon). Nineteen bighorns from British Columbia's Junction Herd were released in the East Fork Owyhee River drainage in 1963, followed by 9 more in 1965 and additional 10 in 1966. Eight ewes and 4 rams were obtained in 1967 and released into Little Jack Creek. The country the sheep were released into was rough, unroaded, and vast, and there were few reports by which success or failure could be evaluated in the early years following release. However, based on reports and sightings, the Idaho Department of Fish and Game assigned a graduate student to assess the Owyhee release in the late 1960s, and his report indicated that the herd had grown to at least 80 individuals. Five hunting permits for California bighorns were allowed in the East Fork Owyhee River in 1969, and two rams were harvested. Hunting of this herd has continued in the Owyhee drainage every year since, and hunting was initiated in Little Jack Creek drainage in 1975 (where it has continued annually as well).

The success of these two initial transplants fueled a demand for more transplants, beginning in 1980 when one ram and four ewes were captured and moved to Granite Mountain in Nevada. Additional captures occurred every year between 1980 and 1993. Over 400 California bighorns were captured and moved as the result of 24 capture operations during that 14-year period, and bighorns were moved into vacant habitats in southwestern Idaho, northwestern Nevada, central Oregon, and

The terraced canyons of Little Jack Creek provide ideal habitat for California bighorn ram sheep in southwestern Idaho.

DALE E. TOWEILL

Startled while feeding, this bachelor group of California bighorn rams flee for the safety of canyon cliffs.

western North Dakota. Sheep management efforts were coupled with extensive research, funded and conducted by the Idaho Fish and Game Department and the Bureau of Land Management, beginning in 1984.

Thirty-five years' experience with California bighorns in southwestern Idaho has revealed some fascinating information. As studies conducted on bighorn sheep elsewhere have indicated, California bighorns rarely disperse more than about 15 miles— but there are exceptions. Even then, dispersal usually follows canyons providing suitable escape/security habitat. California bighorns in Little Jack Creek failed to colonize Big Jack Creek, just a mile to the east across a sagebrush flat, in the twenty years be tween 1967 and 1987. Although there is some evidence of limited exploration, bighorns were no established in Big Jack Creek Canyon until a group of sheep from British Columbia was released there in 1988. This herd was supplemented with sheep from the East Fork Owyhee herd, and it appears (10 years later) that there is regular interchange between all three herds. Populations appear to have reached a level where small groups of sheep do occasionally move into new and unfamiliar territory. Following a wildfire in Oregon's Leslie Gulch bighorn sheep range, a band of 8 to 15 ewes and young rams moved 20 to 25 miles southeastward

Inset: Rocky rims and near-vertical walls of the Owyhee River canyon snake their way through the Great Basin of Idaho and Oregon.

Mature California bighorn ram dashes for cover as biologists conduct a population survey in the Owyhee canyonlands.

DALE E. TOWEILL

Estimated numbers of California bighorn sheep in Idaho.

Herd Unit	1970	1985	1990	1997	Status	Map
Reynolds Creek	0	0	10	25	Increasing	1
Castle Creek	0	0	0	20	Increasing	2
Little Jack Creek	10	140	360	275	Increasing	3
Big Jack Creek	0	0	60	225	Increasing	4
East Fork Owyhee	80	370	600	550	Increasing	5
South Fk Owyhee River	0	10	25	120	Increasing	6
Bruneau/Jarbidge Rivers	0	50	125	225	Increasing	7
Cottonwood Creek	0	0	60	20	Decreasing	8
TOTAL	90	570	1,240	1,460		

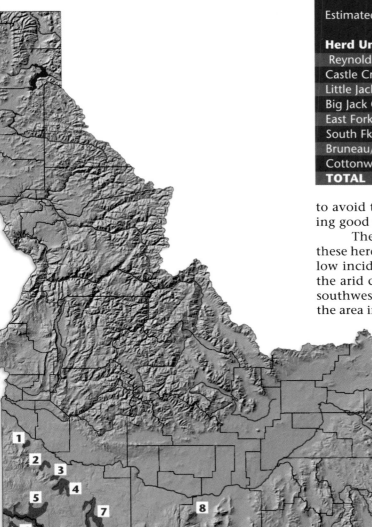

to avoid trees in favor of high, rocky points offering good visibility in all directions.

The high incidence of lungworm common to these herds in the early years has subsided to a very low incidence at present. This may be a result of the arid climate and often bitterly cold winters of southwestern Idaho's high desert, or a reflection of the area in which these bighorns sufficiently range to reduce the heavy parasite loads that can accumulate when small areas are used intensively and rates of reinfection are high. Idaho's experience is that California bighorns appear to have greater resistance to disease than Rocky Mountain bighorns; at least no major die-offs are known to have occurred among California bighorns in Idaho. These sheep coexist with cattle (but not domestic sheep), mule deer, pronghorn antelope, and even a few elk. However, captive animals that have been exposed to direct contact with domestic sheep often die of undetermined causes within a few days.

Idaho plans to continue to transplant California bighorns into historic habitat capable of supporting a herd of 100 or more animals where they are unlikely to come into contact with domestic sheep. Under present management guidelines, hunting of mature rams (over about 3 years of age) will be allowed, on a strictly controlled permit basis, on most herds. Permit numbers will be regulated based on the number of mature rams actually observed in each herd.

into Idaho following a low, rocky ridge south of the Snake River. Although a few were killed (one crossing the highway), this group colonized a rocky portion of Reynolds Creek, and appears to be persisting in their new home.

Not unexpectedly, ewes and lambs occupy the most rugged and broken country. Favored sites include many small shelves among canyon walls, providing forage in the midst of security habitat in the form of climbable cliffs. Rams rarely associate with ewe-lamb groups, often foraging as far as a mile out onto the sagebrush/bunchgrass flats, and finding sufficient security in the proximity of low cliffs or rocky outcroppings. Although California bighorns will occasionally bed in the shade of isolated junipers or rub their horns on trees, they tend

Nevada

California bighorn sheep were apparently widespread in northern Nevada, although there is little evidence that they occurred in large numbers. Trapper and explorer John Work and his party passed through what is now northern and north-central Nevada in May and June of 1831. Field journal accounts of that exploration recorded observations of bighorn sheep tracks along the Humboldt River and South Fork of the Owyhee River, but no bighorn sightings were recorded. Members of John C. Fremont's expedition party recorded observations of 'mountain sheep' near Pyramid Lake in 1844, and immigrants using the Lassen-Applegate Trail observed bighorn sheep in what is now northern Washoe County in 1846. However, even though they were widespread, there is little evidence that California bighorn sheep occurred in large herds anywhere in the northern portion of Nevada. Considering that food supplies were often scarce and that diaries and journals of many of the original travellers through what is now Nevada documented the need to sacrifice their domestic livestock to provide sufficient food to sustain themselves during their travels, one must conclude that large herds of bighorns simply were not present between 1830 and 1850. This has led some scientists to speculate that climatic and vegetation conditions may have been favorable for colonization of much of this area only within the past 2,000 years or so.

Even so, California bighorn sheep populations suffered as immigrants explored and exploited Nevada. With the discovery of the Comstock lode in 1859, a mining and mineral exploration boom led hundreds of individuals to explore every nook and

Nevada's Santa Rosa Range, home of reintroduced California bighorn sheep.

GREGG TANNER

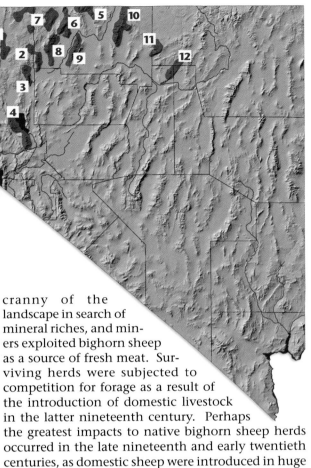

California bighorn sheep herd estimates for Nevada, 1998.

Herd Unit	1970	1985	1990	1992	1998	Map
Hays Canyon Range			15	25	76	1
Calico Range/High Rock Canyon			18	25	53	2
Granite Range		45	60	115	88	3
Northern Virginia/Pah Rah Ranges				32	25	4
Trout Creek/Montana Mountains				23	123	5
Pine Forest Range/McGee Mtn.			98	200	185	6
Sheldon NWR	8	65	—	40	88	7
Black Rock Range				15	92	8
Jackson Mountains		17	110	140	169	9
Santa Rosa Range		50	87	150	219	10
Snowstorm Mountains			27	75	65	11
Sheep Creek Range				25	65	12
Jarbidge Mountains			24	15	0	
TOTAL	8	177	439	880	1,248	

cranny of the landscape in search of mineral riches, and miners exploited bighorn sheep as a source of fresh meat. Surviving herds were subjected to competition for forage as a result of the introduction of domestic livestock in the latter nineteenth century. Perhaps the greatest impacts to native bighorn sheep herds occurred in the late nineteenth and early twentieth centuries, as domestic sheep were introduced in huge numbers (domestic sheep totaled in excess of three million animals by approximately 1910). Domestic sheep were herded across virtually the entire state of Nevada, with only those areas having severely limited supplies of water or forage, or having extremely rugged topography, being spared. Domestic sheep not only competed for forage, but likely introduced diseases and parasites to which native bighorn herds were susceptible.

The Nevada Legislature, in apparent concern for declining bighorn sheep populations statewide, passed a statewide closure on bighorn sheep hunting in 1917. This measure came too late to save the state's native California bighorn sheep herds. By 1940, California bighorn sheep herds in northern Nevada had been eliminated.

Efforts to reestablish California bighorn sheep herds to formerly-occupied ranges were begun in 1967, when the success of Oregon's initial efforts to restore California bighorn sheep was so successful that eight animals from Hart Mountain National Wildlife Refuge in Oregon were made available for a transplant to a 1,700-acre fenced enclosure on Sheldon National Wildlife Refuge in northwestern Nevada. This herd slowly became established.

Twelve California bighorn sheep, obtained from British Columbia in 1978, were released into the northern Santa Rosa Range of Humboldt County. Animals obtained from Idaho were used to establish new herds in the Granite Range and Jarbidge Mountains in 1980 and 1981, respectively, and every year thereafter (through 1998), transplants of California bighorns have been made into suitable habitats, using animals from British Columbia, Oregon, Idaho, or Nevada herds. In 1998, an estimated 1,248 California bighorn sheep occur among 12 herds in northwestern Nevada.

California bighorn sheep restoration efforts have been very successful in Nevada. After initial restoration efforts met with success, a unique partnership of entities interested in bighorn sheep began work on trapping, transplanting, monitoring, and habitat improvement projects to benefit wild sheep restoration efforts. In cooperation with the Nevada Division of Wildlife, sportsmen organized numerous successful fund-raising efforts, and provided generous donations of money, time and effort. Federal agencies including the Bureau of Land Management, Forest Service, and the Fish and Wildlife Service contributed expertise and efforts as well.

GREGG TANNER

Old California bighorn sheep ewe with a very fine ewe lamb, both in winter fur and excellent body condition.

North Dakota

Bighorn sheep in North Dakota occupy an ecotype unique to the Great Plains, the badlands and rough breaks lying adjacent to major river systems. These areas were formerly occupied by the now extinct Audubon bighorn. With Audubon's bighorns no longer available, California bighorns, also adapted to the habitats afforded by badlands and rocky canyons, were obtained from British Columbia, Canada, and translocated to the rugged Magpie Creek area of the North Dakota badlands.

Since that initial reintroduction, 53 additional trap and transplant operations have been conducted by the North Dakota Game and Fish Department. These efforts have involved the capture of 247 bighorn sheep, subsequently released into unoccupied portions of this former Audubon bighorn range. In addition, 71 other California bighorns were captured during three trapping attempts in other jurisdictions, transported to and also released into this area of western North Dakota. These three additional trapping and transplant operations, one in British Columbia, Canada and two in Idaho, were intended to increase the genetic diversity of California bighorns in North Dakota.

Typically, bighorn sheep in North Dakota inhabit topography which includes plateaus that range form 2,500 to 2,900 feet above sea level and encompass areas of 0.6 square miles or more. These plateaus are surrounded by steep cliffs which serve as excellent escape terrain from their only terrestrial predator in North Dakota, the coyote. Most daily movements of bighorns are on or near these plateaus with some use occurring on the flat-topped ridges. Bighorn sheep are now distributed in a number of separate bands over approximately 195 square miles of badlands and, in aggregate, total between 200 and 300 animals.

The first ever recreational hunting season on bighorns in North Dakota was proclaimed in 1975 and (except for the years 1980-1983) have been held

HAROLD UMBER

Alert bighorn sheep, such as this California bighorn ewe, may watch suspicious objects well over a mile away.

California bighorn rams pestering a ewe in North Dakota's badlands. Before the rut, when ewes enter estrus, ewes may lead rams on long arduous chases.

141

annually. During these first eighteen seasons a total of 147 permits were issued (136 to residents of North Dakota and 11 nonresidents), allowing hunters to harvest 141 rams.

Habitat for bighorns in North Dakota is restricted. Bighorn sheep populations are small, and consequently, recreational hunting opportunities are limited. Therefore, to give all North Dakota hunters an equal chance to hunt these animals, all bighorn sheep hunting permits are issued by lottery on a once-in-a-lifetime basis.

Problems that have emerged relative to disease and/or parasite problems of bighorns in North Dakota are most often associated with lungworm loads and with stress from harassment and overcrowding from range constriction. Lungworm probably arrived in North Dakota along with the first bighorns from British Columbia, or it may have persisted as encapsulated larvae that have remained dormant in the soil since Audubon's bighorns occupied these ranges. At any rate, lungworm has been and will continue to be the major disease/parasite problem facing California bighorn sheep management in this jurisdiction, particularly when weather or other stress weakens animals and reduces their resistance. Bighorn losses due to stress can be dramatic. Capture and handling can result in "capture myopathy" or stress disease, and bighorns are also subject to stress due to overcrowding, range constriction and harassment associated with human activities, such as oil development. Regardless, the end result is the same— "fewer bighorns on the mountain."

The North Dakota Game and Fish Department is the principal governmental proponent for all fish and wildlife populations and their habitats in the state, and has an obligation to aggressively conserve and enhance these resources and protect them from irreversible harm to ensure their existence in perpetuity. The goals of the California bighorn sheep program are to maximize populations in areas where feasible and compatible with habitat and people, to provide unique hunting opportunities, and to meet demands for appreciative uses.

Minimum population estimates for California bighorn sheep in North Dakota in 1997, exclusive of Theodore Roosevelt National Park. Total population is believed between 200 and 300 animals. Interstate 94 divides the southern and northern metapopulation.

Herd	1970	1990	1997	Status	Map
Southern Metapopulation					
South Bullion Butte	n/a	11	30	Declining	1
North Bullion Butte	n/a	8	11	Stable	2
Moody-Kinley Plateau	55	25-30	17	Declining	3
Chateau De Mores	25	15-20	21	Stable	4
Northern Metapopulation					
Wannagan Creek	n/a	10-15	20	Stable	5
Magpie Creek	14	40-45	13	Declining	6
Sheep Creek	n/a	10-15	10	Stable	7
NW Lone Butte	n/a	23	12	Stable	8
Lone Butte	n/a	25	2	Declining	9
BLM Tract	n/a	n/a	12	Stable	10
Burnt Creek	n/a	n/a	5	Increasing	11
Total Min. Population	**94**	**167-192**	**153**		

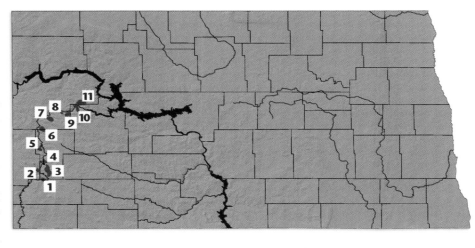

Rams stick together, such as this pair disturbed by the photographer in typical badlands habitat.

California bighorn sheep ewes (and one ram) utilize the eroded slopes of the badlands as well as rocky outcrops to escape predators.

143

Oregon

Historically, two subspecies of bighorn sheep were native to Oregon. Rocky Mountain bighorns inhabited the Wallowa and Blue Mountains of northeastern Oregon north and east of the John Day-Burnt River divide to the Snake River and the Oregon-Washington state line. To the south and west of this boundary were California bighorns, which ranged widely over the John Day and Deschutes River drainages and Great Basin deserts of central and southeastern Oregon. Occupying the canyons, cliffs, rocky buttes, and lava beds typical of this vast area, California bighorns were largely non-migratory and locally abundant.

While California bighorn sheep were both widespread and locally abundant prior to 1850, numbers (which had been showing a steady decline due to unregulated hunting following the first influx of settlers in the 1840s) dropped dramatically about the time domestic sheep were brought into this area following the Civil War. Many of the area's 'old-timers' reported that native bighorns contracted a disease called 'scab' or 'scabies' from domestic sheep. The disease is the result of an infestation of skin mites, which results in loss of hair coat and stress. Tough winters coupled with loss of forage as a result of unregulated grazing by domestic livestock aggravated their condition. These factors, along with unregulated hunting, contributed to the sudden and nearly complete demise of California bighorn sheep from eastern Oregon by 1900. The last native California bighorn sheep known to exist in Oregon disappeared from Steens Mountain about 1915.

HABITAT TYPES

Within Oregon, California bighorn sheep typically occupy shrub-steppe habitats characterized by sagebrush and rocky outcroppings. The low precipitation level (generally less than 12 inches annually) found in these habitats means few areas accumulate substantial overwinter snowpack. With little winter accumulation of snow, California bighorn sheep are not forced to seek out low-elevation wintering areas. And while it is uncertain whether the native herds were migratory, the lack of dramatic topographic relief in much of the Great Basin and central Oregon suggests it is likely that seasonal movements, if they occurred, were limited. Historic reports indicated that California bighorns that summered on Steens Mountain wintered in the lower country east and west of the uplift. Limited interchange between transplants in relative proximity to each other has been observed. This may be viewed as reestablishment of historic movement patterns or as simply exploratory wanderings; in either case, these movements are consistent with historic accounts and current meta-population theory.

Oregon's California bighorn sheep are currently found in three general types of shrub-steppe habitat. Differences between habitats are primarily a function of topography, precipitation, and vegetation. Each will be discussed briefly.

Fault-block Mountain

Fault block mountains were formed by shifts of the earth's crust, which caused huge blocks of underlying rock to be lifted above the surrounding terrain. This uplifting created isolated mountains characterized by a gentle slope on one side of the mountain and a steep, rugged 'face' on the other. The best bighorn sheep habitat is found on these rugged faces which typically provide elevational relief ranging from 1,500 to 5,000 feet above the surrounding desert. Some of the larger fault-block mountains accumulate winter snows to depths that preclude bighorn sheep use in winter, requiring movement (in at least some years) to lower elevations. Vegetation is typically dominated by a sagebrush shrub layer with a perennial bunchgrass understory. Most fault-block mountains are located in the south-central portion of Oregon. Some of the better examples of bighorn sheep ranges in this habitat type occur on Steens Mountain in Harney County, and Hart Mountain, Fish Creek Rim, and Abert Rim in Lake County.

California bighorn ewe with newborn lamb on Steens Mountain.

WALT VAN DYKE

California bighorn sheep rams seek shelter in rocky cave during a helicopter survey of Orejana Canyon. Undisturbed bighorn sheep may venture deeply into caves, although they do not do it often.

Canyon

Habitats of this type are located along river or stream corridors formed by centuries of water erosion. Elevational relief within these canyons is generally less than 1,500 feet, but the protection from winter winds and the solar warming of exposed rocks makes these habitats suitable for year-around use by bighorn sheep. Dominant vegetation in most canyon habitats is composed of bunchgrasses and sagebrush. Some examples of California bighorn sheep ranges of this type are found along the Owyhee River in Malheur County, Burnt River Canyon in Baker County, and the Deschutes and John Day River Canyons in the north-central portion of the state.

Mountain

Most mountain habitats in this area resulted from volcanic activity, and are typically lone high points rising above the surrounding landscape. In southeast and south central Oregon these mountains are dominated by sagebrush with a bunchgrass understory. Further to the north, along the fringes of the Blue Mountains, conifers tend to dominate the north slopes with an understory of shrubs and grasses, while bunchgrasses dominate south slopes. Examples of bighorn sheep habitat include Lone Mountain in Harney County, the Trout Creek Mountains in Malheur and Harney Counties, and Aldrich Mountain in Grant County.

HISTORY OF THE PARENT TRANSPLANT STOCK

The first attempt to restore bighorn sheep to historic California bighorn sheep ranges occurred in 1939, when 23 Rocky Mountain bighorns obtained from Montana were released onto Hart Mountain. This transplant did not fare well; the last survivor was observed in 1947. Oregon's experience with this transplant contributed to the widely-accepted theory that transplant success is in part dependent on reintroducing the subspecies that historically occupied the reintroduction site.

In November 1954, 20 California bighorn sheep were trapped near Williams Lake, British Columbia, and released in a one-thousand-acre fenced enclosure, constructed by the Civilian Conservation Corps

Poker Jim Ridge on the western portion of Hart Mountain Antelope Refuge, typical of California bighorn sheep habitat in southeastern Oregon.

WALT VAN DYKE

(CCC) on the west face of Hart Mountain in Lake County. This population thrived and, in subsequent years as the fence deteriorated, bighorns escaped from the pen and established a free-ranging population on Hart Mountain. The Hart Mountain population has been the source of most subsequent California bighorn sheep transplants in Oregon (stock from Nevada, whose lineage also traces back to British Columbia, was used in a 1997 transplant to Burnt River). All California bighorn sheep in Oregon were derived from stock from British Columbia.

CURRENT DISTRIBUTION AND POPULATION STATUS

Present populations are all the result of reintroduction, and occupy a relatively small percentage of the historic range. Through January 1997, a total of 985 California bighorn sheep in 70 individual releases have been moved within, into, or out of Oregon. A total of 79 California bighorns have been brought into Oregon, 138 have been shipped out of the state, and 768 animals have been moved within the state. The average size of each release has been 14 bighorns (range 1 to 35) and releases have been made into 25 different herd ranges. The estimated 1997 spring population of the 25 established California bighorn herds in Oregon included 2,890 animals. Controlled hunting of rams is currently allowed on 14 of these herds.

Most herds are increasing in number. Several herds are static or show decreasing population trends as a result of poor lamb survival rates and/or high rates of mortality among adult ewes. The reason for this poor population performance is in part due to predation by mountain lions; most herd ranges support healthy mountain lion populations but little alternate prey (deer or elk) that might be selected by these large predators. In some cases, the loss of lambs to coyotes is also suspected. The combination of levels of abundant alternate prey and low numbers of bighorn sheep can mean that even low incidence of predation might result in a significant impact to bighorn sheep herd growth.

MANAGEMENT PHILOSOPHY AND APPROACH

Oregon has officially adopted a Bighorn Sheep Management Plan which identifies management direction within the state. Overall, the plan emphasizes restoration of bighorn sheep to as much of the remaining suitable habitat as possible. More than one transplant is normally made to each identified herd range to increase bighorn sheep distribution, increase the probability that a herd will become viable, and encourage rapid herd growth. Native subspecies are reintroduced within their historic range, and the geographic integrity of bighorn sheep races is maintained within the state and coordinated with adjacent states where interstate herds may become established.

When possible, the genetic diversity of the California bighorn sheep herds will be broadened, although sources of native stock that could be mixed with established herds to increase the size of the gene pool is limited. At present, 23 of the existing 25 herds are direct descendants of the initial population established on Hart Mountain in 1954. Consequently, there is concern that there may be a lack of genetic diversity in most populations.

WALT VAN DYKE

Trapping and transplanting is used to control the population size of those herds which are largest or have reached habitat capacity of suitable ranges. Removing bighorns from these herds provides stock for reintroduction into other suitable vacant habitat. Transplants of bighorn sheep usually are composed primarily of ewes, lambs, and young rams. The Department does not transplant large rams because they are difficult to handle in the capture process and they tend to wander widely. Removing more ewes than rams for transplanting skews the sex ratio of source herds toward rams, so sport hunting of most source herds is allowed to keep the ram-to-ewe ration at or below one-to-one. Where trapping and transplanting is not feasible, hunting of females will be implemented, if necessary, to control population size.

Disease transmission between bighorn sheep and domestic sheep has been a problem in Oregon, and continues to be a major concern within the bighorn sheep restoration program. Bighorn sheep are not transplanted into areas where they may come into contact with domestic sheep. This precludes reestablishing California bighorns into several areas of prime habitat. Any bighorn sheep known or sus-

The eastern face of Steens Mountain, a fault-block mountain rising approximately 5,000 feet in elevation from the surrounding Great Basin.

pected to have had contact with domestic sheep is removed as soon as possible and is never again released where it might contact wild sheep (most of these animals go to zoos or disease research centers). Likewise, if domestic sheep are found within existing bighorn sheep ranges, procedures to remove them are initiated immediately. Funding for the state's Bighorn Sheep Program comes primarily from the annual auction of one tag and raffle of another. These funds are used primarily to fund trapping and transplanting operations, disease research programs, and habitat improvement projects. Where possible, donations are solicited and opportunities for matching grant dollars are pursued through organizations such as the Foundation for North American Wild Sheep.

California bighorn sheep in Oregon.

Herd Range	Year Established	1975	1985	1990	1998	Trend	Map
Hart Mountain	1954	300	400	450	270	Static	1
Steens Mountain	1960	120	200	250	250	Static	2
Lower Owyhee River	1965	100	230	325	225	Declining	3
Strawberry Mountain	1971	40	25	15	10	Declining	4
Abert Rim	1975	3	25	75	140	Increasing	5
Pueblo Mountains	1976		50	80	130	Increasing	6
Alvord Peaks/Black Point	1976		25	50	120	Increasing	7
Aldrich Mountain	1978		85	150	205	Increasing	8
Fish Creek Rim	1980		10	20	80	Increasing	9
Upper Owyhee River	1983		50	250	150	Decreasing	10
Hadley Buttles/Winter Rim	1984		15	75	105	Increasing	11
Burnt River	1987			25	75	Increasing	12
Riverside	1987			25	65	Increasing	13
Trout Creek Mountains	1987			60	100	Increasing	14
Lower John Day River	1989			35	255	Increasing	15
Coglan Buttes	1989			25	70	Increasing	16
Catlow Rim	1989			25	135	Increasing	17
Sheepshead Mountains	1990			20	50	Increasing	18
Diablo Mountain/Sheep Rock	1991				65	Increasing	19
Coleman Rim	1991				30	Increasing	20
Lone Mountain	1992				80	Increasing	21
Rattlesnake/Tenmile Rim	1992				100	Static	22
Deschutes River	1993				125	Increasing	23
Daugherty Rim	1994				25	Increasing	24
Devils Garden	1995				30	Increasing	25
TOTAL		**563**	**1,115**	**1,955**	**2,890**		

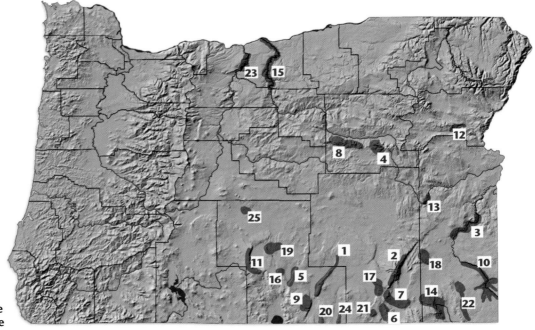

Bachelor group of California bighorn rams feeding among the sagebrush flats near the Owyhee River. Note the typical 'flare' of the horns away from the lower jaw.

Utah

California bighorn sheep were probably not native to Utah. Early records and specimens seem to indicate that Rocky Mountain bighorn sheep occupied the northern mountainous ranges, while desert bighorns were found in arid southern portions of the state. However, Utah received 23 California bighorns from British Columbia's Harper Ranch near Kamloops in 1977, and released them onto Antelope Island in the Great Salt Lake— unoccupied but classic low-elevation bighorn sheep habitat that seemed suited for California bighorns. This herd has apparently become established, and now numbers about 30 animals.

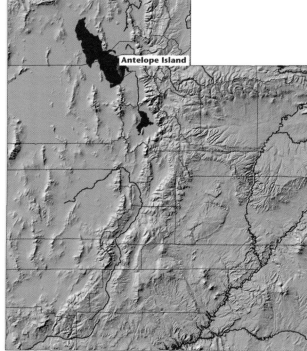

Antelope Island

Inset: Release of California bighorn sheep onto Antelope Island.

Antelope Island in Utah's Great Salt Lake, home to a small herd of California bighorn sheep.

DON PAUL

JIM KARPOWITZ

Washington

Historically, California bighorns occurred on the eastern slopes of the Cascades from the Canadian border south to the Columbia River. Most of Washington's native California bighorn herds were gone from the state before 1900; the last known survivors, on Chopaka, died in 1925.

HABITAT

Washington has only limited habitat for California bighorn sheep. California bighorns typically occupy relatively dry regions, usually associated with climax plant communities featuring grasslands (often maintained, in natural conditions, by periodic wildfire) and shrub-grassland associations in the interior west. High levels of precipitation probably precluded the occurrence of bighorns west of the crest of the Cascade Range in western Washington. California bighorn sheep ranges in Washington occur at elevations ranging from about 1,000 feet along the Columbia River to a maximum of only about 7,000 feet. Vegetation on California bighorn sheep ranges typically consists of bunchgrasses or shrubs interspersed with scattered stands of small trees. This type of habitat is uncommon in eastern Washington, so California bighorn range is limited to islands of suitable habitat located adjacent to suitable rocky escape terrain.

RESTORATION

California bighorn sheep were reintroduced to Washington in 1957, when 18 bighorns were obtained from Williams Lake, British Columbia and released on the Sinlahekin Wildlife Area in north-central Washington. After three years, six bighorns from the Sinlahekin herd were transplanted to Wooten Wildlife Area in southeast Washington. Two

Mixed band of California bighorn sheep ewes and young rams in bunchgrass habitat typical of Washington's Aeneas Mountain.

ROLF JOHNSON

years later (in 1962) eight more bighorns from Sinlahekin were transplanted to Colockum. In these first three releases, bighorns were put in 500-acre enclosures. In subsequent years, releases were made directly to suitable unfenced habitats.

All of Washington's bighorn transplants have been successful except for the Klickitat transplant in 1970. That transplant consisted of only eight bighorns. The only two rams included among the transplanted animals died shortly after release. One ram was killed by a poacher and the other was killed by a vehicle.

One of the concerns associated with Washington's California bighorn sheep reintroduction program has been the limited gene pool. To enhance the genetic diversity of transplant stock, Washington obtained three sheep from a zoological park in Washington State (Northwest Trek) in 1989, and in 1990, obtained 13 California bighorns from John Day, Oregon. The Oregon sheep originated from stock obtained from Williams Lake, British Columbia, but the origin of the Northwest Trek sheep is unknown. In March 1996, 31 California bighorns were secured from Kamloops, British Columbia and spread among the Lincoln Cliff, Mount Hull, Clemons, and Quilomene herds. These supplemental introductions will provide additional genetic diversity to existing herds, and hopefully will rejuvenate 'stagnant' herds helping them to grow and fill available habitats. Washington now has California bighorns in 12 areas of the state.

MANAGEMENT

Bighorn sheep management has focused primarily on restoring bighorn sheep to native habitats. One of our earliest reintroduction efforts involving California bighorns was a transplant to southeastern Washington (the Tucannon area) resulted in establishing a herd of California bighorns in an area now believed to have been occupied by Rocky Mountain bighorn sheep. A subsequent transplant of four bighorn sheep from the Tucannon area to Cottonwood Creek started the Cottonwood Creek herd. Since then, Rocky Mountain bighorns from other herds in Blue Mountains of southeastern Washington have populated the Cottonwood Creek area. Washington has reclassified this herd as Rocky Mountain bighorns, and manages it as part of the Asotin herd.

Washington is also interested in providing bighorn sheep-associated recreation opportunities in conjunction with restoration of native wildlife. The Clemon Mountain herd is provided supplemental feed on its winter range, providing a popular opportunity for wildlife viewing and photography. A limited-entry hunting program was initiated in 1966. Washington uses a very conservative approach to bighorn sheep harvest and strictly limits the number of hunting permits issued annually. Currently, half of he bighorn herds in the state meet the established criteria to allow limited hunting (e.g., minimum herd size and number of rams, among other measures).

A statewide bighorn management plan was completed in 1995. This plan identifies individual bighorn sheep herd management plans, with specific management objectives. Washington had about 745 California bighorns in 1998.

California bighorn sheep numbers in Washington. Herd estimates from are from Washington Department of Fish and Game files.

Location	Established	1960	1969	1975	1984	1990	1998	Map
Sinlahekin	1957	35	78	150	100	70	30	1
Tucannon River/Wooten	1960	6	60	15	35	50	50	2
Clemans	1967		8	30	35	45	100	3
Swakane	1969		9	18	30	30	30	4
Umtanum	1970			25	130	180	180	5
Klictitat	1970			0	0	0	7	6
Mt. Hull	1970			20	50	85	45	7
Vulcan Mtn.	1971			20	85	160	80	8
Cottonwood Creek*	1973			12	45	30	20	9
Lincoln Cliffs	1990					8	100	10
Quilomene	1993						120	11
Tieton	1998						10	12
TOTAL		41	155	290	510	658	772	

*The initial herd was California bighorn. It is now classified as a Rocky Mountain bighorn sheep herd.

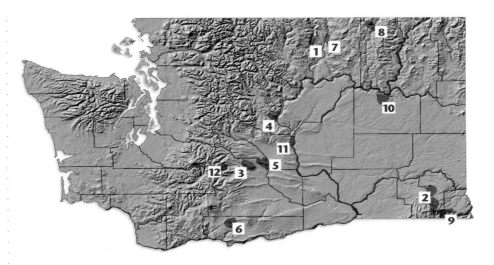

153

Chapter Six

DESERT BIGHORN SHEEP

esert bighorns are generally believed to be 'relict' populations (i.e., populations isolated as a result of climate or habitat change), holdouts from a geologically earlier period, when glaciation in continental North America forced ancestral populations southward into habitats much like those occupied by Rocky Mountain bighorn sheep in Colorado today. Retreat of the glaciers and formation of southwestern deserts stranded these ancestral populations in isolated mountain ranges, where the animals gradually adapted to drier habitats.

Adaptations of the desert bighorns make them unique among bighorn sheep. Unlike their northern counterparts which developed massive, blocky bodies to conserve body heat during periods of extreme cold, desert bighorn sheep are routinely subjected to heat stress. One adaptation to deal with heat stress was to reduce the amount of hair covering the body. By reducing this layer of insulation, desert bighorns maximize their surface area relative to body mass, thereby increasing their ability to lose excess heat. Since horn size in rams has remained about the same as among ancestral populations (and those of Rocky Mountain bighorns today), desert bighorn rams often give the appearance of having horns that are disproportionately large relative to body size. Horn size is important to social organization, an indicator of reproductive fitness, and is more resistant to change than many other organs. Horns of mature desert bighorns measure about 35 to 40 inches in total length, with basal circumference of 13 to 16 inches. Horns of ewes are less important as social signals, but (although they are much smaller than those of rams)

JIM DEFORGE

Nelson's desert bighorn in brushy habitat of California's San Gabriel Mountains.

the horns of desert bighorn sheep ewes are relatively large compared to those of Rocky Mountain bighorn sheep ewes. Horns of ewes are typically 13 to 15 inches long, with bases 5 to 6 inches in circumference. Ears of desert bighorns are also relatively large, especially in the Mexican subspecies.

Desert bighorns also adapted to the stresses typical of deserts worldwide— lack of water. To

155

deal with this problem, the desert bighorns specialized their digestive process to become especially proficient in extracting water for metabolic requirements from their forage. Desert bighorns can exist for up to six months without drinking water, although where water is available bighorns will typically drink every two or three days. Bighorns are also adapted to take particular advantage of water when it is available (sometimes a rarity in the desert). Desert bighorns have been reported as drinking over two gallons per minute, and they have developed large water retention organs. Desert bighorns can withstand the loss of up to one-third of their body weight due to dehydration. To help conserve water, desert bighorns perspire very little, relying instead on respiration and energy conservation to regulate body temperature within a relatively wide range. Body temperatures of desert bighorns may be allowed to climb as high as 107°F.

Desert bighorns have adapted to desert environments in many other ways as well. The breeding period is very long when compared with the typical November breeding period of Rocky Mountain and California bighorn sheep. The more northerly Nelson's bighorns typically breed between July and October, with a peak of rutting activity in August; the more southerly Mexican bighorns typically breed between June and September. This wide range of dates is important for a species which is widely distributed in low numbers, reducing the rate of contact between individuals; it is also important in that it helps insure that at least some of the lambs (usually a single lamb is born, although twins have been reported) will be born during a period when forage conditions are at their best. Birth of the 8 to 10-pound precocious lambs will occur 179 days later, sometime between January and April. Lambs are able to walk and run among the cliffs within hours after birth. The ewe is dependent on an adequate supply of nutritious forage to ensure the production of sufficient milk to raise a healthy lamb able to survive the stress of transition to a diet of desert foliage. Mortality

is high among lambs; about half of all lambs born die before six months of age.

Lambs remain with the maternal band into which they were born for the first two years of life— if they survive. Although ewes typically remain with the same band for life, the growing horns of young rams result in their expulsion from ewe/lamb bands at about two years of age. The young rams search out older, mature rams (typically those with large horns) and follow them, learning the best places to feed and secure routes of travel from the older animals.

The desert bighorn sheep are typically widely but thinly distributed in the isolated mountain ranges of the southwestern United States and northern Mexico. There are four generally recognized 'races' or subspecies of desert bighorn sheep. The northernmost of these is Nelson's desert bighorn (subspecies *nelsoni*). This is an animal of the southern Great Basin desert of Nevada, the Painted Desert of southern Utah and southwestern Colorado, the Mojave Desert of the southern one-third of California and Nevada and northwestern Arizona, and the Colorado Desert of southern California. This is a relatively small bighorn, standing about 33 to 35 inches at the shoulder. Rams are typically much larger than ewes, weighing 125 to 200 pounds; the smaller ewes typically weigh 75 to 115 pounds. The Mexican desert bighorn (subspecies *mexicana*) occurs east of the Colorado River in Arizona, New Mexico, Texas, and Sonora; this subspecies also occurred in earlier times westward into Coahuila and Chihuahua, Mexico. This is a relatively large-bodied bighorn sheep, noted for its unusual (for a bighorn) long, pointed ears. Rams often weigh 160 to 200 pounds. This subspecies also includes the Texas bighorns of eastern new Mexico, and Gaillard's bighorns of southern Arizona and northern Sonora as identified by James Clark in his book, *The Great Arc of Wild Sheep*. The Peninsular desert bighorn (subspecies *cremnobates*) occurs in extreme southern California's San Diego and Imperial Counties and southward along eastern portions of Baja California Norte, and Weem's desert bighorn (subspecies *weemsi*) occurs still further south, in the eastern portions of Baja California Sur. Taxonomy of desert bighorn sheep has historically been based on only a few individuals, and differences of skeletal measurements and body size and coloration were viewed as distinctive. In fact, we now know that these characteristics are controlled at least in part by habitat and diet, and wide differences may

Oasis-like vegetation often develops around permanent water sources in the mountains of southern California and Baja California Norte, a beacon to thirsty animals.

DALE E. TOWEILL

Mature peninsular desert bighorn ram in southern California's northern Santa Rosa Mountains.

occur within any given population. This is especially true when a species, such as the desert bighorns, tend to live in small isolated groups. New techniques have become available for assessing genetic differences between populations, and the taxonomy of bighorn sheep will no doubt be substantially revised in the near future. For that reason, although the subspecies are mentioned here, the desert bighorns are treated as a single group.

Habitats occupied by desert bighorns, generally lumped together as 'desert,' vary widely. Nelson's bighorns occupy the greatest variability of habitat types. At the southern fringe of the Great Basin in Nevada, Nelson's bighorns occupy sagebrush-covered mountain ranges at elevations of 2,000 to 6,000 feet, characterized by cold winters and hot summers— habitat much like that of California bighorns. The Painted Desert is a land of sandstone mesas and canyonlands at elevations of 3,500 to 7,000 feet. This area is characterized by hot, dry summers and cold winters with occasional snow. Vegetation typically includes sagebrush, shadscale, and four-wing saltbush. Mojave desert habitats are characterized by Joshua trees and creosote bush at elevations from 2,000 to over 11,000 feet in Death Valley. Winters are mild and summers are hot, and the climate is characterized by only 1 to 5 inches of annual rainfall except in the Transverse Range of southern California, where rainfall may reach 20 to 30 inches annually. Desert bighorns typically occupy rough, broken mountains characterized by steep rocky slopes. The Colorado desert, which lies immediately west of the Colorado River in southern California, is very hot and dry, with annual precipitation (usually summer mon-

GREGG TANNER

Inset: Nelson's bighorn ram and ewe in Nevada.

Mexican desert bighorn ram follows a ewe to check on her breeding condition in Arizona's Kofa National Wildlife Refuge. Note the long thin horns of the ewe, typical of the desert bighorn sheep.

BOB MILES

soonal rains) of less than 5 inches. Elevations range from below sea level to 7,000 feet. Creosote bush, burro bush, brittle bush, and smoke trees dominate the vegetation.

The Mexican bighorn is an animal of the Chihuahuan desert. This vast area is the southernmost of North American deserts. It is characterized as high (over half of this desert lies between 4,000 and 6,000 feet in elevation) and hot; rainfall occurs primarily during the summer and totals 3 to 10 inches annually. Vegetation is sparse, characterized by creosote bush, lechuguilla, sotol, barrel cactus, ocotillo and mesquite.

Peninsular bighorns occupy Baja California mountain desert. This area ranges from sea level at the western shore of the Sea of Cortez to 10,000 feet at San Pedro Martir. Topography includes eastern slopes of volcanic and granitic mountains, washes, and isolated mountain ranges. Temperatures are very warm year-around. Rainfall (typically less than 5 inches annually) occurs primarily in the summer and early fall. Vegetation consists largely of various cacti and shrubs. Some common species include cardon, prickly pear, cholla, ocotillo, palo verde trees, creosote bush, brittle bush, and mesquite.

By contrast, the habitat of the Weem's bighorn is almost tropical. Palo blanco and palo verde trees are interspersed with extensive stands of cardon, prickly pear and organ pipe cacti.

Wherever they occur, desert bighorn face many challenges to their continued survival. Habitats are harsh, and bighorns must compete with domestic livestock and feral burros, horses, cattle, or goats for limited vegetation and water. Lamb survival is typically low due to limited forage and stress, and predators (including mountain lions, coyotes, bobcats, and eagles) also kill many lambs annually. Predation on adult bighorns is typically low in many ranges because there are too few large animals (such as bighorns, deer, and feral or domestic livestock) to support mountain lion populations, but where mountain lions find sufficient food to survive, predation on adult bighorns may be very significant, limiting bighorn population size. Finally, poaching— the illegal harvest of both rams and ewes for meat or trophies— can also become a significant limitation to herd growth and maintenance if allowed to continue unchecked. Although the remote and rugged habitats occupied by desert bighorns afford some measure of protection, bighorns attracted to desert water holes become especially vulnerable to both predators and humans.

Population estimates of desert bighorn sheep in North America in 1998. Numbers appear in Buechner (1960), Trefethen (1975), Monson and Sumner (1981), Hoefs (1985), and Desert Bighorn Council reports (1993). Totals for 1975 and 1992 not estimated because key data not available.

State	1960	1975	1980	1985	1992	1998
Arizona	3,000-5,000	2,350	2,100-2,600	4,000	5,550	5,910
California	1,800-2,100	3,642	3,250-3,750	4,000	4,470	3,326
Colorado	0	0	0	60	425-485	460
Nevada	1,500-2,000	2,200	3,700-4,200	5,200	2,027	5,175
New Mexico	400-500	300	350-390	100	278	310
Texas	12	—	50	120	304	277
Utah	—	250	350-500	2,500	—	2,560
Subtotal	**6,712-8,112**	**8,742**	**9,800-11,490**	**15,980**	**13,054-14,114**	**18,018**
Baja	—	—	4,560-7,800	4,500-7,800	—	2,500
Sonora	—	935	900	1,000	880-1,760	2,000
Coahuila	—	—	100	0	—	0
Subtotal	—	—	5,560-8,800	5,500-8,800	880-1,760	4,500
TOTAL	**12,000**	**—**	**15,360-20,290**	**21,480-24,780**	**—**	**22,518**

Arizona

Beaver trapper James Ohio Pattie entered into his journal that on January 1, 1825, he and a band of fellow trappers moved up the San Francisco River from the confluence with the Gila River. He wrote that "upon the high and rugged mountains we saw multitudes of mountain sheep." While Mr. Pattie was an excellent observer of wildlife, he was not a taxonomist. Currently, the proper classification of the sheep originally seen by these early beaver trappers is under some debate.

Early explorers generally traveled along river bottoms and valleys. Therefore, most did not report seeing large numbers of bighorn sheep. These early travelers did report a bighorn sheep distribution greater than that of today. In 1859, Schott described bighorn range in Arizona as the "rocky, waterless sierras." Coues stated in 1867 that the "mountain ram has a very extensive range, which includes nearly all the elevated mountains and broken regions."

There were numerous observations of bighorn sheep in mountains from which the species was later extirpated. In the 1850s, Whipple and Kennerly reported bighorn sheep in the Aquarius, Cottonwood, and Artillery mountains; ranges in which bighorn sheep are now absent. Mearns reported bighorn sheep in the 1880s in the Peloncillo, Pajarito, Atascosa, and Santa Rita mountains; the mountains bordering the Verde Valley; and on Bill Williams Mountain and the San Francisco Peaks. Nelson reported bighorn sheep in the 1880s along the cliffs bordering the Little Colorado River below Springerville. He also noted bighorn sheep near Springerville, and along the rocky canyons of Chevelon and Clear creeks north of the Mogollon Rim. According to Nelson, bighorn sheep disappeared from all of these areas and the San Francisco Peaks by 1911.

There are no records of bighorn sheep from much of what is now the Navajo Indian Reserva-

Nelson's desert bighorn ewe with lamb on Black Mountain.

RAYMOND LEE

Nelson's desert bighorns on Superstition Mountain.

tion, and many of the wooded mountains in southeastern Arizona were sparsely inhabited, if at all. That bighorn sheep were scarce in southeastern Arizona is shown in a December 1888 article in the Arizona Weekly Star:

"The first mountain sheep ever seen in the Tombstone market were brought in by Pete Bute yesterday from the Winchester Mountains. One of them was dressed and hanging in front of the Cummings meat market... There were but four in the herd, the successful hunters getting the whole of them."

The original distribution of bighorn sheep in Arizona's mountain ranges is not well known because many bighorn sheep populations declined rapidly and disappeared at an early date. As early as 1867, Elliot Coues wrote:

"In America it [the bighorn sheep] has been formerly much more abundant than now, for though it still exists in the more inaccessible portions, it is rarely to be seen. But its great horns may be found scattered about the bases of nearly every cliff and precipice."

The decline of bighorn sheep in Arizona was so rapid that in 1893 the Territorial Legislature passed a five year moratorium against the taking of bighorn sheep, while retaining an open season on deer and pronghorn antelope. Bighorn sheep existed in good numbers after 1900 only in the arid southwestern regions and in the Grand Canyon, where established ranches were absent. Despite total protection, once thriving populations were still declining. Arizona's bighorn sheep population received additional protection with the establishment of a State Game Code in 1913. Although enforcement of the game laws may have been lax, those populations in desert ranges too arid or steep for livestock persisted. Isolated populations continued to be extirpated, however; the last native bighorn sheep reported from the Virgin Mountains was in 1915. By 1930, the only sizeable bighorn sheep populations remaining outside of western Arizona were in the Grand Canyon and the Santa Catalina and Superstition mountains. The late 1930s found Arizona's desert bighorn sheep population reduced still further, to only about 1,000 animals, most of which were found along the Colorado River and its tributaries.

Settlers, miners, and market hunters were held accountable for low bighorn sheep numbers after the

RAYMOND LEE

161

1880s, but the question remains why bighorn sheep persisted in the most arid regions, while disappearing entirely from better-watered areas. The answer lies not with the miner or the market hunter, but with the introduction of domestic livestock - especially sheep and goats. It is well documented that sheep and goats transmit diseases to bighorn sheep. The evidence linking the reduction and elimination of bighorn sheep populations with the arrival of domestic livestock is overwhelming. Domestic sheep were recognized as a source of disease as early as 1895 when a Territorial Act established an inspector with authority to inspect all domestic sheep entering the territory, and to impound any sheep with infectious disease.

In 1937, Nichol conducted a statewide inventory to determine why bighorn sheep numbers were declining and to make recommendations on how the species could be saved from extinction. Nichol's study estimated that no more than 700 bighorn sheep remained in Arizona outside of the Grand Canyon and Lake Mead areas. Nichol emphasized that poaching and predators were the primary reasons why bighorn sheep were not making a comeback.

Concern for the Southwest's bighorn sheep gained national attention. Federal Wildlife Refuges were established in Nevada (Desert Game Range), New Mexico (San Andres National Wildlife Refuge), and in Arizona. In 1939, the creation of the Kofa and Cabeza Prieta game ranges set aside 1.5 million acres of southwestern Arizona for bighorn sheep and other wildlife. Although then Governor Hunt ridiculed these "federal takeovers" as "billy goat pastures," these actions were considered essential if the bighorn sheep was going to be saved from extinction. Game ranges were patrolled, and most importantly, livestock grazing was eliminated. Habitat, the primary means of retaining viable populations of any wildlife species, had been protected.

Populations outside these refuges, however, continued to decline. Poaching and predation were believed the main reasons for continued losses. There were other speculations, but it wasn't until 1950 that a systematic survey of bighorn sheep populations and a comprehensive life history study were initiated.

Modern bighorn sheep management in Arizona began with John Russo's study. Started in 1950

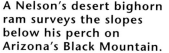

A Nelson's desert bighorn ram surveys the slopes below his perch on Arizona's Black Mountain.

Estimated number of desert bighorn sheep in Arizona by area, based on helicopter survey data.

Herd Area	1998	Map
Virgin River/Beaver Dams	185	1
Northern Grand Wash Cliffs	95	2
Kanab Creek/Hacks Canyon	230	3
Paria Canyon	105	4
Blacks	1,815	5
Southern Grand Wash Cliffs	195	6
Cataract Canyon	50	7
Chemehuevis	70	8
Mojaves, Rawhides, Artilleries	125	9
Dome Rocks	50	10
Plomosa	125	11
Harcuvar/Buckskins	70	12
Trigos	205	13
Castle Domes	180	14
Kofas	460	15
New Waters	105	16
Tanks	110	17
Eagletails	150	18
Gila Bends	150	19
Maricopas	185	20
Stewart and Goat Mountains	80	21
Superstitions	80	22
Tinajas Altas	50	23
Mowhawks	75	24
Sierra Pintas	310	25
Growlers	205	26
Saucedas	195	27
Silverbells	85	28
Catalinas	5	29
Aravaipa Canyon	80	30
Galiuros	35	31
Peloncillos	50	32
TOTAL	**5,910**	

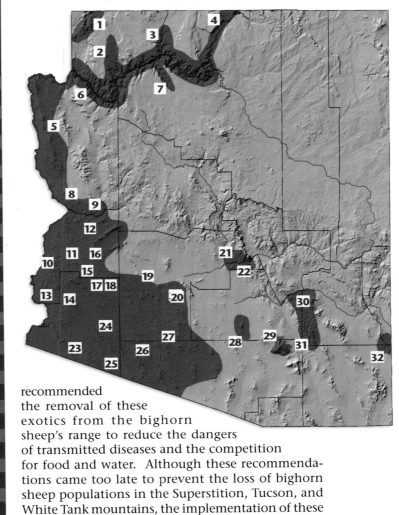

and continued for five years, this study sought to locate and document bighorn sheep distribution, determine the animal's food, water, and habitat requirements; determine its limiting factors and the effects of predation; develop survey techniques and methods of indexing the populations; recommend beneficial management practices; evaluate the effects of removing excess rams through limited hunting; and investigate the feasibility of transplanting bighorn sheep to suitable unoccupied ranges.

Several recommendations resulting from Russo's investigations were to be the cornerstone for the successful increase in bighorn sheep numbers enjoyed today. Russo emphasized the need to separate bighorn sheep from livestock and feral burros, and recommended the removal of these exotics from the bighorn sheep's range to reduce the dangers of transmitted diseases and the competition for food and water. Although these recommendations came too late to prevent the loss of bighorn sheep populations in the Superstition, Tucson, and White Tank mountains, the implementation of these recommendations in other areas resulted in a steady increase in bighorn sheep populations.

Russo's most important contribution was to initiate hunting and reintroduction programs. The first hunt in 1953 intensified interest in bighorn sheep management among the state's sportsmen. To date nearly 2,000 bighorn rams have been harvested.

In 1955, the Arizona Game and Fish Department began efforts to reintroduce bighorn sheep into historic ranges. Since that time over 1,200 animals have been captured in areas of relatively abundant populations and released into historic habitat. Arizona's desert bighorn sheep population is now estimated at approximately 6,000 animals.

Additional captures have been made to provide transplant stock to other states to augment their bighorn sheep populations. To date, 208 desert bighorn sheep have been provided to other states, including 99 sheep sent to Colorado in trade for Rocky Mountain bighorn sheep.

Baja California

Bighorn sheep in Baja California were first referred to by their native name *taye* (mountain sheep) by Jesuit missionaries as early as 1702. These initial accounts of bighorns in Baja California remained the only published account of wild sheep in North America for over 100 years. Little was known of the abundance or distribution of wild sheep in Baja California, although most observers of the early twentieth century reported large numbers.

Two subspecies or races of desert bighorn sheep occur in the states of Baja California Norte and Baja California Sur, which together comprise the Baja peninsula. To the north, the Peninsular desert bighorn extends its range southward from southern California, while the Weem's desert bighorn occurs at the southern end of the peninsula. The boundary between the two is not clearly differentiated, and there is a zone of intergradation in the area of the Sierra San Borjas. Recent data indicates that the taxonomic distinction between these races needs further investigation.

Early information on the distribution of wild sheep in Baja is derived from such hunters as A. W. North and W. E. Humphrey, who published detailed accounts of their experiences. Using information from hunters, E. T. Seton estimated that at least 28,000 desert bighorn inhabited the Baja peninsula in 1928. Humphrey reported that he observed bighorn on the desert floor during his hunting trips in the early 1900s, and he noted that bighorn regularly crossed the desert plains in northern Baja to move between the Sierra Juarez to the Sierra Las Tinajas— a pattern that continues today.

The history of bighorn sheep in Baja parallels that of the United States. Stories reported by early hunters and naturalists paint images of abundant bighorn herds and unregulated hunting. Biologist E. W. Nelson conducted biological surveys of the peninsula in 1905 and 1906. In publishing the information he collected during these trips, he deplored the large numbers of desert bighorns killed to provide jerky for mining camps and other commercial markets. Nelson was informed of one party of market hunters that killed more than 100 bighorn sheep in a single season. Several naturalists identified the potential for over-exploitation of these herds, and cautioned that poaching should be controlled. Nevertheless, the early chronicles of Baja overflowed with the thrill of hunting the desert sheep, 'the most noble of game animals,' in a vast, pristine region.

Hunting, and especially guiding Americans on trophy hunts, was a flourishing business in the Baja of the early 1900s. The prestige and adventure of a wild sheep hunt was considered a worthy challenge to many American sportsmen, able to experience an exotic locale without overseas travel. It wasn't long before uncontrolled killing of wildlife in Mexico was recognized as a serious problem. The massacre of 17 sheep east of Magdelena Bay, as reported in a 1908 Los Angeles *Times* newspaper article, incited the distinguished naturalist William T. Hornaday to contact the Mexican government and urge enactment of hunting regulations for the protection of desert bighorns. Hornaday received a prompt and favorable reply from the Mexican government— but the laws protecting bighorns were established without the resources for enforcement, and were largely futile. Bighorn sheep in Mexico were fully protected by law against all hunting for 10 years beginning in 1921. Hunting seasons, allowed after 1931, were again closed in 1944. Ten years later, in 1954, the Minister of Agriculture and Livestock Gilberto Flores Munoz signed a decree that wild sheep were among the list of animals for which hunting was permanently prohibited. Even so, A. Starker Leopold wrote in 1959 that effective protection from hunting was the most critical need of the bighorn sheep in Mexico. In another attempt to improve bighorn management and focus attention on the remaining populations, Mexico offered a limited number of permits (50) for desert bighorn sheep and provided a controlled hunting season in 1963. Despite established hunting seasons, widespread poaching continued.

Biologist Jim DeForge of the Bighorn Institute with blindfolded Weem's desert bighorn ram captured in the Sierra las Tarabillis for transplant to Isla del Carmen.

STACEY OSTERMANN

Peninsular desert bighorn ram in Baja California Norte seen from a helicopter.

In the early 1970s, an earnest and relatively well publicized attempt was made to improve wild sheep management in Mexico. Under the leadership of Mario Luis Cossio Gabusio, field technicians accompanied hunters during the 1974 hunting season specifically to gather data on the abundance and habitat of bighorn in Baja. The resulting population estimate of 4,500 to 7,800 bighorn in all of Baja was based on 279 man-days in the field covering 2,000 square kilometers. The highest density of bighorns, estimated at 1.5 animals per square kilometer, was found in the Matomi area, south of San Felipe and west of Puertecitos. This field survey was the first of its kind in Baja. Based on this estimate, permits allowing the harvest of bighorn sheep in Baja were relatively abundant, with 625 issued in the decade from the 1980-81 through the 1989-90 seasons. Although hunter success was relatively high (about 75 percent), there was growing concern about bighorn population status and possible declines in sheep numbers. As a result, the President of Mexico issued a decree halting bighorn sheep hunting in Baja in 1990.

Following the President's order halting bighorn sheep hunting, efforts were initiated to obtain bighorn sheep population data. The Bighorn Institute conducted the first systematic helicopter survey of desert bighorn sheep ranges in Baja California Norte in the spring of 1992. Mountain ranges surveyed included the Sierra Cucapa, Sierra Juarez, Sierra Las Tinajas, Sierra Pinta, Arroyo Grande, Sierra San Felipe, Sierra San Pedro Martir, Sierra Santa Rosa, and Sierra Santa Isabel. Vegetation, which featured encelia, agave, creosote, cholla cactus, and a variety of grasses was plentiful in most of these northern Baja ranges with the exception of the arid region of the Sierra San Felipe. Numerous *tinajas* (natural water tanks) with capacities up to an estimated 45,000 liters were noted, especially

Area	Map
Peninsular Desert Bighorn	
Sierra Cucapa	1
Sierra El Mayor	2
Sierra de Juarez	3
Sierra Las Tinajas	4
Sierra Las Pintas	5
Sierra San Felipe (North)	6
Sierra San Felipe (South)	7
Sierra Santa Rosa	8
Sierra San Pedro Martir	9
Sierra Santa Isabel	10
Sierra La Asamblea	11
Sierra San Francisco	12
Las Virgenes	13
Weem's Desert Bighorn	
Loreto	14
Isla Del Carmen	15
Sierra De La Giganta	16
Sierra Las Tarabillis	17

Areas occupied by Peninsular and Weem's desert bighorn sheep in Baja California.

in the Sierra Las Tinajas, Sierra San Pedro Martir, and Sierra Santa Isabel. A total of 116 groups of sheep, and 603 individual animals, were recorded, and the population for northern Baja was estimated to include 780 to 1,170 adult sheep. Bighorns were observed at elevations ranging from 700 feet near the coast in the Sierra Santa Isabel to over 4,500 feet in the Sierra San Pedro Martir. Greatest densities of bighorns were found in the Sierra Santa Rosa, while the Sierra San Pedro Martir contained the highest percentage of lambs and rams as components of the total population. Results of this survey indicated that either bighorn numbers in the northern and central portions of the Baja California peninsula had been previously overestimated, or that there had been significant declines in populations since the 1970s. Extensive damage to vegetation from livestock was noted in several ranges, and more than 200 burros were observed in desert bighorn sheep habitat. A second survey, including many of the same ranges, was conducted by both U.S. and Mexican biologists in the fall of 1995. The survey reported higher portions of lambs and mature rams in Baja populations. While this may be due in part to the season of observation, this survey confirmed earlier findings and indicated that numbers of bighorn sheep in northern Baja were stable or maybe increasing. Surveys of desert

Biologists pause in desert sheep habitat of the rocky Sierra Juarez ranges of Baja California Norte. The helicopter provides scale.

bighorn sheep habitat in Baja California Sur were initiated in 1995, when Bighorn Institute personnel conducted a cursory survey of Weem's desert bighorn habitat in the Sierra de la Gigantia near Loreto and the Sierra Las Tarabillis west of Punta el Mechudo. Subsequent surveys funded by FNAWS and Mexico were conducted annually, 1996 through 1998. Habitats occupied by the Weem's bighorns were vastly different than those of Peninsular desert bighorns to the north. Vegetation was much more abundant, increasingly so toward the southern end of Baja California Sur, where the foliage became subtropical brilliant green and the soils changed from desert tans to deep, rich blackish-browns. Water was

plentiful and well-distributed. The landscape was dominated by palo blanco trees, organ pipe cacti, and palo verde trees interspersed with prickly pear cacti and elephant trees. Extensive stands of cardon cacti were also common. In contrast with the pale Peninsular bighorns, Weem's bighorns were typically a rich chocolate brown, almost blackish, with black hairs on their legs and on the dorsal line along their spine. However, as in the desert bighorn sheep habitats of Baja California Norte, feral livestock were numerous. Large numbers of feral goats as well as numerous cattle, burros, and horses were observed within bighorn sheep habitat. Near Loreto, roads and feral animals were especially prevalent. Bighorn

Inset: Weem's desert bighorn sheep habitat in the southern Sierra la Giganta.

Mountain lions, such as this large male in the Sierra San Pedro Martir, prey heavily on desert sheep, and have been implicated in reducing or eliminating desert bighorns from many areas.

JIM DEFORGE

sheep observed near Loreto were generally seen in dense vegetation, isolated from roads and feral animals; bighorn sheep seen west of Punta el Mechudo were in less heavily-vegetated habitat, but were also typically seen in areas away from roads, human dwellings, and feral livestock. It appears that these populations have declined since the 1974 surveys, when field technicians observed 194 bighorns in 15 days near Loreto, despite the fact (as recorded by Alvarez) that bighorn sheep were difficult to observe from the ground in this area because of the steep terrain and thick sub-tropical vegetation.

Additional helicopter surveys of desert big-horn sheep habitats in Baja California Sur and Baja California Norte are being conducted to determine complete population estimates and to assess demo-graphic trends. However, the recent surveys serve to identify some of the problems facing these herds and the critical need for management and protec-tion of remaining populations. Populations are believed to total approximately 2,500 Peninsular bighorns and 500 Weem's bighorns.

The distribution and the abundance of desert bighorn sheep in Baja today is undoubtedly seri-ously reduced compared to historical accounts. Law enforcement is poorly funded and difficult in the remote areas inhabited by bighorns, and their re-mote, rugged and harsh environment remains their best protection. Desert bighorns of the San Pedro Martir are believed to have maintained viable popu-lations because of their inaccessible habitat, and the steep and isolated slopes of the Punta el Mechudo likewise offer wild sheep some protection from poachers. Another less obvious threat is the lack of baseline distribution and abundance data on which to base sound management programs. Recent surveys have identified competition with feral livestock (which compete for food, water and living space, and which may harbor diseases to which bighorn sheep are susceptible) and poach-ing for meat (which removes animals, including ewes of reproductive age, from the population) as serious current problems.

Desert bighorn sheep management in Baja has been the responsibility of the Secretaria de Medio Ambiente, Recursos Naturales y Pesca (SEMARNAP) since 1994. Hunting of bighorn sheep has been prohibited in Baja California Norte since 1991, and seasons were closed one year (1995) in Baja California Sur. Specific, research-based man-agement actions such as law enforcement, public education, technical training for wildlife manag-ers, habitat management, con-trol of feral animals, and bighorn census efforts have been recommended for bighorn in Baja. Surveys have been con-ducted annually since 1995, and training for Mexican biologists has been provided in Mexico as well as in the United States.

The only nationally-pro-tected desert bighorn sheep habitat in Baja California is within the San Pedro Martir National Park and the Vizcaino Biosphere Reserve. The conservation value of these areas may be limited by a lack of both public awareness and law enforcement. In 1995, a pri-vately-funded effort to promote the recovery of Weem's bighorns was initiated with the translocation of 26 bighorns to Isla del Carmen near Loreto, with the objective of allowing these animals to increase their numbers on the predator-free island. Offspring of these animals in excess of population maintenance needs will be available for eventual transplant back to the main-land to replenish diminishing stocks.

Management of desert bighorn sheep in Baja, based on a solid conservation ethic and reliable data and supported by local citizens and sportsmen, is essential if these populations are to survive the twenty-first century. Private and community-based conservation initiatives are also necessary to sup-port and ensure the future welfare of wild sheep in Baja. Public education and distribution of economic gain from carefully managed ram-only hunts encour-ages local people to remove feral livestock from bighorn range and reduce poaching. Such hunts occurred in 1997 and 1998, and generated over $500,000 for wildlife conservation and social devel-opment projects.

JIM DEFORGE

Peninsular desert bighorn sheep habitat in the Sierra Santa Isabel range, looking eastward to the Sea of Cortez.

California

Desert bighorn sheep inhabit the southeastern part of the state. Populations of desert bighorns occur in most of southern California's arid mountain ranges, from the White Mountains in the north to the extremely arid Chocolate Mountains of Imperial County in the southeast and the Peninsular ranges of San Diego County in the southwest. Desert bighorns are even found in the Transverse Ranges of Los Angeles and Ventura Counties.

Habitat occupied by desert bighorn sheep ranges from less than 1,000 feet to over 10,000 feet in elevation in California. These areas are typified by steep, open rocky slopes that provide opportunities to escape from most predators. Access to water is important, although these animals can go days at a time without drinking, getting most of their required moisture from the plants they eat. Sensitive to disturbance and habitat degradation, desert bighorn sheep make an excellent ecological indicator of quality desert and mountain ecosystems, and the conservation effort dedicated toward bighorn sheep has therefore played a role in assessing ecosystem structure and biodiversity.

Occupation of such 'harsh' habitats as these has provided desert bighorn sheep a measure of protection from humans in today's world, but this was not true historically. Unregulated hunting for meat and trophies during the period of early settlement and mineral exploration associated with California's 'gold rush' days resulted in the complete elimination of many isolated populations. Natural springs and habitats that bighorns had relied upon for centuries were altered, and many of the animals that escaped the hunter's gun fell to disease epidemics associated with the range-wide grazing of domestic livestock, particularly domestic sheep. Concern about the welfare of desert bighorn resulted in a moratorium on all taking of bighorns for a period of over 100 years, following passage of legislation by the State legislature in 1878.

Unfortunately, this moratorium failed to protect the remaining herds from alterations to their habitat, and herds continued to decline. Records indicate that where once at least 97 populations of desert bighorns occurred in California, today only 61 populations (63 percent) remain, and many of these at but a fraction of earlier numbers.

CURRENT POPULATIONS

An inventory of desert bighorn sheep distribution is maintained by the California Department of Fish and Game's 'Mountain Sheep Conservation Program.' This program includes an assessment of bighorn sheep populations as part of a long-term management plan. 'Metapopulations' of desert bighorn sheep (i.e., somewhat isolated herds that constitute an effective 'gene pool' by occasional exchange of individuals) are monitored, as are individual herd units. Metapopulations are important biologically, as habitat conditions may change from site to site between years, and survival of herds may depend on exchange with other habitats or herds.

Highways, which often mark major valley drainages between groups of mountains, are used to demarcate the boundaries between metapopulation units. Major boundaries are U.S. Highway 395 and Interstate Highways 10, 15, and 40. Not so obvious on this map are vegetation and geographic boundaries that were also identified as restricting bighorn sheep movement. This regional approach recognizes the importance of inter-mountain areas that allow movement and exchange of individuals between populations, recolonization of vacant habitat, and interagency coordination of land management. Management by metapopulation emphasizes the regional importance of both herds and habitats for the future well-being of sheep populations. This concept allows agencies to consider the long-term implications of population size and genetic variability to the long-term survival of populations over a period spanning generations, and helps emphasize the importance of maintaining bighorn sheep habitat even if it is currently unoccupied.

Ten metapopulations of bighorn sheep have been defined within California; of these, seven metapopulations are desert bighorns (Table 1). These

Petroglyph of desert bighorn sheep in California's Coso Range.

BIGHORN INSTITUTE

Peninsular desert bighorn ram.

metapopulations include three subspecies defined by early taxonomists: California bighorns of the Sierra Nevada; Peninsular bighorns of the western Sonoran Desert of Riverside, Imperial, and San Diego Counties; and Nelson's bighorn of the eastern Sonoran Desert, the Mojave Desert, the Transverse Ranges, and the Great Basin Desert of Mono and Inyo Counties. Of these three subspecies of sheep, the first two are listed as 'Threatened' by the State of California (Peninsular bighorns were also listed as nationally 'Endangered' under the Endangered Species Act in 1998), and Nelson's bighorn are fully protected by California law. Taxonomy of wild sheep (and especially desert bighorns) is confusing, and new methods (such as using various genetic markers) are helping to redefine this field of science. Recent taxonomic evidence indicates that Nelson's bighorn and Peninsular bighorn belong to the same subspecies, but scientists continue to examine this question. This same research has found that California bighorn in the Sierra Nevada are very unique and are most similar to the desert subspecies of bighorns— certainly not a surprising result given the potential for some genetic interchange over past centuries.

Given the need to understand the status and dynamics of regional populations of bighorn sheep, we have utilized historic and current data from ground counts, water hole surveys, and aerial surveys to monitor herd size and trend. Although a complete census is impossible and estimates vary in precision, we believe that sample data are sufficiently large to provide an accurate and conservative assessment of populations. Individual herd sizes are summarized in Table 1,

Inset: Desert bighorn sheep often nearly disappear in their arid surroundings, despite the apparent lack of vegetation. Note the bedded Peninsular desert bighorn ewes in the center of this photograph.

Nelson's desert bighorn rams in the San Gabriel Mountains.

DALE E. TOWEILL

JIM DEFORGE

172

and metapopulation estimates provided in Table 2. California is currently believed to have about 3,500 bighorn sheep distributed among 61 mountain ranges. Most of these (an estimated 2,963 animals) are Nelson's bighorns; Peninsular bighorn are believed to total about 364 animals, with the balance (about 170 animals) being California bighorns of the Sierra Nevada, discussed earlier.

Table 1. Number of desert bighorn sheep populations within each herd size class (number of individual animals) for each metapopulation in 1998. Metapopulations of the Sierra Nevada and northeastern California refer to California bighorn sheep.

Metapopulation	0	<25	25-50	51-100	101-150	151-200	201-300	>300	No. Viable
Peninsular Ranges	4	0	3	0	2	0	0	0	5
San Gabriel	0	0	0	0	1	0	0	0	1
West. Transverse Range	1	1	0	0	0	0	0	0	1
Sonoran	2	0	1	1	2	0	0	0	4
South Mojave	7	7	3	5	3	0	0	0	18
Central Mojave	0	1	6	2	0	0	0	0	9
North-central Mojave	1	0	1	3	0	0	0	0	4
North Mojave	3	3	3	7	0	1	0	0	14
Southern Sierra Nevada	8	2	2	0	0	0	0	0	4
TOTAL	26	14	19	18	8	1	0	0	60

MANAGEMENT

California's Mountain Sheep Conservation Program features two primary objectives: (1) maintain, improve, and expand bighorn sheep habitat, and (2) reestablish bighorn sheep populations on historic ranges. Naturally, population reintroduction projects are a major activity used to restore historic populations. Since 1983 the California Department of Fish and Game has moved 387 bighorn sheep (273 ewes and 114 rams) in projects designed to restore and augment historic populations of Nelson's bighorns.

Efforts are currently underway to develop bighorn sheep metapopulation plans based on inventory data and to evaluate the population status of all bighorn sheep herds and populations in the state. As part of this effort, managers will identify and prioritize management activities to ensure the long-term viability of bighorn sheep herds. Efforts will focus on protection of important habitats and inter-mountain travel corridors, identification of potential reintroduction sites, and the development, maintenance, and improvement of water sources ('guzzlers') in bighorn habitats.

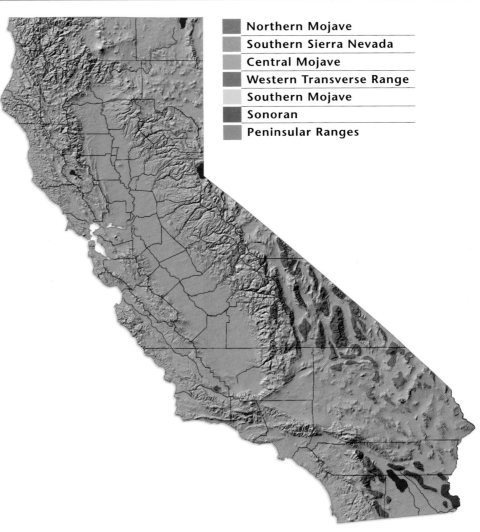

Northern Mojave
Southern Sierra Nevada
Central Mojave
Western Transverse Range
Southern Mojave
Sonoran
Peninsular Ranges

Table 2. Desert bighorn sheep population estimates by metapopulation in 1998.

Metapopulation	Low	Medium	High
Peninsular Ranges	277	364	450
San Gabriel	101	126	150
West. Transverse Range	1	13	24
Sonoran	278	364	450
South Mojave	640	954	1,268
Central Mojave	253	389	524
North-central Mojave	178	264	350
North Mojave	586	854	1,122
TOTAL	2,314	3,326	4,338

Colorado

There is scant scientific evidence that desert bighorn sheep existed in Colorado prior to 1970. Monson mistakenly reported in 1980 that the bighorn sheep population on Battlement Mesa represented desert bighorns, but recent analysis of blood and body tissue collected from some of these by Dr. Ramey has shown this population to be a remnant herd of Rocky Mountain bighorns. Nevertheless, in the 1970s wildlife managers believed that arid, low-elevation portions of western Colorado could support desert bighorn sheep, and began a program of introducing desert bighorn sheep from other states into suitable habitats.

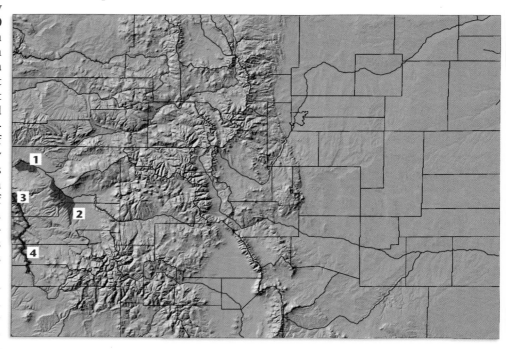

The first release of desert bighorn sheep occurred November 8, 1979, when 11 sheep from the Yuma-Kofa Mountains of Arizona were released into Devils Canyon, just west of the boundary of Colorado National Monument. Subsequent releases have brought the total number of desert bighorns released into Colorado to 212 animals, resulting in the establishment of four herds that now total about 460 desert bighorns. Three of the four herds are considered static or increasing, and one has declined in recent years due to predation, disease, or other unknown cause.

Desert bighorn sheep herds in Colorado.

Herd Name	Population	Map
Black Ridge	70	1
Dominguez Canyon	175	2
Middle Delores River	35	3
Upper Delores River	180	4
TOTAL	460	

Nevada

Desert bighorn sheep apparently occurred on most if not all southern Nevada mountain ranges prior to the time of exploration and settlement in the nineteenth century. Indian pictographs and petroglyphs are widely scattered, particularly in southern Nevada mountain ranges, and archaeological evidence in the form of bones and tools has been recovered from many sites. Mormon settlers, writing about wildlife near the Muddy River settlement along the Colorado River in 1855, mentioned bighorn sheep. However, remarkably few references to bighorn sheep appear in the journals of explorers and settlers in this area, suggesting that although bighorn sheep occurred widely, they were not common, at least during the period of 1830-1850.

The arid desert ranges occupied by desert bighorn sheep in Nevada were forbidding, and attracted few visitors prior to the discovery of the Comstock lode in northern Nevada in 1859. However, the lure of mineral wealth attracted miners to the sun-baked and exposed mineral outcrops of Nevada's desert ranges, and bighorn sheep no doubt provided meat to hungry prospectors. In addition, desert sheep populations were no doubt affected as prospectors and settlers preempted formerly remote (and often important) springs and seeps of water for livestock and personal use. Feral livestock (especially burros) adapted to desert conditions competed with desert bighorns for water supplies. Reports of damage to springs and tanks and of fouling of the water in these areas by carcasses is not uncommon. Hunting of all bighorns in Nevada was eliminated by action of the Nevada legislature in 1917, but this action came too late to stop the decline in bighorn sheep numbers. By 1940, desert bighorns remained in only 12 mountain ranges of southern Nevada. Based on herd estimates published by E.R. Hall in 1946 and those published by the U.S. Forest Service for the Toiyabee and Grant-Quinn Ranges, it is be-

GREGG TANNER

Southern Nevada desert bighorn sheep habitat.

Desert ram and ewe group of skyline.

Population estimates of desert bighorn sheep in Nevada, 1998.

Herd Unit	Population	Map
Stillwater/East Ranges	121	1
Grant Range	15	2
Pancake Range	233	3
Toquima Range	200	4
Hot Creek Range	70	5
Toiyabe Range	147	6
Clan Alpine Range	90	7
Desatoya Range	110	8
Wassuk Range	81	9
Gillis/Gabbs Valley Ranges	244	10
Excelsior Range	110	11
Silver Peak/Monte Cristo Ranges	230	12
Lone Mountain	112	13
Egan Range	81	14
Hiko/South Pahroc Ranges	118	15
Meadow Valley Range	27	16
Arrow Canyon Range	150	17
Pahranagat Range	87	18
Stonewall Mountain	102	19
Bare Range	59	20
Specter Range	91	21
Spotted Range	73	22
Last Chance Range	135	23
Red Rock/La Madre/South Spring/ Bird Spring Ranges	127	24
McCullough/Highland Ranges	129	25
Newberry Mountains	30	26
El Dorado Mountains	355	27
Muddy/Black Mountains	744	28
River Mountains	207	29
Mormon Mountains	284	30
Virgin/Cold Butte Ranges	74	31
Pintwater Range	185	32
Desert Range	79	33
Sheep Range	147	34
Las Vegas Range	128	35
TOTAL	**5, 175**	

sheep hunting, and has continued every year except 1955. Harvest regulations were used to focus attention on bighorn sheep as a highly desirable trophy animal, and on collecting biological information necessary to improve management systems. Regulations were designed to provide strictly limited harvest of a few adult rams each year, providing a few hunters opportunity for a unique, high quality hunting experience.

Sportsman support for bighorn sheep restoration in Nevada was revitalized in 1967, with the introduction of California bighorns to former habitat in northern Nevada. This effort was quickly followed by reintroduction of desert bighorns to suitable historic habitat in 1968, when 21 desert bighorns were captured and moved to an enclosure located on Mt. Grant (near Walker Lake) in Mineral County. Success in these early efforts provided the spark necessary to bring together a coalition of concerned sportsmen to encourage the Nevada Department of Fish and Game and a number of federal agencies (including the U.S. Bureau of Land Management, U.S. Forest Service, U.S. Fish and Wildlife Service, and National Parks Service) to continue aggressive efforts to restore bighorn sheep to historic habitats throughout Nevada.

The future of desert bighorn sheep populations in Nevada appears bright. The Nevada Division of Wildlife continues a very active program of bighorn sheep management, and all federal agencies are increasingly aware of bighorn sheep as a critically important public resource. Much of the funding for transplants and range improvement activities is provided by sportsmen, many of whom also volunteer time and other resources to assist wildlife management personnel in meeting management objectives. Threats in the form of continued competition with feral and domestic livestock, and increased recreational use and development of desert lands, will continue. There is an emphasis on ensuring that bighorns remain a perpetual part of Nevada's wildlife legacy to future generations.

lieved that only about 700 to 1,000 desert bighorn sheep remained in Nevada by 1940.

Restrictive regulations aimed at rebuilding desert bighorn sheep populations were an early and continuing priority of the Nevada Fish and Game Commission. Limited hunting of desert bighorns was begun in 1952, 35 years after the legislature had eliminated bighorn

The rocky, arid mountains of Nye County in southern Nevada provide nearly ideal habitat for Nelson's desert bighorn sheep.

New Mexico

Desert bighorn sheep occurred historically in most if not all of the arid desert mountain ranges of southern and central New Mexico. Coronado reported bighorn sheep in the Zuni Mountains in 1540. Evidence indicating the existence of bighorn sheep, in the form of skeletal remains, petroglyphs, or historic accounts, has been located in 14 mountain ranges. However, by the early 1900s only a few native herds remained following a period of unregulated hunting, extensive grazing of critical bighorn sheep habitats by domestic livestock, and loss of wild sheep to diseases introduced by domestic sheep and goats brought in by settlers. By 1955, only the San Andreas and Big Hatchet populations remained.

During settlement of New Mexico, desert bighorn sheep populations declined rapidly due to indiscriminate hunting, competition with domestic livestock for forage, and diseases introduced by domestic livestock, according to Buechner (1960). The decline in numbers followed a north-to-south trend that correlates with the progressive intrusion of man and livestock. Spanish settlers introduced domestic sheep into the Rio Grande Valley in the mid-1500s, and the adoption of sheep herding by both the Navajo and Pueblo people spread the impacts of domestic sheep throughout central and northern New Mexico. These flocks of domestic sheep were huge, estimated to total three million animals by 1820. Between 1860 and 1900, large-scale cattle operations controlled the open range in southern New Mexico, and the desert grassland deteriorated to desert shrub. By 1900, the large cattle companies disbanded and homesteaders stocked domestic goats and sheep.

One of the first written accounts of bighorn sheep in New Mexico was provided by the explorer James O. Pattie. While trapping beaver in the San Francisco River in 1825, Pattie wrote that he saw "...multitudes of mountain sheep. One of them that we killed had the largest horns that I ever saw on any animal." Bighorn hunting was prohibited in 1889, but unregulated hunting continued to be an important cause of mortality in some areas. In the early 1900s, 40 bighorn sheep were brought to a Deming meat market from the West Potrillo Mountains, 32 were killed in the Guadalupe Mountains, and 20 bighorns were killed in the Hatchet Mountains. Bighorns also died after being roped by cowboys when found away from precipitous terrain.

State Game Refuges were established in the Hatchet and Guadalupe Mountains during the mid-1920s in the belief that, if bighorn sheep were protected from illegal killing, they would increase and colonize former ranges. Livestock, however, were not prohibited in the refuges. Unregulated cattle grazing exacerbated by the drought of the 1950s contributed to the decline of the Hatchet bighorns from 125 animals to 20 animals by 1960. Diseases, overgrazing by domestic sheep and goats, and continued illegal hunting contributed to the loss of Guadalupe bighorn sheep by 1946.

Rather than remove additional bighorns from small and declining herds for transplant elsewhere, the New Mexico Department of Game and Fish established a bighorn sheep propagation program at the Red Rock Wildlife Area in 1972. Beginning with a nucleus of 22 desert bighorns from the San Andreas Mountains in New Mexico and the Loma Prieta Range in Sonora, Mexico, this herd has been managed to enhance its population growth. Excess animals (those over what was needed for program maintenance) were released into the wild. Bighorns at the Red Rock Wildlife Area roam freely through over 1,300 fenced acres of canyons and cliffs, feeding on native vegetation and drinking at natural springs. And while efforts are undertaken to remove most predators, the occasional coyote or mountain lion does get into the area, keeping the herd alert and wary. Partially as a result of predator control, lamb survival within the enclosure has averaged over 70 percent most years, as compared with about 30 percent for New Mexico's fully wild herds of desert bighorn. As a result, this successful program has provided over 200 animals used to augment declining herds and to reestablish herds in vacant habitats.

Despite these efforts, desert bighorn were listed by New Mexico as 'Endangered' in 1980 following a scabies mite epizootic in the San Andreas Mountains, which reduced the herd from 200 animals to 75 within one year. The mites weaken bighorns, and cause infected sheep to lose patches of skin. Masses of mites can multiply to the point where they physically plug the animal's ears, causing induced deafness. The combination of effects makes bighorns increasingly susceptible to accidents and predation.

A small band of rams at New Mexico's Red Rock Wildlife Area.

HABITAT

Most of New Mexico's desert bighorn are found in Chihuahuan Desert habitats dominated by a prickly mix of agaves, yuccas, prickly pear, acacia, and ocotillo on stony, shallow soils. Desert bighorns frequent open, steep, and rocky canyonlands and mountains, generally avoiding areas with tree canopies that exceed 30 percent, such as occur on deeper soils where mountain-mahogany, oaks, pinyon pine, and juniper are found. Common ground-level plants include grama grass, drop-seed, muly, globe-mallow, and crown-beard. Protected riparian areas found in the bottom of canyons are often shaded by cottonwoods, Arizona sycamores, desert willow, and apache plume. Although the ewes and their lambs are usually found in the rugged and broken country year-around, rams often venture into gentler terrain if it offers both food and access to steep escape cover.

Shrubs dominate the diet of desert bighorns, although bighorn sheep will eat a wide variety of plant foods. Diet selection varies, based on the nutritive value of available forage. Newly-sprouted grasses and forbs are favored during the summer and fall monsoon season, while shrubs predominate in the winter and early spring as grass quality declines. Plants high in protein content, like mountain-mahogany and winter fat, are often selected as are succulents like prickly pear.

Although desert bighorns can endure long periods without access to water, most herds are located within one mile of an open source of water (and even closer during extended periods of hot, dry weather). While some native populations of desert bighorns may have depended solely on moisture obtained through their diet and ephemeral water sources, availability of water is obviously an important factor in habitat selection by desert bighorns.

PRESENT OUTLOOK AND MANAGEMENT

In 1997, an estimated 335 desert bighorn occurred in seven ranges in New Mexico (including 60 bighorns at Red Rock Wildlife Area). All of these populations are small (less than 100 individual animals) and only one large interbreeding

Alerted, a mixed group of desert bighorn ewes and rams at the Red Rock Wildlife Area watches intently before deciding whether to flee.

Herd Name	Year Established	1998	Map
Red Rock	1972	75	1
Peloncillo Mountains	1981	65	2
Animas Mountains	1997	15	3
Hatchet Mountains	1979	65	4
Fra Cristobal Mountains	1995	47	5
Ladron Mountain	1992	37	6
San Andres Mountains	Indigenous	1	7
Alamo Hueco Mountains	1986	5	8

Population estimates for desert bighorn sheep in New Mexico, 1998.

metapopulation has been established. The state's long-term objective is to increase the numbers and distribution of desert bighorn sheep in New Mexico, and removal of the species from New Mexico's list of 'Endangered' species. This will require a free-ranging herd of at least 500 desert bighorns in at least three geographically-distinct populations or metapopulations, each of which would contain no less than 100 animals. It will take time before New Mexico's herds grow to sufficient size to allow de-listing (the target date is the year 2010) and to ensure the inter-mountain movements necessary to prevent inbreeding and to confer knowledge of alternate habitats in the case of local habitat deterioration. Preservation of potential bighorn sheep movement corridors is crucial to the eventual establishment of metapopulations, and will require close coordination between landowners and management agencies.

Habitat surveys and biologist evaluations of desert bighorn sheep needs have resulted in an estimate of a potential for at least 1,500 desert bighorn sheep in New Mexico. However, transplants of bighorns into currently vacant habitats will be critical to achieving management objectives. Twelve suitable transplant sites have been identified, and transplant stock is expected to come from the Red Rock Wildlife Area (and ultimately from other wild herds as they become well-established). The San Andres Mountains offer the largest and most continuous habitat area for desert bighorn sheep in New Mexico, but the persistence of scabies and fear of losing newly-transplanted animals has caused reintroduction efforts to be placed on hold for 17 years. Desert bighorns are almost extinct in the San Andres Mountains at present, and with the loss of sheep it is expected that the scab mite may be gone as well. If so, the opportunity to reestablish desert bighorns in this mountain range may soon be a possibility once again.

Recovering bighorn sheep herds is expensive, and costs of reestablishment by the state wildlife management agency are not offset by hunting license and tag fees from the severely limited hunting opportunities offered. Much of New Mexico's bighorn sheep management program is financed by sportsmen, through auction of a bighorn sheep hunting permit sold annually at the convention of the Foundation for North American Wild Sheep. Proceeds are matched with federal funds for wildlife restoration available through the Pittman-Robertson Act. This program has raised nearly half a million dollars since 1990. Beginning in 1995, two permits became available annually for desert bighorns in the Peloncillo Mountains, the only free-ranging herd in New Mexico not classified as 'Endangered.'

Threats now facing desert bighorns in New Mexico differ from those of a century ago. Regulation of livestock grazing, reduction of domestic sheep herds, elimination of market hunting and control of illegal harvest have all decreased the severity of these types of impact on bighorn populations. Currently, competing public interests and increasing human pressure in desert environments are among the most important threats to bighorn sheep.

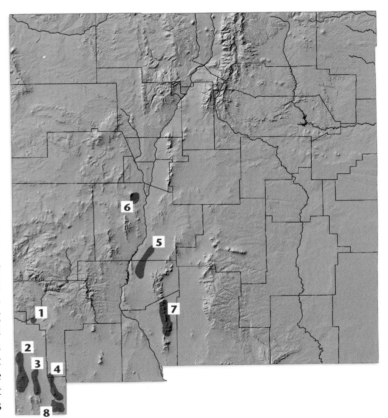

Human activities can stress bighorn sheep and alter their environments. These kind of impacts exacerbate problems for managers dealing with desert bighorn sheep, and coupled with the desert bighorn sheep's inherently low rate of population increase, difficulty in colonizing new habitat, and sensitivity to disease and disturbance, can make recovery of populations very slow. As a result of these factors, recovery of desert bighorn herds in New Mexico will take time and extraordinary effort.

Sonora

The isolated, rocky, mountain ranges of western Sonora have long been known as a stronghold for desert bighorns, protected in their rugged ranges by the harsh climate, scarcity of drinking water, and few primitive roads. Desert bighorn sheep are found in nearly all of the mountainous areas of northwestern Sonora, particularly those ranges along the Sea of Cortez north of Kino Bay to Caborca. Desert bighorns frequent Sonoran desert scrub habitats, characterized by creosote bush-white bursage, palo verde-saguaro, and torchwood-cardon plant associations. The climate generally features warm winters, with temperatures averaging about 40-45 degrees Fahrenheit, and hot summers, when temperatures average the mid-90° range and often exceed 100 degrees Fahrenheit. Rainfall is bi-seasonal (winter rains and summer monsoons) but low amounts of precipitation (3 to 7 inches) occur annually. The dew resulting from fog rising from the Sea of Cortez may be an important source of moisture for both plants and animals.

The remote nature of these environments has prevented biologists from gathering much more than anecdotal information on desert bighorn sheep population status until recently. As late as 1976, Mendoza stated that "very little has been published with respect to this desert species in Mexico." In his report on the status of bighorn sheep in Sonora, Mendoza gave a "conservative" population estimate of 935 animals. He further provided population estimates ranging from 350 animals in Sierra Viejo to 20 in El Marmol. In 1980, Monson and Sumner, relying heavily on Mendoza's earlier work, offered a similar estimate of 900 sheep in all of Sonora.

More current work centered on the mountain ranges in west central Sonora, near Caborca. Ground surveys in 1989 and 1991 resulted in estimates of a bighorn sheep population in this area which fluctuate between 200 and 500 animals.

Mexican desert bighorn in Sonora's Sierra Julio watches biologists in a helicopter hovering above.

RAYMOND LEE

These estimates are consistent with the work done by Mendoza.

Prior to recent helicopter surveys it was felt that the bighorn sheep population in Sonora probably did not exceed 1,000 animals. Some feared the population may have fallen considerably below this number. To address those concerns, helicopter surveys were conducted to evaluate the present distribution of desert bighorn sheep and to provide population estimates for Sonora.

In 1992, 25 mountain ranges were surveyed for desert bighorn sheep. A total of 155 groups were seen, resulting in 528 individual classifications. In 1993, 17 mountain ranges (14 were different from those flown in 1992) were surveyed for desert bighorn sheep. A total of 132 groups was seen in 11 of the areas flown, resulting in 442 individual classifications. A total of 365 observations of desert bighorns made in 1993 were from areas not covered during 1992. This results in a 2-year total of 893 individual sheep observed. Desert bighorn sheep were seen in 32 of the 39 ranges surveyed.

In 1996, 11 mountain ranges were surveyed for desert bighorn sheep. A total of 523 sheep were classified, including 287 on Tiburon Island. Observation rates in both Sierra Viejo and Sierra Kun-Kaak exceeded 90 bighorn sheep per hour. These 11 ranges had been flown in the past, and the 1996 observation rates were higher in the majority of ranges flown. It is likely that the bighorn population in Sonora, therefore, is at least stable, if not increasing. The ratio of lambs (37:100 ewes) and yearlings (20:100 ewes) indicate a very productive population.

Data from surveys conducted where sheep population size is well-known indicates that surveys dependent upon direct observations tend to underestimate the total number of animals in an area. In fact, studies indicate that only 30-60 percent of the population is typically seen during a helicopter bighorn sheep survey. Using these observation rates, the desert bighorn sheep population in that portion of Sonora surveyed was estimated to range between 1,488 and 2,977 animals. It should be noted that even these surveys did not cover all of each mountain range, nor did they cover all of the potential sheep habitat. These considerations produce a conservative estimate of 2,000 desert bighorn sheep in Sonora.

Current desert bighorn sheep populations in Sonora are large enough to support a limited sport hunting program with the resulting revenue used to support not only work for bighorn sheep, but also provide the means for wildlife conservation work throughout Sonora.

The bighorn sheep in Sonora are primarily a native population. One transplant occurred in 1975 from the adjacent mainland to Tiburon Island. This transplant has resulted in a large population of bighorn sheep on the island. Other areas in Sonora also have exceedingly dense sheep populations. These areas could serve as sources for transplant into previously occupied historic habitat. In the last 2 years, 3 transplants to- taling 110 animals have occurred from Tiburon Island to the mainland.

There are a number of factors limiting the distribution and abundance of bighorn sheep in Sonora. Illegal hunting of desert bighorns is not uncommon in Sonora. Rams are highly sought because of their relative scarcity. Ewes may be taken to provide sustenance for poor families. Loss of these animals can keep populations from increasing, and may lead to a decline in populations. However, these animals are a valuable national resource. The potential for local landowners to receive income from management to provide sport hunting is slowly taking root in

RAYMOND LEE

Inset: Mature desert bighorn ram on Tiburon Island in the Sea of Cortez.

Mexican desert bighorns on Pico Johnson flee from a helicopter.

RAYMOND LEE

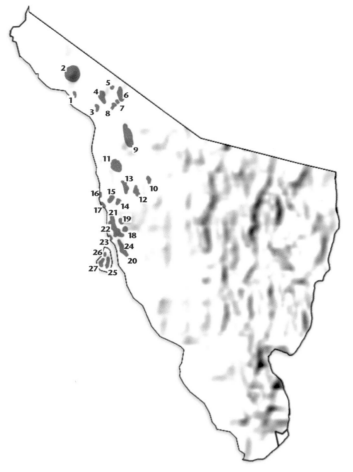

Estimated number of desert bighorn sheep in Sonora by area, based on helicopter surveys conducted in 1992, 1993, 1996, and 1997.

Herd Area	1998	Map
Sierra Blanca	10	1
Sierra El Pinacate	55	2
Sierra Pinta	15	3
Sierra San Francisco	90	4
Sierra Cipriano	10	5
Sierra Cubabi	20	6
Cerro la Silla	35	7
Sierra San Antonio	35	8
Sierra las Hojalatas	25	9
Sierra el Rajon	5	10
Sierra el Alamo	55	11
Cerro la Verruga	35	12
Sierra el Viejo	280	13
Sierra Picu	20	14
Sierra Aguirre	65	15
Sierra Julio	35	16
Cerro Santa Maria	25	17
Sierra los Lobos	15	18
Sierra los Mochos	80	19
Sierra Pico Johnson	150	20
Sierra Cirio	175	21
Sierra la Tordilla	70	22
Sierra Punta Tepoca	40	23
Sierra la Tinaja	15	24
Sierra Kun-Kaak*	415	25
Sierra Tiburon*	35	26
Sierra Menor*	125	27
TOTAL	**1,935**	

* Tiburon Island

Mexico, encouraging some landowners to zealously guard their herds. As the economic value of these animals becomes more widely known and the economic proceeds more widely distributed, losses associated with poaching will be reduced. In some instances, private landowners (many of whom fully realize the value of bighorn sheep) have developed breeding facilities for the bighorn sheep which occur on their land holdings. Unfortunately, this, too, can result in problems since many landowners have constructed fences to ensure that the bighorn sheep stay on their holdings. This precludes the bighorn sheep from using seasonally important habitat, reduces genetic exchange, and increases susceptibility to catastrophic events, such as range deterioration and susceptibility to disease outbreaks. Cattle, sheep, and goats often compete with bighorn sheep for limited food and water in these restricted areas, as well.

Presently, there is no statewide desert bighorn sheep management program in place in Sonora. The National Institute of Ecology is working toward development of a nationwide recovery plan for desert bighorn sheep populations, but implementation of this plan will be difficult given the high economic value associated with the species, patterns of land ownership, and limited population data. Hunting of desert bighorns can contribute to the conservation of existing herds if a portion of the funds derived can be channelled into a program that emphasizes habitat management, protection, and public education.

Texas

Historically, desert bighorn sheep occupied most of the arid ranges of the Trans-Pecos region of Texas (that portion west of the Pecos River). Bighorn sheep are pictured in many Indian pictographs throughout this region, although archaeological evidence indicates that populations were probably never very high due to the paucity of natural water holes and the harsh, arid environment. The number of desert bighorns in the mountains around Van Horn, Texas was estimated at about 1,000 to 1,500 animals in 1884 by pioneer rancher R. P. Bean.

The year 1881 marked the beginning of a series of events which resulted in total extinction of the native desert bighorn sheep in Texas. That year the railroad was built through Van Horn, in the heart of Texas' bighorn sheep range. (Prior to that time, human pressure on bighorn sheep herds was low, as few Spanish or American settlers ventured into the harsh and remote habitats occupied by bighorn sheep and native Indian tribes.) The following year, 1882, the Hazel Silver Mine opened between the Sierra Diablo, Beach, and Baylor Mountains— those ranges most heavily occupied by bighorn sheep (and ultimately their last stronghold in Texas). Railway work crews and miners demanded fresh meat, and bighorn sheep were favored. Market hunters supplying this market quickly reduced bighorn sheep herds in this area, and soon thereafter ventured into the mountains around Van Horn— especially after the great southern buffalo herd was diminished. These market hunters typically worked all winter, while the weather was cold enough to allow meat storage. They then hauled meat of desert bighorns as well as deer and pronghorn antelope by the wagon-load to Van Horn, where much of it was loaded onto refrigerated railroad cars and shipped cross-country to supply northern markets. Unregulated harvest of desert bighorn sheep continued until 1903, when hunting of bighorns in Texas was prohibited.

A mature desert bighorn ram watches the photographer from his bed in the shade of a large boulder in Texas' Sierra Diablo Wildlife Management Area.

DOUG HUMPHREYS, TEXAS PARKS AND WILDLIFE

Two rams on the Chilicote Ranch in Texas' Sierra Vejas Mountains.

Bighorn sheep populations persisted in these ranges, although at low numbers. However, in 1938 domestic sheep were introduced into this last stronghold of desert bighorns. By 1941 the population of Texas desert bighorn sheep was estimated by Butch Carson of the U.S. Bureau of Biological Survey at only about 150 animals, half the number believed present before arrival of domestic sheep.

Concerned about potential extermination of bighorn sheep from Texas, the Texas legislature established the Sierra Diablo Wildlife Management Area in 1945 as a sanctuary for the last remaining animals. No attempt was made to manage these herds, however, and populations continued their decline. In 1955 the population was estimated at 25 bighorns, all in the Sierra Diablo Range. The last observation of native desert bighorns in Texas occurred in 1960, when two ewes were sighted by Department personnel in Victoria Canyon in the Diablo Mountains.

RESTORATION

Once it became apparent that Texas' native desert bighorns were in danger of extinction, efforts to reintroduce bighorns to ranges formerly occupied by the species were initiated. This project, resulting from an agreement between the U.S. Fish and Wildlife Service, Boone and Crockett Club, The Wildlife Management Institute, and the Game and Fish Commissions of both Texas and Arizona, was a significant achievement in trapping and transplanting bighorn sheep in the United States, and has continued since its inception in 1954. A 427-acre 'brood pasture' was constructed on the Black Gap Wildlife Management Area. Trapping and transplanting operations were conducted in Arizona's Kofa Game Range in 1957, 1958, and 1959, which resulted in 16 desert bighorn sheep released into the Black Gap pasture. This herd increased steadily, to an estimated 68 animals in 1970. Twenty of these animals were released from the enclosure into the Black Gap Wildlife Management Area in January 1971. That year at least 16 lambs were produced (both in and outside the enclosure), bringing the population to a minimum of 84 bighorns. Unfortunately, later in 1971, disaster struck. Eighteen of the desert bighorns in the enclosure died due to nutritional stress believed

brought about by poor range conditions and the rigors of the breeding season. Disease organisms causing pneumonia and bluetongue were isolated and identified.

The captive herd was supplemented in 1977 with six ewes captured by Department personnel in Mexico, but problems continued to plague the project. Despite extension of the fence and predator control efforts, a total of 21 bighorns were killed by mountain lions and bobcats in the Black Gap enclosure between 1975 and 1977, and in the late 1970s it was determined that predation on this herd made it virtually impossible to achieve management goals there.

Concurrent with propagation efforts at Black Gap Wildlife Man-

agement Area, a second enclosure had been built (in 1970) at the Sierra Diablo Wildlife Management Area. Three rams and five ewes from the Black Gap herd were placed in this 8-acre enclosure between 1971 and 1978. From this small herd, four rams and three ewes were released into the Sierra Diablo in 1973, and these were supplemented with three rams and four ewes in 1979. These free-ranging bighorns survived and increased to an estimated 100 bighorns in 1989.

A new brood facility was constructed at the Sierra Diablo Wildlife Management Area in June 1983 by the Texas Bighorn Society, a donation to the Texas Parks and Wildlife Department. This facility consisted of four 10-acre pens designed to hold 40 ewes

Inset: Mature ram in the Sierra Diablo Wildlife Management Area.

Newly-collared young ram in the Sierra Diablo Wildlife Management Area flees from biologists.

Desert bighorn sheep population estimates for Texas.

Herd Unit	1995	1996	1997	Map
Sierra Diablo/Baylor/Beach Mountains	160	160	132	1
Elephant Mountain	54	60	66	2
Van Horn Mountains	5	13	4	3
Sierra Vieja Mountain	25	21	30	4
Black Gap Wildlife Management Area	14	9	45	5
TOTAL	**258**	**263**	**277**	

and 4 rams as brood stock. Stocking of these pens began in July 1983 with 17 desert bighorn sheep obtained from Nevada. These animals were supplemented in subsequent years with the addition of 10 bighorns from Arizona, two rams from Utah, and two more rams obtained from the free-ranging herd on the Sierra Diablo Wildlife Management Area. All sheep were released from the brood facility in 1998. The Sierra Diablo herd now numbers about 180 free-ranging animals.

Twenty bighorns from the Sierra Diablo brood facility were released onto the Elephant Mountain Wildlife Management Area, approximately 26 miles south of Alpine, in February 1987. Most stayed on the 8,000-acre Elephant Mountain. This herd was supplemented with three yearling rams from the Sierra Diablo herd in 1988 and continues to grow, although drought in 1988 and 1989 temporarily slowed its growth. The Van Horn Mountains, approximately 12 miles southwest of the city of Van Horn, were stocked with 25 desert bighorns captured in the Mormon Mountains of Nevada in October 1987. These animals were supplemented with 15 wild bighorns, also from Nevada herds, in 1988. High predation losses were documented among this herd; at least 12 ewes and two rams were killed by mountain lions. An additional nine ewes are also known to have died, probably from nutritional stress. Range conditions were very dry in the spring and both 1988 and 1989, and several bighorns were observed to be in very poor condition. The future of this herd appears grim. No lambs are known to have survived in 1989 or 1990 although two survived in 1991 and six in 1992. Only about four bighorn sheep are known to exist from this effort at present.

An effort to restore desert bighorn sheep to the Baylor Mountains was begun in October 1988, when ten bighorns from Nevada were released approximately 7 miles north-northeast of Van Horn. These animals were supplemented with 11 more, obtained from the Chilicote Ranch, in December 1988. (The Chilicote Ranch herd, established with three rams and four ewes in late 1977 and early 1978, had increased to 29 animals by March 1987 despite predation by mountain lions.) Two of the animals released into the Baylor Mountains are known to have moved to the Sierra Diablo Range, but the remainder continue to occupy the Baylor Mountains.

The nearby Beach Mountains were stocked with 16 rams (14 of them lambs) and nine ewes (four lambs) in December 1990. These animals originated from the Sierra Diablo facility, and were originally moved into a holding facility in the Beach Mountains. All were released in May 1991. Because of some known movements between ranges, the Sierra Diablo, Baylor Mountain, and Beach Mountain herds are believed to function as a metapopulation (i.e., a population wherein distinct herds exist but with some interchange among members) at present.

Limited harvest of older rams has been allowed in Texas beginning in 1990. Harvest to date totals 13 rams, seven from the Sierra Diablo Range (1990-1993), and two each from the Beach (1995-1997), Baylor (1997), and Elephant Mountain (1996-1997) herds.

DESERT BIGHORN

Utah

Desert bighorn sheep are native to the deserts of southern Utah. Archaeological evidence indicates that desert bighorns were well-known to the prehistoric inhabitants of Utah, since bighorns are depicted in pictographs and petroglyphs more than any other form of wildlife.

The presence of desert bighorns was noted by Father Escalante in 1776, who recorded in his journal that, where he crossed the Colorado River, "Through here wild sheep live in such abundance that their tracks are like those of great herds of domestic sheep." Explorers, trappers, pioneers and settlers also recorded numerous observations of bighorn sheep throughout the state. However, native populations of desert bighorns declined suddenly and dramatically soon after settlement in the mid-1800s. The decline is usually attributed to unregulated hunting and introduction of domestic livestock, which competed for food and brought diseases that could be transmitted to wild bighorns. Remote herds persisted in some areas after the turn of the century, but by the mid-1960s the only viable population of desert bighorn sheep in Utah occurred in the steep canyon country of San Juan County, along the Colorado River.

Desert bighorn sheep habitat in Utah's North San Raphael Unit.

JIM KARPOWITZ

RESTORATION EFFORTS AND MANAGEMENT

Efforts to restore bighorn sheep to native habitats began in the mid-1970s. From 1973 through 1997, a total of 528 desert bighorn sheep were moved into areas of historic habitat, resulting in the reestablishment of several populations. Nearly all desert bighorn transplant operations were successful, resulting in establishing herds that continue to expand and merge into larger 'metapopulations.' It is believed that approximately 2,500 desert bighorn sheep existed in Utah in 1997.

However, despite these efforts, there have been problems. Disease outbreaks have occurred

Desert bighorn sheep in canyonlands of the South San Juan Unit in Utah.

in several native herds, causing rapid declines in numbers. One of the most serious of these occurred in the herds east of the Colorado River beginning in the 1980s, affecting desert bighorn sheep herds in the Needles, North San Juan, and South San Juan areas. Although 259 bighorns were observed in surveys of this area conducted in 1976, by 1988 only eight animals were seen, and only six in 1989. It is hoped that this herd will recover.

Several of Utah's desert bighorn sheep herds live in close proximity to domestic sheep grazing areas, and there is fear that contact with domestic sheep may initiate further disease transmission. The Utah Division of Wildlife and the Foundation for North American Wild Sheep have been working closely with domestic sheep permittees, landowners and managers to resolve conflicts and reduce the risk in some of these areas.

Dramatic increases in recreation use have occurred in recent years in much of the desert bighorn sheep habitat of southern Utah. Beginning in the early 1990s, thousands of mountain bikers, off-highway vehicle owners, hikers, and tourists began flocking to Utah's 'red rock' country. Much of that recreational activity has occurred during the spring lambing season, and the effect of this disturbance to bighorn sheep is a concern but the actual impacts are unknown.

Pending designation of several million acres of desert bighorn

Inset: Desert bighorn ram in southeastern Utah.

Desert bighorn sheep habitat near Moab, Utah.

JIM KARPOWITZ

JIM KARPOWITZ

sheep habitat on public land in southern Utah as a 'Natural Area' may also present management challenges to the Utah Division of Wildlife. While such a designation might afford a degree of protection to bighorns, there are also concerns that it may also limit management options such as helicopter use for bighorn census and water hole development. However, wildlife managers are cautiously optimistic about the future of desert bighorn sheep in southern Utah. There is hope that the current upward trend in populations will continue well into the twenty-first century.

Estimated population size and trend in Utah's desert bighorn sheep herds in 1997.

Herd Unit	1997	Trend	Map
North San Rafael	350	Up	1
South San Rafael	350	Up	2
Westwater	20	Down	3
Professor Valley/Arches	150	Up	4
Potash/Island-in-the-Sky	500	Stable	5
Lockhart	75	Up	6
Maze	80	Stable	7
Needles/North San Juan	50	Stable	8
Dirty Devil	50	Up	9
South San Juan	150	Stable	10
Navajo Tribe	70	Up	11
Capitol Reef	75	Up	12
Escalante	300	Up	13
Kaiparowits	150	Up	14
Paria/Coyote Canyon	60	Up	15
Zion	70	Stable	16
Beaver Dam	60	Up	17
TOTAL	**2,560**		

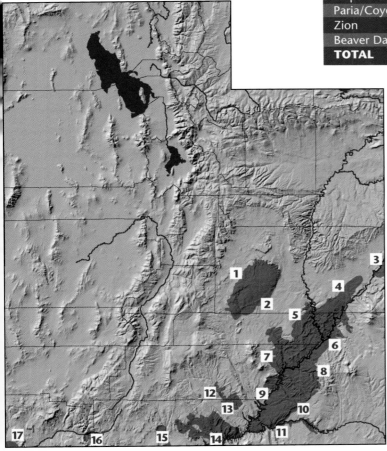

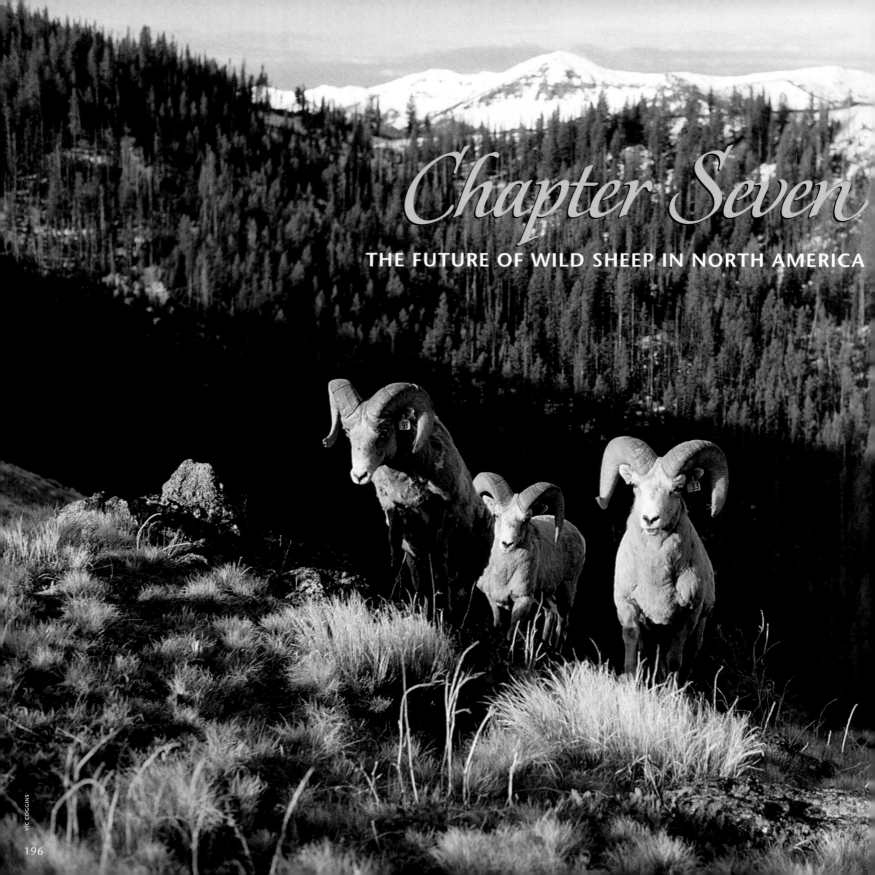

Chapter Seven

THE FUTURE OF WILD SHEEP IN NORTH AMERICA

The wild sheep of North America have experienced a tumultuous past, from great abundance to complete extermination from vast portions of their range. Recovery of wild sheep populations in North America— the return of royalty to North American mountainlands— has been termed as one of the greatest conservation stories of this century. Tremendous human resources are still being directed toward restoration of this magnificent species. Yet, the wild sheep of North America still face an uncertain future.

Many of the adaptations of wild sheep— those very features that enabled them to survive dramatic climate change across the tens of centuries— increase their vulnerability in today's world. Unlike deer and other ungulates that live alongside man in changing suburban environments, wild sheep select and survive in only specialized habitats characterized by steep, rough and open terrain. While that might seem an advantage, in that it keeps them distant from people and human development, in reality it is often a disadvantage. Such areas are typically relatively small and localized, and in a warm climatic period such as we are currently experiencing in North America, subject to change from suitable to unsuitable within a human lifetime as forests encroach on critical grassland ranges. Even more seriously, the mountain ranges and canyonlands wild sheep find necessary for survival are often political boundaries between states, complicating management. Idaho's populations are a good example, bounded on the west by the tri-state Hells Canyon herds managed in conjunction with the states of Oregon and Washington, and on the east by herds that occupy the Rocky Mountain crest on the border with Montana. In between, wild sheep occupy the vast canyons along the Salmon River, the 'River of No Return,' a huge wilderness playground for thousands of

DALE E. TOWEILL

Nearly one mile deep and bounded by rocky cliffs and rims, Hells Canyon is the focus of one of today's most aggressive bighorn population restoration efforts, the Hells Canyon Initiative.

people attracted by recreational pursuits— floating wild white-water rivers, hiking and hunting the canyon trails. Idaho is not unique— in every western state and province, wild lands needed as homes by wild sheep are also magnets for recreationists. With their requirement for open habitats, sheep are relatively easy to spot, and are often an irresistible attraction for wildlife enthusiasts and photographers. Although wild sheep adapt readily to the presence of humans, it seems humans rarely coexist well with wild animals, trying to approach too closely or even poaching the habituated animals. While managed levels of human activity in sheep habitat are probably acceptable, too much disturbance is almost always harmful to wild sheep. Many affected herds are hunted seasonally, and in these, especially, too much human disturbance may result in abandonment (and therefore, loss) of some critical habitats.

Wild sheep are habitat specialists, animals with a high level of home range fidelity. They not only do not disperse well or easily across the landscape, but populations depend— for their very existence— on transmittal of learned behaviors through successive generations. This kind of behavior, useful in a species which has adapted to a landscape that changes on the order of centuries, can be critically limiting to a population subject to large or wide-scale population losses, the sort of losses associated with disease outbreaks. In these situations, large-scale die-offs have become an all-too-familiar pattern to wildlife managers. Every adult that dies takes with it a portion of the herd's ability to survive, in the form of individual knowledge about when to migrate between ranges, and which paths offer the greatest degree of security. We know many of the managers of wild sheep in western North America— and we know all too well the heartbreak of watching decades of wild sheep restoration efforts destroyed in weeks or months by an outbreak of pneumonia or some other disease.

Management of sheep is complicated by the fact that sheep, again unlike deer, have low rates of reproduction. Even though wild sheep popula-

tions have the inherent ability to double within three years, such growth is, in reality, exceptional. Most herds grow very slowly, with much lower than optimum reproductive rates— and wildlife managers rarely know why. Compounding the low rates of reproduction, often only a small portion of the annual lamb crop survives its first year. Survival means not only escaping predators, but also disease and the rigors of weaning. Thus population growth in wild sheep populations typically occurs at a virtual snail's pace, making recovery from setbacks a long, often tedious, process.

However, even with all of these problems, the immediate future of North America's wild sheep looks bright. Many of the efforts to restore bighorn sheep, begun in the 1960s and still accelerating, have been successful in restoring wild sheep populations to native habitat. As the preceding tables state-by-state accounts show, even though there have been many failures and setbacks, herds have grown dramatically. This is especially true for the period of the past two decades, as funding from such organizations as the Foundation for North American Wild Sheep (FNAWS) has enabled wildlife management organizations to capture and relocate animals.

Growth in individual herds has resulted, in many instances, in reestablishment of widely dispersed interbreeding populations capable of withstanding onslaughts of disease and habitat degradation that would have eliminated smaller, local herds. Research has identified key habitat requirements and biological factors affecting herd growth, allowing managers to make better and more timely management decisions affecting both wild sheep herds and habitats. And perhaps most importantly, sportsmen have developed national, state, and provincial organizations capable of focusing attention on bighorn sheep issues in national and local political decision-making processes, and able to provide the necessary manpower and financial resources to see their desires implemented. This chapter will identify some of encouraging projects underway nationwide.

One of the most impressive single-focus projects is the Hells Canyon Initiative. This initiative is the result of a cooperative partnership involving the United States Forest Service, the individual states of Oregon, Idaho, and Washington, and private organizations and individuals dedicated to the restoration of Rocky Mountain bighorn sheep to the 5 million acres of potential

Reclaimed coal mine headwalls offer escape cover and security for bighorn sheep.

DALE E. TOWEILL

Biologists examine bighorn sheep habitat in Idaho's Hells Canyon.

wild sheep habitat in the tri-state Hells Canyon area. Once Rocky Mountain bighorns were abundant throughout this area, as evidenced by a Shoshone Indian culture (the "Sheep-eaters") closely associated with bighorn sheep as both a staple of diet and an essential element of tribal culture and beliefs, much as the plains tribes were associated with the American bison. Herds of bighorns were reduced by a century of hunting and domestic livestock invasion of their habitats, and finally extirpated in the middle of the twentieth century. Although individual herd restoration efforts were begun by each of the three participating states in the early-to-middle 1970s, this area has suffered a series of devastating dis-

ease setbacks since 1984. The Hells Canyon Initiative was conceived in 1995 to overcome these problems of wild sheep restoration in this area. The Foundation for North American Wild Sheep pledged millions of sportsmen's dollars to this effort, money generated by private citizens anxious to restore wild sheep populations. This commitment of funding has been supplemented by a commitment from the U.S. Forest Service (through the Hells Canyon National Recreation Area program and land management policy), and wild sheep restoration objectives and management activities of the Oregon Department of Fish and Wildlife, Idaho Department of Fish and Game, and Washington Department

DALE E. TOWEILL

Inset: Mining leaves some patches of the original mature coniferous forest intact to provide cover for mule deer, increasing the effectiveness of restoration efforts.

A small band of rams feeds on a reclaimed mine slope planted to legumes.

of Game. Additional support comes from the Nez Perce Tribe and sportsmen nationwide.

The Hells Canyon Initiative consists of several key elements, each necessary to achieve final objectives. Critical components include restoration of wild sheep into suitable habitat and development of a comprehensive program to minimize the risk of future outbreaks of disease.

The first component, restoration and expansion of Rocky Mountain bighorn sheep within the Hells Canyon area, is comprised of four separate programs: (1) habitat identification, protection and restoration; (2) reestablishment of individual herds into suitable habitat; (3) research into past and any future outbreaks of disease; and (4) habitat acquisition. The second component consists of a focussed bighorn sheep disease research program, involving wildlife veterinarians, research biologists, and pharmaceutical companies working together to isolate, identify, and respond quickly to the biological and management challenges posed by disease outbreaks in this area. As a wildlife research biologist faced with such a die-off in this area in 1984-85, I (Toweill) know first-hand the feeling of helplessness in dealing with a silent killer of bighorn sheep. This component of the problem includes the development of necessary funding to support an emergency response team and establishment of procedures to isolate any future disease outbreaks, thereby protecting the investments in reestablishment of this resource. The potential payoff, for bighorn sheep, sportsmen, and local economies, is huge, as this 5 million acre National Recreation Area could potentially hold the greatest single population of Rocky Mountain bighorn sheep south of Canada.

Further north, near the northern boundary of Alberta's Jasper National Park near Hinton, Alberta, another program has been quietly revolutionizing bighorn sheep management. Vast deposits of coal have been strip-mined from Alberta's Nianassin Range, in and near Rocky Mountain bighorn sheep habitat. The mines and companies involved, the Cardinal River Mine of Cardinal River Coals Ltd. and the Gregg River Mine of Manalta Coal Ltd., Alberta Environmental Protection and Jasper National Park jointly developed mineland restoration plans, wherein the open pits are backfilled with rock, covered with topsoil, and replanted with a mixture of grasses, legumes, shrubs and trees. Concern about the impacts of mining on bighorn sheep resulted in research to restore and create bighorn sheep escape habitat on mine pit walls exposed to sunlight and wind, as part of habitat restoration activities. Building on research I (Geist) had completed, Beth MacCallum, as a student of mine in Environmental Design at the University of Calgary, applied that information to on-site design of the new and potential habitat created following coal removal. Beth truly completed an 'environmental design' project, turning knowledge of biological requirements into functional structures and highly desirable sheep habitat.

The success of this program has been astounding. Bighorn sheep have adopted these newly-created habitats as part of their home ranges, as have many other kinds of wildlife: mule deer, elk, grizzly bears, wolves, and wolverines, as well as dozens of songbirds and smaller species. While some ewes selected reclaimed mine walls as lambing habitat, others used them year-around, since they afford secure habitat near good forage areas in the winter months when weather conditions are often severe. While there's no evidence that wild sheep have abandoned other habitats to move to these areas, many animals routinely travelled to and through these areas. Not only has the bighorn sheep population level in this region increased, but so has average body and horn size of both ewes and rams as sheep have been able to utilize the abundant forage close to their new-found security terrain. These sheep are the largest bodied, on average, of any population in North America, a result of the abundant high-quality (and highly favored) forage made available on the fertilized slopes. The success of this program has clearly identified the possibility to design habitat modifications to benefit wild sheep herds, and this knowledge can be widely applied, allowing managers to design landscape restoration efforts with wild sheep and human activities in mind.

Another success story, still in progress, is the restoration of bighorn sheep metapopulations in National Park units of the U.S. National Park Service. This cooperative effort, involving the National Park Service, Biological Resources Division of the U.S. Geological Survey, and Colorado State University, featured two phases. The first, including research, population surveys, and planning was conducted during 1991-1993, and the second featured assessment bighorn sheep habitat using Geographical Information Systems (GIS) technology, development of herd restoration plans, and restoring and monitoring bighorn herds at selected locations.

Of the 18 national park units (national parks, national recreation areas, and national monuments) initially surveyed, large and secure metapopulations occur in only four (Glacier, Yellowstone, Rocky Mountain, and Canyonlands National Parks). A GIS-based analysis of occupied or potential bighorn sheep habitat near the remaining units was conducted, and 73 potential habitat units were identified— of which only 36 sites (22 percent of the identified areas) were currently occupied. Thirteen park units were judged capable of supporting populations of 300 to 700 bighorns, populations large enough to be biologically secure. As a result of this work, restoration efforts have begun in seven of the national park units: Capitol Reef National Park, Dinosaur National Monument, Badlands National Park, Glen Canyon National Recreation Area, Colorado National Monument, Curecanti-Black Canyon National Recreation Area, and Theodore Roosevelt National Park. These efforts will be completed and restoration of bighorn sheep to additional areas will be initiated as funding becomes available. This kind of program provides a necessary and critical supplement to the efforts of individual western state fish and wildlife agencies. Just as the vast Rocky Mountain National Parks of the western Canadian provinces provides security for unhunted core populations of Rocky Mountain bighorns, this effort can assure that unhunted populations of Rocky Mountain, California, and desert sheep will be provided secure habitats into the future.

In addition to these few programs, a review of projects funded by the Foundation for North American Wild Sheep (provided in the book, **Putting Sheep on the Mountain**) reveals the tremendous scope of work currently underway to protect and enhance wild sheep populations. Funding has been provided for hands-on habitat restoration, transplants, and critical research on the biology and diseases of wild sheep. Other sources of information about wild sheep appear in research and management reports published by such groups as the Northern Wild Sheep and Goat Council, Desert Bighorn Council, and The Wildlife Society.

With so much being done to benefit wild sheep, what are the major challenges facing sportsmen wildlife managers as they strive to continue to restore populations of these majestic animals in the twenty-first century?

One of the foremost concerns is the development of metapopulations— developing the small discrete herds of wild sheep (typical of most reintroduction efforts) into larger, interbreeding populations. Although the numbers are still controversial, most scientists believe that a population consisting of a minimum of 300 to 500 animals is necessary to ensure the long-term viability of a population, and at least 100 to 300 animals are necessary to ensure the security of a population over a period of at least several decades. A review of state-by-state herd units reveals few populations of that size south of Canada. Although this is cause for some concern, many herds are in the range of 75 to 100 animals and moderately secure for the short-term, and most of these have been in existence for a relatively short period— one or two decades at most. Efforts to restore wild sheep herds are still relatively young, and early successes and commitments to herd restoration are promising.

Disease continues to be concern. Devastating die-offs can quickly undo the success of years of restoration efforts. Bighorn sheep in particular, and likely northern 'thinhorn' sheep as well, are notoriously susceptible to a variety of disease organisms that affect domestic sheep little if all. Attempts to reestablish wild sheep in an area used by domestic sheep may be jeopardized, particularly if free-ranging wild sheep ever come into direct, animal-to-animal contact with domestic sheep or goats. As a result, many land management and wildlife management agencies are working with grazing permittees to determine the feasibility of changing the class of domestic livestock from sheep and goats to cattle, in some key areas, and some private groups are examining opportunities to purchase and retire public land grazing permits where the operator and agency are willing to do so. On private lands, conservation easements may be established that stipulate the type of livestock grazing allowed. One bright note in this regard is the development of bighorn sheep-domestic sheep management guidelines that provide policy direction to Forest Service and Bureau of Land Management personnel in western states.

As habitat specialists, wild sheep populations may suffer as a result of competition with other animals, wild as well as domestic. Cattle, burros, horses, and goats compete for limited water as well as food in arid rangelands, and there is some evidence emerging that such competition may be even more detrimental to sheep populations than the limitations of water. Desert bighorns in particular, adapted as they are to the arid conditions typical of many desert mountain ranges, may actually survive better without water hole developments than with them— and the attendant competition for limited forage.

While these are all critical concerns, the greatest threat to wild sheep restoration is competition, not with other wild or even domestic animals, but with humans themselves. Wild sheep cannot alter their habitat; in order to survive in a changing world, sheep must be able to find areas that provide as least the basic elements of food, water, and security from predators and disturbance. Human development, not only in or adjacent to sheep habitat but also in the valley bottoms used only rarely as travel routes by sheep crossing from one mountain range to another, fragments sheep populations into individual herds, isolated from others of their kind as effectively as if bounded by an ocean. It is these small populations, cut off from one another, that are most vulnerable to the random kinds of events that can completely eliminate herds. Extinction is often neither a sudden or dramatic event; rather, it is the inevitable outcome of changes in the environment that cause it to become too limited to support sustainable populations. Those of us who value wild sheep (and other wild creatures) must find a way to ensure that our own population requirements and expansions incorporate considerations for other living things.

This brings us, in full circle, to our beginnings and to the Roosevelt Doctrine. Wildlife in North America is, and must remain, a public resource. Managers must remain accountable for their management, and decisions must be based on the best foundation of knowledge that current research tools and approaches can provide. The citizens of our nations have a critical role to play, for it is only through citizen concern, involvement, and support that truly sustainable populations will result.

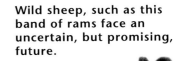

Wild sheep, such as this band of rams face an uncertain, but promising, future.

DALE E. TOWEILL

Creating Sheep Habitat

By Beth MacCallum

April 1997 was a memorable day— the kind of day that makes the struggle of working in often hostile environments worthwhile. As a biologist, I had been darting bighorn sheep rams, so that I could remove non-functioning radio-collars when, while waiting for the drug to take affect on one of the darted rams, a pack of wolves moved out of the forest and began a cacophony of howls. Despite any anti-predator response that this may have elicited on the part of the ram as he was slipping from consciousness, I had to stop and admire the wolves. Earlier in the day a bald eagle had passed below us as it flew over the still ice-covered lake during its migration northward. And while I did not see a grizzly bear that day, bears had been observed nearby in other seasons. These symbols of wilderness—bighorn sheep, gray wolves, bald eagles and grizzly bear—might have been expected had I been in a remote and protected area, but the rumble and hum of large trucks and machinery in the distance reminded me that I was, instead, in the centre of an active open pit coal mine in the Alberta foothills.

The impacts of mining on wildlife—especially open-pit coal mining—has often been controversial. In fact, in 1972 the coalition of provincial and state biologists which comprised the Northern Wild Sheep and Goat Council issued a formal statement of concern regarding detrimental effects of coal mining on wild sheep in Alberta's foothill and mountain regions. Bighorn sheep are among the least tolerant of all big game animals to human intrusions of their habitat, and that habitat is naturally limited in distribution. Thus the biologists identified the need for economic, social and ecological evaluation of important biological resources on ranges where coal might be found, and formulation of multiple use plans for these lands. So how did it happen that wildlife—and bighorn sheep—could flourish in an active mine site?

The concerns of biologists did not go unheeded; various jurisdictions passed relevant legislation in the early 1970s, which laid the framework for industrial development within a larger social and environmental responsibility. Wildlife habitat needs were to be identified and addressed. Thus, when Cardinal River Coals Ltd. submitted one of the first end land use plans for wildlife in the late 1970s, restoration of the affected lands for wildlife was accepted as an objective for reclamation of open pit coal mines in Alberta.

The Luscar Mine of Cardinal River Coals Ltd. and the Gregg River Mine are situated about 50 km south of the town of Hinton, in the northern foothills of Alberta. This is an area characterized by warm winter 'chinook' winds, which clear the slopes of accumulated snow, thus providing feeding areas for a wide variety of wild animals. Mining began in 1969 at Cardinal River Coals' Luscar Mine, and in 1982 on the nearby Gregg River Mine.

Mining is a very predicable human activity, characterized by heavy machinery removing coal from seams in the mountains and heavy trucks transferring that coal to a central depot. Work is concentrated in specific locations, and vehicle activity is restricted to driving on roads from the pits to the plants. Once mining activity is completed, it is followed by progressive reclamation of the land, covering exposed mineral soil with topsoil and re-seeding affected areas with desirable plants. Reclamation really begins prior to mining, with identification of restoration objectives, clear statements of the desired end uses of the lands affected, and selection and scheduling of restoration activities. A pragmatic ecosystem approach to reclamation is often adopted, one which attempts to integrate procedures that restore pre-mine habitat condition, replace habitat function, and exchange certain components for others of similar benefit.

Wildlife reclamation techniques which are known to maintain wildlife use of the site during and after mining are identified and employed. These techniques include tree retention, topographic manipulation, topsoil handling, highwall modification, brush and rock pile placement, shape and spatial distribution of revegetation communities, shrub and tree planting, ground cover revegetation, use of seed mixes favourable to a variety of wildlife species, edge effect, special structures, impoundments and reconstruction of stream channels. As well as reclamation activities, several initiatives are undertaken to promote the wildlife use of the final reclaimed landscape during active mining. These initiatives include hazard identification, maintenance of undisturbed or partially disturbed ground, wildlife education pro-

DALE E. TOWEILL

Bighorn sheep have learned to adjust to human activities – and coal miners have learned to give bighorn sheep right-of-way at crossing areas.

grams, annual monitoring, and liaison with wildlife management agencies. The objectives of the annual monitoring program include documenting species presence before, during, and after mining disturbance as well as changes in abundance and distribution of different species, and generation of population indices to be used for management purposes. The seasonal distribution of bighorn sheep, mule deer, and elk are mapped, the locations of carnivore observations are plotted, and observations of all other wildlife are recorded. Knowledge of wildlife movement patterns and habitat use gained from annual wildlife monitoring programs is integrated with mine planning through its reclamation program.

Reclamation of the Luscar and Gregg River Mines began near timberline, adjacent to occupied bighorn range. As a result of the location of the mines and the presence of nearby healthy bighorn sheep populations, bighorn sheep were one of the first large ungulates to colonize the newly created landscapes. Because mine activities were very predictable and posed little direct threat to wild sheep, these animals quickly learned to tolerate the disturbance even as they quickly learned to make use of the feed provided on fertilized and newly revegetated areas. Winter counts of bighorn sheep on the reclaimed landscapes increased from 198 in 1985 to 635 in 1997. Increased

DALE E. TOWEILL

Reclaimed portions of the Cardinal River Coals Ltd. Luscar Mine feature stabilized rocky slopes and fertilized feeding areas for bighorn sheep.

numbers are also reflected in the regional population. Another indicator of the success of this program is that bighorn sheep in the vicinity of the mines have grown large-bodied (average fall weight for 69 ewes 2.5yrs = 75 kg) even for bighorns. Lamb survival has consistently been high—high enough that the population of bighorn sheep in the area has increased at a rate near theoretical maximum.

In addition to bighorn sheep, mule deer have been consistent and regular occupants throughout the life of the mines. Mountain mining results in a discontinuous disturbance of the surface, which leaves patches of the original mature coniferous forest intact. These tree-covered areas are sufficient to fulfill mule deer hiding and thermal cover requirements within the disturbed landscape. Elk populations had been locally suppressed, and so elk were relatively slow

to take advantage of the reclaimed landscapes. However, by 1992, 14 elk (cows and calves) began to systematically use the mine habitat as winter range. Elk using the area rapidly increased in number (to about 70 by 1997) and use has expanded to include calving and summer grazing.

Wolves, which had always been present in small numbers in the areas of the mines, began to systematically hunt bighorn sheep, mule deer and elk among the reclaimed sites—frequently enough that wolf status was recently changed from 'occasional visitors' to 'regular occupants.' Coyotes are present throughout the year, and grizzly bears move through the mine seasonally, often stopping to graze on the legumes planted with the reclamation mix.

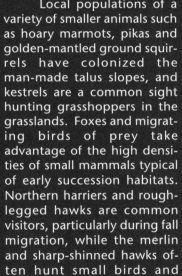

Occasionally a wolverine track can be found in winter.

Local populations of a variety of smaller animals such as hoary marmots, pikas and golden-mantled ground squirrels have colonized the man-made talus slopes, and kestrels are a common sight hunting grasshoppers in the grasslands. Foxes and migrating birds of prey take advantage of the high densities of small mammals typical of early succession habitats. Northern harriers and rough-legged hawks are common visitors, particularly during fall migration, while the merlin and sharp-shinned hawks often hunt small birds and insects on reclaimed sites during the summer and fall, while a wide variety of waterfowl have been observed on various settling ponds and man-made lakes during migration.

The fact is, reclamation activities of these two coal mines in the Alberta foothills has resulted in range expansion and increased population of bighorn sheep, as well as new habitat for other species. These modified habitats, designed specifically to benefit wildlife displaced during mining activities, take on increased significance when considered in context with range losses experienced by bighorn sheep elsewhere in North America during settlement. The presence of a range of species, representing every stage of the food chain, on reclaimed mine sites is an indication of successful reclamation, monitoring and management programs.

Suggested Reading

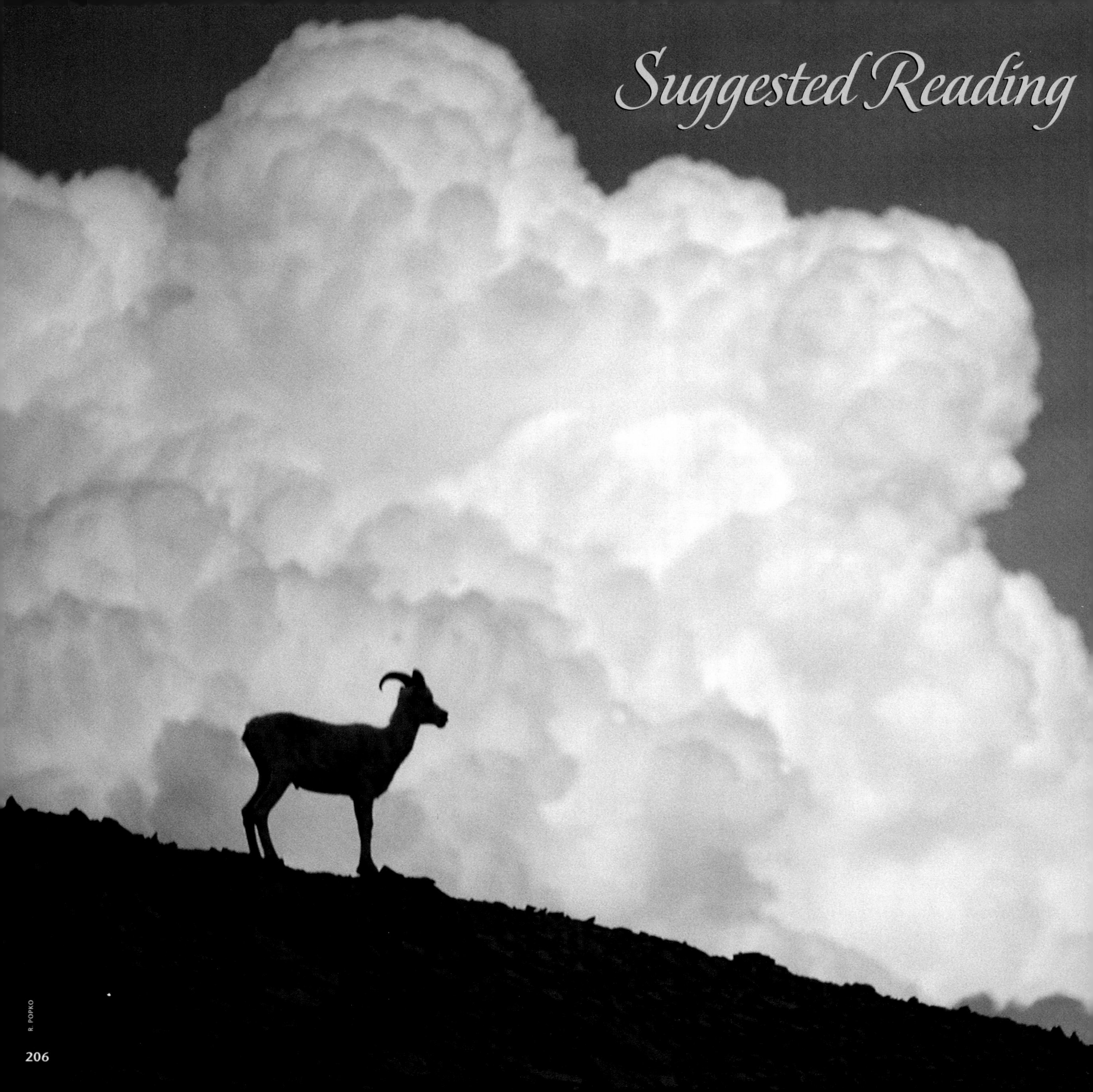

R. POPKO

GENERAL

Bleich, V. C., R. T. Bowyer, and J. D. Wehausen. 1997. Sexual segregation in mountain sheep: resources or predation? Wildlife Monograph 134, The Wildlife Society, Washington, D.C. 50 pp.

Buechner, H. K. 1960. The Bighorn Sheep in the United States: Its Past, Present, and Future. Wildlife Monograph 4, The Wildlife Society, Washington, D.C. 174 pp.

Clark, J. L. 1964. The Great Arc of the Wild Sheep. University of Oklahoma Press, Norman. 247 pp.

Cowan, I. M. 1940. The distribution and variation in the native sheep of North America. American Midland Naturalist 24:505-580.

Foundation for North American Wild Sheep. 1998. The Wild Sheep Journal. The Foundation for North American Wild Sheep, Cody, Wyoming. 192 pp.

Geist, V. 1971. Mountain Sheep: A Study in Behavior and Evolution. University of Chicago Press, Chicago, Illinois. 383 pp.

Geist, V. 1975. Mountain Sheep and Man in the Northern Wilds. Cornell University Press, New York. 170 pp.

Geist, V., and M. H. Francis. 1993. Wild Sheep Country. NorthWord Press Inc., Minocqua, Wisconsin. 176 pp.

Hoefs, M., editor. 1985. Wild sheep: distribution, abundance, management and conservation of the sheep of the world and closely related mountain ungulates. Northern Wild Sheep and Goat Council, Whitehorse, Yukon Territory, Canada. 218 pp.

Krausman, P., and R. Valdez, eds. 1999. Wild sheep of North America. University of Arizona Press, Tucson.

Lawson, B., and R. Johnson. Mountain Sheep. Pp. 1036-1055 in J. A. Chapman and G. A. Feldhamer, editors. Wild Mammals of North America: Biology, Management, Economics. Johns Hopkins University Press, Baltimore, Maryland. 1147 pp.

Rawley, E. V. 1986. Early records of wildlife in Utah. Publ. 86-2, Div. Wildl. Division of Wildlife Resources, Department of Natural Resources, Salt Lake City, Utah.

Schultz, R., D. A. Pedrotti, and S. C. Reneau. 1998. Putting Sheep on the Mountain. The Foundation for North American Wild Sheep, Cody, Wyoming.

Shackleton, D. M., ed., and the IUCN/SSC Caprinae Specialist Group. 1997. Wild Sheep and Goats and Their Relatives. Status Survey and Conservation Action Plan for the Caprinae. IUCN, Gland, Switzerland and Cambridge, UK. 390 pp.

Seton, E. T. 1909. Lives of game animals. Charles T. Branford Co., Boston, Massachusetts. 780 pp.

Trefethen, J. B., editor. 1975. The Wild Sheep in Modern North America. Boone and Crockett Club. 302 pp.

Valdez, R. 1982. The Wild Sheep of the World. Wild Sheep and Goat International, Mesilla, New Mexico. 186 pp.

Valdez, R. 1988. Wild Sheep and Wild Sheep Hunters of the New World. Wild Sheep and Goat International, Mesilla, New Mexico. 270 pp.

THINHORN (DALL'S AND STONE'S) SHEEP

Hoefs, M., and I. M. Cowan. 1979. Ecological investigation of a population of Dall sheep (*Ovis dalli dalli* Nelson). Syesis 12(1), The British Columbia Provincial Museum.

Murie, A. 1944. The Wolves of Mt. McKinley. U.S. Fauna of the National Parks, Fauna Series No. 5, USDI National Park Service, Washington, D.C. 238 pp.

Nichols, L. Jr. Dall's Sheep. Pp. 171-189 in Schmidt, J. L., and D. L. Gilbert, editors. Big Game of North America: Ecology and Management. Stackpole Books, Harrisburg, Pennsylvania. 494 pp.

Sheldon, C. 1911. The Wilderness of the Upper Yukon. Charles Scribner's Sons, New York, New York.

Sheldon, C. 1930. The Wilderness of Denali. Charles Scribner's Sons, New York, New York.

ROCKY MOUNTAIN BIGHORN SHEEP

Couey, F. M. 1950. Rocky Mountain bighorn sheep of Montana. Bulletin 2, Montana Fish and Game Commission. 90 pp.

Gilchrist, D. 1994. Quest for Giant Bighorns. Outdoor Expeditions and Books, Corvallis, Montana. 224 pp.

Hells Canyon Restoration Committee. 1997. Restoration of bighorn sheep to Hells Canyon: The Hells Canyon Initiative. Technical Bulletin No. 97-14, Idaho Bureau of Land Management, Boise. 60 pp.

Mosier, C. 1962. The bighorn sheep of Colorado. Colorado Game and Fish Dep. Tech. Bulletin 10, Denver. 49 pp.

Mussehl, T. W., and F. W. Howell. 1971. Game management in Montana. Montana Fish and Game Dep., Helena, Montana. 238 pp.

Singer, F. J., and M. Gudorf. 1998. Restoration of bighorn sheep metapopulations into and near 15 National Park units: Conservation biology of a severely fragmented species. USDI National Park Service, Washington D.C.

Smith, D. R. 1954. The Bighorn Sheep in Idaho: Its Status, Life History, and Management. Wildlife Bulletin No. 1, Idaho Department of Fish and Game, Boise. 154 pp.

Stemp, R. 1983. Heart rate responses of bighorn sheep to environmental factors and harassment. Master of Environmental Design, University of Calgary, Alberta. 313 pp.

Wishart, W. 1978. Bighorn Sheep. Pp. 161-171 in Schmidt, J. L., and D. L. Gilbert, editors. Big Game of North America: Ecology and Management. Stackpole Books, Harrisburg, Pennsylvania. 494 pp.

AUDUBON'S BIGHORN

Audubon, M. R. 1986. Audubon and His Journals, with Zoological and Other Notes by Elliott Coues. 2 vols. Dover Books, New York.

Bailey, V. 1926. A biological survey of North Dakota. North American Fauna No. 49. U.S. Bureau of Biological Survey.

Knue, J. 1991. The Audubon Bighorn. Pp. 62-81 in Big Game in North Dakota: A Short History. North Dakota Game and Fish Department, Bismarck.

CALIFORNIA BIGHORN SHEEP

Hebert, D., and M. Evans. 1991. A Proposal to Institute a Separate Trophy Status for California and Rocky Mountain Bighorn Sheep in North America. Wildlife Programme, Ministry of Environment, Williams Lake, British Columbia. 33 + 15 unnumbered pp.

Knue, J. 1991. The California Bighorn. Pp. 220-249 in Big Game in North Dakota: A Short History. North Dakota Game and Fish Department, Bismarck.

Nevada Department of Wildlife. 1985. Proceedings California Bighorn Workshop. Reno, Nevada. 78 pp.

Sugden, L G. 1961. The California Bighorn in British Columbia, with particular reference to the Churn Creek Herd. British Columbia Department of Recreation and Conservation. 58 pp.

DESERT BIGHORN SHEEP

Cook, R. M. 1991. A Historical Review of Reports, Field Notes and Correspondence on the Desert Bighorn Sheep in Texas. Special Report to the Desert Bighorn Sheep Advisory Committee, Texas Parks and Wildlife Department, Austin. 68 pp.

Irvine, C. A. 1969. The Desert Bighorn Sheep of Southeastern Utah. Publication No. 69-12, Utah State Division of Fish and Game, Salt Lake City. 99 pp.

Krausman, P., B. D. Leopold, R. F. Seegmiller, and S. G. Torres. 1989. Relationships between desert bighorn sheep and habitat in western Arizona. Wildlife Monograph 102, The Wildlife Society, Washington, D.C.

Lee, R. M., editor. 1989. The Desert Bighorn Sheep in Arizona. Arizona Game and Fish Department, Phoenix. 265 pp.

Leopold, A. S. 1959. Wildlife of Mexico. Univ. of California Press, Berkeley. 568 pp.

Leslie, D. M. Jr., and C. L. Douglas. 1979. Desert bighorn sheep of the River Mountains. Nevada Wildlife Monographs 66. 56 pp.

McQuivey, R. P. 1978. The Desert Bighorn of Nevada. Biological Bulletin 6, Nevada Department of Fish and Game, Reno. 86 pp.

Mendoza, J. 1976. The bighorn sheep of the state of Sonora. Desert Bighorn Council Transactions 20:25-26.

Monson, G. and L. Sumner, eds. 1981. The Desert Bighorn: Its Life History, Ecology, and Management. The Univ. of Arizona Press, Tucson. 370 pp.

Nabhan, G. P., editor. 1993. Counting Sheep: Twenty Ways of Seeing Desert Bighorns. The University of Arizona Press, Tucson.

Russo, J. P. 1956. The Desert Bighorn Sheep in Arizona: A Research and Management Study. Arizona Game and Fish Department, Phoenix.

Seegmiller, R. F., and R. D. Ohmart. 1981. Ecological relationships of feral burros and desert bighorn sheep. Wildlife Monograph 78, The Wildlife Society, Washington, D.C. 58 pp.

Sheldon, C. 1979. The Wilderness of Desert Bighorns and Seri Indians. Arizona Desert Bighorn Sheep Society, Phoenix.

Welles, R. E., and F. B. Welles. 1961. The Bighorn of Death Valley. Fauna of the National Parks of the United States, Fauna Series No. 6. USDI National Park Service, Washington, D.C. 242 pp.

HISTORICAL RECORDS

DeVoto, B. 1953. The journals of Lewis and Clark. Houghton Mifflin and Co., Boston, Massachusetts. 504 pp.

Haines, A. L. 1955. Osborne Russell's Journal of a Trapper. University of Nebraska Press, Lincoln. 191 pp.

Haines, F. D. 1971. The Snake Country Expedition of 1830-31: John Work's Field Journal. University of Oklahoma Press, Norman. 172 pp.

Spaulding, K. A. 1956. Alexander Ross: The Fur Hunters of the Far West. University of Oklahoma Press, Norman. 304 pp.

Townsend, J. K. 1978. Narrative of a Journey Across the Rocky Mountains to the Columbia River. University of Nebraska Press, Lincoln. 259 pp.

AUTHOR'S NOTE

There are two organizations of professional wildlife managers whose work involves wild sheep and goats. These are The Northern Wild Sheep and Goat Council and The Desert Bighorn Sheep Society. Both organizations publish proceedings containing papers and discussions of wild sheep research and management. To learn where these proceedings may be purchased or reviewed, interested readers should contact the fish and wildlife management agency of any western state or province.

Scientific names of animals identified in text. Asterisks denote extinct species.

addax *Addax nasomaculatus*
African lion *Panthera leo*
American camel* *Camelops herspernus*
American cheetah* *Miracinonyx trumani*
American lion* *Panthera leo atrox*
American llama* *Paleolama sp.*
American long-horned bison* *Bison latifrons*
American horse* *Equus sp.*
aoudad *Ammotragus lervia*
arctic fox *Alopex lagopus*
arctic hare *Lepus acticus*
argali sheep *Ovis ammon*
bald eagle *Haliaeetus leucocephalus*
bighorn sheep *Ovis canadensis*
bison (or buffalo) *Bison bison*
black bear *Ursus americanus*
black-tailed deer *Odocoileus hemionus columbianus*
blue grouse *Dendragapus obscurus*
blue sheep *Pseudois nayaur*
bobcat *Lynx rufus*
bull-dog bear* *Arctodus simus*
burro *Asinus asinus*
California bighorn sheep *Ovis canadensis californiana*
caribou *Rangifer tarandus*
cattle *Bos sp.*
Columbian mammoth* *Mammuthus columbi*
Conklin's pronghorn* *Stockoceros conklingi*
coyote *Canis latrans*
Dall's sheep *Ovis dalli*
desert oryx *Oryx dammah*
dire wolf* *Canis dirus*
dog *Canis familiaris*
domestic sheep *Ovis sp.*
elephant *Elaphus sp.*
elk *Cervus elaphus canadensis*
fox *Vulpes sp.*
goat *Capra sp.*
golden eagle *Aquila chrysaetos*
golden-mantled ground squirrel *Spermophilus lateralis*
gorilla *Gorilla gorilla*
gray wolf *Canis lupus*
Greenland caribou *Rangifer tarandus groenlandicus*
grizzly bear *Ursus arctos*
ground sloth* *Nothrotheriops shastensis*

hare *Lepus sp.*
hoary marmot *Marmota caligata*
horned lark *Eremophila alpestris*
human *Homo sapiens*
ibex *Capra sp.*
Indian rhinoceros *Rhinoceros unicornis*
Irish elk* *Megaloceros giganteus*
jaguar *Panthera onca*
Kamchatka snow sheep *Ovis nivicola nivicola*
kestrel *Falco sparverius*
long-billed curlew *Numenius americanus*
mammoth* *Mammuthus sp.*
marmot *Marmota sp.*
merlin *Falco columbarius*
Mexican desert bighorn sheep *Ovis canadensis mexicana*
moose *Alces alces*
mouflon sheep *Ovis orientalis* subspecies
mountain deer *Navahoceros fricki*
mountain goat *Oreamnos americanus*
mountain lion *Felis concolor*
mule deer *Odocoileus hemionus*
muntjac *Muntiacus muntjak*
musk ox *Ovibos moschatus*
Neanderthal man* *Homo sapiens neanderthalensis*
Nelson's desert bighorn sheep *Ovis canadensis nelsoni*
northern harrier *Circus cyaneus*
Okhotsk snow sheep *Ovis nivicola alleni*
orangutan *Pongo pygmaeus*
Peary's caribou *Rangifer tarandus pearyi*
peccary *Tayassu tajacu*
pika *Ochotona princeps*
polar bear *Ursus maritimus*
pronghorn *Antelocapra americana*
ptarmigan *Lagopus sp.*
Putorean snow sheep *Ovis nivicola borealis*
rabbit *Sylvilagus sp.*
red deer *Cervus elaphus*
reindeer *Rangifer tarandus*
Rocky Mountain bighorn sheep *Ovis canadensis canadensis*
roe deer *Capreolus capreolus*
rough-legged hawk *Buteo lagopus*
saber-toothed cat* *Smilodon fatalis*
saiga antelope *Saiga tatarica*
scimitar-toothed cat* *Homotherium serum*
serow *Capricornis sp.*

sharp-shinned hawk *Accipiter striatus*
shrub ox * *Euceratherium collinum*
Siberian moose *Alces alces pfitzenmaier*
Siberian steppe bison* *Bison priscus*
Siberian tiger *Panthera tigris altaica*
snow sheep *Ovis nivicola*
spadefoot toad *Scaphiopus sp.*
Stag moose* *Cervalces scotticus*
Stone's sheep *Ovis dalli stonei*
sun bear *Ursus malayanus*
thar *Hemitragus sp.*
thinhorn sheep *Ovis dalli*
urial sheep *Ovis orientalis*
Weem's desert bighorn sheep *Ovis canadensis weemsi*
white-tailed deer *Odocoileus hemionus*
wolf *Canis lupus*
wolverine *Gulo gulo*
woodland musk ox *Symbos cavifrons*
woolly mammoth* *Mammuthus primigenius*
woolly rhinoceros* *Coelodonta antiquatis*
Yakut snow sheep *Ovis nivicola lydekkeri*

Wild Sheep Conservation Organizations

HARVEY BROWN

BOONE AND CROCKETT CLUB

Telephone: 406-542-1888
FAX: 406-542-0784
E-mail: bcclub@boone-crockett.org
250 Station Drive
Missoula, Montana 59801-2753
Website: www.boone-crockett.org

FOUNDATION FOR NORTH AMERICAN WILD SHEEP

Telephone: 307-527-6261
Telefax: 307-527-7117
E-mail: fnaws@wyoming.com
720 Allen Avenue
Cody, Wyoming 82414
Website: www.iigi.com/os/non/fnaws/fnaws.htm

ARIZONA DESERT BIGHORN SHEEP SOCIETY

Telephone: 602-854-8950
P.O. Drawer 7545
Phoenix, Arizona 85011

BIGHORN INSTITUTE

Telephone: 760-346-7334
FAX: 760-340-3987
51000 Highway 74
P.O. Box 262
Palm Desert, California 92261

ROCKY MOUNTAIN BIGHORN SHEEP SOCIETY

Telephone: 970-493-0016
FAX: 970-224-3726
P.O. Box 853
Las Porte, Colorado 80535

SOCIETY FOR THE CONSERVATION OF BIGHORN SHEEP

Telephone: 213-256-0463
P.O. Box 94182
Pasadena, California 91109-4182

TEXAS BIGHORN SOCIETY

Telephone: 806-799-6816
5003 21st Street
Lubbock, Texas 79407

THE GRAND SLAM CLUB

Telephone: 205-674-0101
FAX: 205-674-0190
P.O. Box 310727
Birmingham, Alabama 35231

WILD SHEEP SOCIETY OF BRITISH COLUMBIA

Telephone: 604-944-4429
34A-2755 Lougheed Highway
Suite 539
Port Coquitlam, British Columbia V3B 5Y9

About The Authors

DUNCAN GILCHRIST

DR. DALE E. TOWEILL

As a wildlife research biologist, Dr. Dale Toweill has conducted and published original research findings on Rocky Mountain and California bighorn sheep as well as elk, mule deer, pronghorn antelope, mountain lions, bobcats, coyotes and many other species. Dr. Toweill holds advanced degrees in wildlife management and ecology from Oregon State and Texas A&M Universities. He is past president of the Northwest Section of The Wildlife Society, and a Certified Wildlife Biologist. Currently Wildlife Program Coordinator for the Idaho Department of Fish and Game, Dr. Toweill has also worked for the Oregon Department of Fish and Wildlife, Oregon Cooperative Wildlife Research Unit, and U.S. Forest Service. Currently, Dr. Toweill serves as a Technical Advisor to the Foundation for North American Wild Sheep, Bighorn Institute, and on the Board of Directors for Idaho's ZooBoise. He is also a Professional Member of the Boone and Crockett Club.

JACK RENEAU

DR. VALERIUS GEIST

Valerius Geist is Professor Emeritus of Environmental Science in the Faculty of Environmental Design, at the University of Calgary. He was a founding member of that graduate faculty and its first Programme Director for Environmental Science. He is certified as a Professional Biologist by the Alberta Society for Professional Biologists. His research interest focused on the evolution of large mammals, humans included, during the Ice Ages. Author of over 300 hundred technical and popular articles, reviews, book chapters and encyclopedia entries, Dr. Geist has published 14 books that deal in part with wildlife ecology, behavior and evolution, but also with wildlife conservation policy and the biology of health. These books have been honored with six 'book of the year' awards for original contributions to science and policy analyses, as well as for popularizing science. Dr. Geist has served on numerous editorial boards of learned journals, encyclopedias, and with conservation organizations such as the International Union for the Conservation of Nature. He is a fellow of the American Association for the Advancement of Science, a member of the European Conseil International de la Chasse and a Professional Member of the Boone and Crockett Club.